Radical, Religious, and Vic

Radical, Religious, and Violent
The New Economics of Terrorism

Eli Berman

The MIT Press
Cambridge, Massachusetts
London, England

First MIT Press paperback edition, 2011
© 2009 Massachusetts Institute of Technology

For information about special quantity discounts, please e-mail special_sales@ mitpress.mit.edu

This book was set in Sabon by SNP Best-set Typesetter Ltd., Hong Kong. Printed and bound in the United States of America.

Library of Congress Cataloging-in-Publication Data

Berman, Eli.
Radical, religious, and violent : the new economics of terrorism / Eli Berman.
  p. cm.
Includes bibliographical references and index.
ISBN 978-0-262-02640-6 (hbk. : alk. paper)—978-0-262-51667-9 (pb.)
1. Terrorism—Economic aspects. 2. Terrorism—Religious aspects. I. Title.
HV6431.B478 2009
363.325—dc22

2009014105

10 9 8 7 6 5 4 3

Contents

Acknowledgments

If you tell almost anyone that you study religion and terrorism, they typically have a few thoughts to share. I am grateful for most of those insights, but feel particularly obliged to the following people.

The soldiers and officers of the Golani Brigade taught me counterinsurgency many years ago. They are some of the most talented and impressive colleagues I've ever worked with. It's a tribute to their training, bravery, and professionalism—and to good luck—that I returned home unscathed; many of my comrades did not return at all.

When Ruth Klinov and I first started puzzling over ultra-Orthodox economics we received critical guidance from Menachem Friedman of Bar Ilan University, the world's expert on the Israeli ultra-Orthodox community. Since then I've drawn many times from his deep well of knowledge. Friedman has also let me accompany him as he conducted fieldwork and interviews in ultra-Orthodox neighborhoods of Jerusalem.

Several research assistants have cleverly managed data and contributed original ideas to this project over the years, including Liang Choon Wang, Lindsay Heger and Tiffany Chou of UC San Diego, who deserve special thanks.

My friend Susan Shirk and my agent, Jill Marsal, enthusiastically encouraged me to write a book accessible to a broad audience, even when I was just as happy to follow the safer path of writing academic articles. My editor, John Covell, and the staff of the MIT Press are responsible for keeping this project moving when I strayed from the chosen path. They also enforced high standards of production and guided the manuscript in the direction of accessibility. Any remaining obscure academic formulations are the result of my own stubbornness, not of any failure on their part.

David Berman—who managed to complete an excellent book on ethical graphic design in the time it took me to revise a draft—has been a generous sibling rival, improving and accelerating my work.

Andrea Hill of the UC Institute on Global Conflict and Cooperation, and Lindsay Heger of the UC San Diego Political Science Department, read patiently through the manuscript more times than I care to mention. They provided fresh pointers each time. Shier Berman provided critical insights on the writing of the first draft.

My colleagues at Boston University, Rice University, UC San Diego, and at the National Bureau of Economic Research have supported my forays into territory not usually considered economics with cheerful and constructive advice. I've been fortunate to be surrounded by unusually clever and creative social scientists, but I'm especially indebted to Kevin Lang and Roger Gordon, who have been generous mentors.

This book would not have been written (at least by me) were it not for the influence of two daring scholars who unfortunately are no longer with us. Yoram Ben-Porath of the Hebrew University, who taught me introductory economics and later mentored me, demonstrated to his students the broad landscape that economists can aspire to explore. The late Zvi Griliches, one of my dissertation advisors at Harvard, greeted my initial decision to study the economics of ultra-Orthodox Jews with his usual excited curiosity and perceptive questions; at our next meeting he produced a pile of relevant and excellent books from his own library, both fiction and nonfiction. I like to think that Ben-Porath and Griliches would have enjoyed reading this work.

My coauthors have selflessly shared their intellectual contributions, which pervade this book. I've tried in the text to note the major contributions of Laurence Iannaccone, Ruth Klinov, David Laitin, and Ara Stepanyan. I'd like to acknowledge that the aggregate mass of their minor contributions is also critical.

Any mistakes of omission or commission are of course my own.

My parents, Shirley and Shier Berman, have supported all my adventures, however far they have taken me from home.

There is only so much time. My remarkable wife Linda Oz and our two terrific children have been generous and patient with their affection as I've taken time that was rightfully theirs to write this book. I'm especially grateful to them for letting me work quietly, even when I've secluded myself to write on weekends and family vacations.

San Diego 2009

Preface to the Paperback Edition

When this book first went to press in the summer of 2009, Osama Bin Laden was still active, hiding out in a safe house in Abbottabad. U.S. troops were patrolling Iraq. NATO was conducting a "surge" in force strength in Afghanistan. I was actually in Afghanistan that summer with a team of academic researchers studying how development fits in a counterterrorism or counterinsurgency effort, the subject of chapter 7. Much has changed since then, yet the basic arguments of this book remain unfortunately relevant.

What has changed? Al Qaeda is weaker, so much so that at this writing Western societies are reconsidering the privacy we've surrendered to our own governments in the name of protection from terrorism. The geography of the threat has also shifted. With Western forces out of Iraq and drawing down in Afghanistan, we're removing targets and inevitably reducing media attention. The sources of terrorism are now less likely to be Somalia, the West Bank, or Sri Lanka, while violence against civilians is more likely to be unleashed from ungoverned spaces in Yemen, Libya, or Mali, with new bases of operation possibly emerging in Syria and the Sinai Peninsula.

Religious radicals remain the world's most lethal terrorists, the puzzle highlighted in chapter 1. Hezbollah, the Taliban, and Hamas are still very much with us. The first has been critical in preserving the Assad regime in Syria, by effectively countering rebel forces. The second seems set to expand their control of southern Afghanistan as NATO forces withdraw, and remains active in western Pakistan. The third governs Gaza without challenge. Not only do radical religious "clubs" remain relevant, recent events have reinforced a lesson reviewed in the history of the Muslim Brotherhood (chapter 5): though religious radicals seldom start revolutions, they are extremely adept at increasing their power when government falters, as we've seen recently in Egypt, Syria, and Yemen; over the last decade in Gaza, Somalia, and western Pakistan; and historically in Iran. That pattern suggests an organizational advantage that goes beyond collective violence to include political mobilization as well, all consistent with the internal discipline provided by clubs.

The operational logic of suicide attacks remains unfortunately with us, as those attacks continue to exact a lethal toll, especially in Pakistan, Afghanistan, and Iraq.

As scholars, we know a lot more about the functioning of violent organizations in general, and of religious terrorists in particular, than we did even a few years ago. For instance, the "defection constraint" and other organizational vulnerabilities discussed in chapter 2 are subject to a more general analysis by Jacob Shapiro of Princeton in a new volume, *The Terrorist's Dilemma.*

The empirical analysis of counterterrorism and counterinsurgency, which our team led in Afghanistan in the summer of 2009, has now replaced some of the speculative and anecdote-based analysis of chapter 7 with empirically grounded findings. Fortunately, the basic proposition holds true: development programs that enhance governance and deliver basic services in particular ways are extremely cost effective in reducing violence. That finding is strongly supported by analysis of data on development projects in Iraq. In that sense chapter 7 now serves as a good introduction to a set of academic papers on constructive approaches to counterinsurgency now collected at our "Development and Conflict" website, igcc.ucsd.edu/DACOR. I hope that these results will be useful to practitioners.

More generally, analysis of the social science of conflict has blossomed over the past few years. I urge the interested reader to check out the Empirical Studies of Conflict site at esoc.princeton.edu for the latest working papers, many of which are accessible to the general public. That research group is now actively studying conflicts in at least a dozen countries, developing new empirical tools, and testing new theories. As the World Bank and the development community increasingly confront the challenge that dysfunctional states pose for human well-being, I hope that research by the Empirical Studies of Conflict collaborative will play an important role in shaping policy.

Returning to the original source of my own interest in clubs, Israeli politics has recently tipped the balance of power away from the ultra-Orthodox, allowing policymakers and community leaders an opportunity to grapple with the unsustainable dynamics implied by the combination of low employment rates and high fertility among the ultra-Orthodox. The logic presented in chapter 4 continues, I think, to be borne out: norms of fertility, employment, and military service are plastic, but only when discriminatory subsidies that strengthen sacrifices are reduced. How that reduction can be humanely achieved is a challenge for Israeli public policy.

One delightful reward of scholarship is the debate, exchange, and new ideas that it encourages. For instance, David Skarbek has used the club concept to analyze prison gangs in Los Angeles, while Rachel McCleary and Leonard van der Kuijp have applied these ideas to understanding sixteenth century Tibetan Buddhist monks. This book is now available in libraries throughout the world, including university and public libraries in the Middle East and Asia, so there's reason to hope for more rewards from an increasingly diverse group of scholars.

Eli Berman
La Jolla, California
August 2013

Rescue operations at U.S. Marine barracks after a Hezbollah suicide attack, Beirut, October 1983 (AP Photo/Zouki).

1

Why Are Religious Terrorists So Lethal?

In the tense days after the horrific attacks of September 2001 the United States vowed a "global war on terrorism," with the support of almost all the world's governments. Since then the United States and most of the world have massively increased their counterterrorism effort. Has the threat from terrorism diminished?

Counting casualties from terrorism since September 11 provides a clear answer. In the six years *following* those attacks, starting in October 2001, terrorists killed about 11,800 people worldwide. In the three years and eight months before 9/11, starting from January 1998, when the first comparable data are available, the world suffered approximately 4,800 fatalities resulting from terrorist attacks.[1] These numbers paint a stark and sobering picture. *From an average of 109 people killed per month by terrorists before the attacks of September 11, the global death rate rose to about 158 people killed per month in the six years following, an increase of 45 percent.* That figure excludes fatalities resulting from terrorist attacks in the active conflicts in Iraq and Afghanistan.[2] If the toll included Iraq and Afghanistan the global fatality rate in the six years after September 11 would be much higher—529 people killed monthly in terrorist attacks.

These striking figures are consistent with what we see and read in the media. Al-Qaeda has not managed another day as devastating as September 11, 2001, but the bombings in Madrid, London, Bali, Sinai, and Amman, the attacks in Turkey, Chechnya, and Mumbai, and the ongoing carnage in Iraq, Afghanistan, and Pakistan provide stark evidence that global terrorism is worsening. The death toll has risen despite our monumentally expensive counterterrorism effort. That effort forced

Al-Qaeda to reorganize and reduced its potential. Yet the threat from more localized terrorists has only increased. Hezbollah, Hamas, the resurgent Taliban, and even Muqtada al-Sadr's militia (the so called "Mahdi Army") each constitute more of a threat to governments in their own countries than Al-Qaeda ever did.

These four radical religious organizations, Hezbollah, Hamas, the Taliban, and the Mahdi Army, continue to surprise established militaries with both their resilience and their lethality. Eight years after their expulsion by Coalition forces, the Taliban has re-established itself in most provinces of Afghanistan and in neighboring regions of Pakistan. Muqtada al-Sadr has built a militia out of a religious charity and used it to become a kingmaker in Iraqi politics, favoring coalition forces with a ceasefire when he sees fit. The Lebanese Hezbollah, who invented the modern high-casualty suicide attack in Lebanon in 1982, withstood a month of Israeli air strikes in the summer of 2006 while unleashing daily rocket fire on northern Israeli towns. It is currently a partner in Lebanon's coalition government, with veto power. Hamas has built the most potent militia in Palestine, won national elections in January 2006, and defeated tens of thousands of Palestinian security forces to take military control of the Gaza Strip in June 2007. It took them only three days. At this writing they are negotiating a power-sharing agreement to create a unity government in the Palestinian Authority.

The experience of these four groups frames a puzzle common to all four organizations: Why are religious radicals, who often start out appearing benign and charitable and generally avoid conflict, so effective at violence when they choose to engage in it?

Hezbollah

For Americans, Israelis, French, and Lebanese, radical religious terrorism is by now an old wound, dating back to the first deadly attacks by Hezbollah in the early 1980s. Hezbollah seemed to emerge from nowhere in the aftermath of the Israeli invasion of south Lebanon in 1982. It surprised Israeli forces, as well as American and French peacekeepers with a consistently deadly series of attacks, including the Marine barracks attack of October 1983 in Beirut. The remains of those barracks are displayed in the photograph that opened this chapter. That suicide attack claimed the lives of 241 servicemen.[3]

Hezbollah was formed by a group of former seminary students. Many had studied in the Shiite holy cities of Najaf and Qom and had subsequently been expelled—either by the Iranian government of the Shah or by the Iraqi government under Saddam Hussein. In the eastern Lebanese city of Baalbek, and later in the poor Shiite neighborhoods of Beirut, Hezbollah organized mosques, schools, and charities, with generous support from the Islamist government of Ayatollah Khomeini that had just seized power in Iran. Between 1982 and 1987 Iran spent more than $100 million annually on hospitals, mosques, schools, and charitable organizations affiliated with Hezbollah. Baalbek, a picturesque city in the Bekaa valley east of Beirut, which had been tolerant enough to attract secular tourists of all denominations, was radicalized over a few short years. The *burka*, a loose garment worn by traditional Muslim women, became ubiquitous, first in Baalbek, then in the Shiite neighborhoods of Beirut, and after that in south Lebanon, as Hezbollah displaced the more secular Shiite *Amal* movement. This religious radicalization was accompanied by massive increases in social service provision, all because of Hezbollah. In 1996 Lebanese sociologist Waddah Sharara dubbed this network the *Hezbollah State* in a book bearing that title, arguing that the institutional base that Hezbollah established was functioning as a sort of alternative government.[4]

Hezbollah developed and improved many of the tactics that currently torment Coalition troops in Iraq and Afghanistan: roadside bombs, suicide attacks, and rocket attacks. Those tactics were battle-tested, from the treacherous mountain roads of southern Lebanon to the putrid alleyways of South Beirut. Hezbollah demonstrated their tactical prowess again in this decade, successfully kidnapping Israeli soldiers patrolling Israel's northern border, in October 2001 and again in July 2006. When Israel retaliated against that second kidnapping with air strikes within Lebanon, Hezbollah responded with a month of rocket attacks on Israeli civilians. Entrenched in fortified bunkers camouflaged by the terraced hills and olive trees of southern Lebanon, Hezbollah retained their tactical capacity to fire rockets into Israel despite relentless strikes by Israeli fighter planes and constant artillery fire. On the political front Hezbollah has been even more successful, displacing Amal as the leading representative of Lebanese Shiite Muslims, effectively undermining the authority of Western-oriented governments, and eventually negotiating its way into the governing coalition.

The Taliban

In 1994 another apparently benign group of clerics suddenly achieved remarkable success at violence, organizing a small insurgency in southern Afghanistan. They called themselves Taliban—"students" in Arabic—and they changed the course of modern history. The Taliban began as a motley collection of former seminary students from the dusty, squalid Afghan refugee camps scattered across the border in Pakistan. Their background was typical of religious radicals: they were pious and mostly poor. As far as we know, their aspirations were also typical. They sought to provide services, both spiritual and tangible, to local residents. The most important of these services was, by their own lights, *safety*. In the Taliban's own version of their origins they organized to prevent school-children from being abducted and raped on their way to school in the impoverished villages around Kandahar in southern Afghanistan.[5]

Amazingly, a ragged band of religious radicals with little military experience, poor training, and no particular theological motivation for conquest managed to do what for centuries the strongest military powers in the world had struggled with and mostly failed at. The Taliban conquered Afghanistan, hill by hill, village by village, road by road, and province by province, and then they held it.

Though they could not have known it at the time, the Taliban conquest of Afghanistan would be a catalyst for conflicts in the new century. They went on to provide a safe haven in Afghanistan for foreign radical Islamists, including Osama Bin Laden. The foreigners were free to organize and set up training camps. Al-Qaeda grew and thrived with Taliban protection, using Afghanistan as a base to plan and train for a chain of terrorist attacks, including eventually the attacks of September 11, 2001.

Coalition forces from Western countries responded to the 9/11 attacks within months; an overwhelming barrage of high-tech attacks from the air supported the expulsion of the Taliban by the Northern Alliance and other domestic forces. Eight years later those Western forces remain mired in Afghanistan for the foreseeable future in support of its new government. Had the Taliban not managed to conquer Afghanistan, and then make the fateful decision to provide a haven for Al-Qaeda, facilitating the attacks of 9/11, there would most likely never have been a "global war on terrorism." Recalling that countering terrorism provided a rationale for the United States and its allies to invade Iraq in March 2003, it is already difficult to imagine how the first decade of the twenty-first century might have developed had the Taliban not first conquered Kandahar, and then gone on to control the country.

The subjugation of Afghanistan by the Taliban in the last decade of the twentieth century was not only a catalyst but also a prelude—to other violent campaigns by resilient Islamist rebels against Western countries and their allies. It demonstrated quite dramatically that a radical religious group has the potential to be an amazingly potent and violent force. In conquering Afghanistan the Taliban managed to tame an ethnically diverse country whose stark, breathtaking mountains and decrepit roads made it scarcely passable, much less governable. Afghanistan was ruled by a patchwork of well-armed local warlords, each more experienced than the Taliban in guerilla warfare, having spent years in active conflict during their victorious insurgency against the Soviet Union and its proxies. In Kabul, in the north, and in the east the Taliban defeated well-organized militias with foreign allies, formal command structures, and ample revenue bases. At this writing, the reconstituted Taliban threaten both the Afghan and Pakistani governments despite a concerted Coalition effort, so much so that some experts now suggest negotiating an interim truce with moderate Taliban rather than continuing to try to suppress them.

The Taliban began like many other radical religious groups, with noble aspirations and limited ambitions. They sought to improve their own lives and those of local community members through personal piety and local Islamic government. Following their initial conquests in the southern provinces, they developed an aspiration to become a national Islamic government. However, to achieve even their initial successes, these clerics and seminary students had to somehow outmaneuver and outfight their Afghan rivals. How did they acquire that tactical skill?

Hamas

The Palestinian radical Islamic group Hamas is puzzling for the same reason. Why are they so effective at violence? For almost four decades, beginning with their founding in the 1950s, the Islamic Brotherhood (*al-Ikhwan al-Moslemoon*, or simply *al-Ikhwan*) in the Gaza Strip was a benign, nonviolent religious organization. Like other branches of the Brotherhood worldwide, they complemented the spiritual services provided in mosques with social and welfare services, delivered through a network of clinics, schools, charities, drug treatment centers, and even sports clubs. In 1988 the Islamic Brotherhood in the Gaza Strip changed course. The *Intifada* (the common Arabic name for the Palestinian revolt against Israeli occupation), which had just begun, was immensely popular among Palestinians. The rank and file organizers of the Brotherhood suddenly found themselves politically impotent because their popular following was drawn away by the young secular leaders of the rebellion. Though it had traditionally treated the national conflict as a secondary issue, the Brotherhood realized that it had to reinvent itself or become irrelevant. It established a militia, naming it *Hamas*. Almost overnight Hamas became the single deadliest terrorist organization in the Israel-Palestine conflict. It was hard to penetrate, disciplined, adequately funded, trained, and committed. Among Palestinian terrorist organizations it has carried out the most deadly attacks on civilians. By January 2006 Hamas had become the most potent *political* force among Palestinians as well, with its victory in Palestinian national elections. By June 2007 it had taken Gaza by force. In January 2009 Hamas survived an all out assault by Israeli ground forces on Gaza, aimed at halting rocket fire from Gaza on Israeli settlements. While at this writing it is too soon to judge the long-term effects of that incursion, first indications are that by surviving the incursion (and continuing the intermittent rocket attacks), Hamas has been strengthened politically and is now well positioned to negotiate a position of partnership in the government of the Palestinian Authority.

As with Hezbollah and the Taliban, the effectiveness of Hamas at violence came as an awful surprise to its targets. Hamas entered the conflict with less experience than either of its secular rivals, Fatah (the major component of the Palestine Liberation Organization) and the Popular Front for the Liberation of Palestine (PFLP). Both of these were experienced fighters by the late 1980s, with two decades of rebellion, hijackings, guerilla warfare, and terrorism under their belts. Hamas also had less experience than the Palestinian Islamic Jihad, which shares the same radical Islamist ideology but has proven to be far less dangerous than Hamas, both in the number of attacks it carries out and in the number of casualties it inflicts per attack.

The Lethality of Religious Radicals

If the initial victories of Hezbollah, Hamas, and the Taliban were preludes, September 11, 2001, was the opening act of a much larger drama. Suddenly the United States and Europe were engaged in a "war" with radical religious terrorists, simultaneously, and on multiple fronts. Al-Qaeda's ability to plan and execute those audaciously deadly attacks will disturb our sleep for generations. It planned the operations, financed them, recruited operatives, trained them for months, controlled them in foreign countries, and successfully executed the attacks, all without being discovered.

Despite increased security and heightened public awareness, Islamist terrorists continue to kill hundreds of civilians in high-profile attacks. Al-Qaeda in Iraq, reportedly organized by the late Abu Musab al-Zarqawi until his assassination in June 2006, is responsible for large numbers of civilian casualties in Iraq and Jordan. It has killed numerous U.S. troops and has even struck at the United Nations headquarters in Baghdad, claiming twenty dead. The effectiveness of Al Qaeda Iraq is less of a surprise than that of the Taliban, Hezbollah, or Hamas. The core group of insurgents were seasoned militants, reportedly imprisoned together in Jordan, and bonding with al-Zarqawi during his jail sentence from 1992 until 1999 for conspiring against the Jordanian Kingdom. Muqtada al-Sadr's militia, the so-called Mahdi Army, is more like the Taliban, Hezbollah, and Hamas. It evolved quickly from a benign religious organization, providing welfare services to Shiite residents of Baghdad's slums, into a potent militia with substantial political power.

Radical Islamists are particularly lethal terrorists. Looking at organizations designated as international terrorists by the U.S. State Department, we have information on 3,932 terrorist attacks carried out worldwide over the forty years between 1968 and 2007. Excluding attacks in Iraq and Afghanistan, the nineteen secular terrorist organizations on the State Department list committed 2,077 attacks, claiming 2,668 lives, an average of 1.3 fatalities per attack. (Those groups include the Basque separatists (ETA), the National Liberation Army and the Revolutionary Armed Forces (FARC) in Colombia, the Shining Path in Peru, the Kurdistan Workers' Party (PKK) in Turkey, and the Liberation Tigers of Tamil Elam (LTTE) in Sri Lanka.) During the same four decades religious terrorists perpetrated fewer attacks, 1,265, but killed far more people, 3,784, averaging almost three deaths per attack. If we include the 587 attacks reported in Iraq and Afghanistan in that calculation, the death toll resulting from religious terrorism rises to 6,706, or 3.6 fatalities per attack. Adding in the three attacks of 9/11 raises the number of deaths resulting from religious terrorism to 9,689, and the lethality per attack to 5.2, four times as lethal on average (per attack) as the secular organizations.[6]

Of the twenty religious terrorist organizations on that list, eighteen are radical Islamists. The other two are *Kahane Chai*, a Jewish group with two attacks recorded, and the Japanese cult *Aum Shinrikyo*, which launched the infamous sarin gas attack on the Tokyo subway system, killing twelve people and injuring about five thousand. These figures reflect a general pattern in global terrorism over the past few decades: radical religious terrorists of the early twenty-first century have become extremely dangerous to citizens and pose an existential threat to some governments.

The threat from modern religious terrorist organizations is unprecedented. In retrospect, the secular terrorist organizations of the 1960s and 1970s did not pose nearly as potent a threat. The militant leftist Baader-Meinhof Group in West Germany, the Japanese Red Army, the Canadian FLQ (Front de Libération du Québec), and even the Fatah under the young Yasir Arafat, kidnapped, hijacked, inflicted casualties, and drew attention but were brought under control long before they threatened sovereign states.

Before examining the reasons why religious terrorism is so dangerous, it is worth noting that not all religious terrorists succeed. The so-called Jewish Underground was a group of Orthodox Jewish settlers living on the occupied West Bank in the 1980s. They had a messianic theology and political/terrorist agenda. The conspirators hoped that by targeting civilian Arabs and Muslim holy sites they could provoke a war that would prevent Israel from withdrawing from the Palestinian West Bank. So extreme was their ideology that they aspired to extort the Almighty into dispatching the Messiah to prevent that withdrawal—by triggering Armageddon. Yet, despite theological commitment, military experience, and a pool of like-minded potential recruits among Jewish settlers, the Jewish Underground was quickly infiltrated and suppressed by Israeli intelligence. In a very important way the Jewish Underground was typical of violent conspiracies, religious or secular—its members leaked information, leading to infiltration by the authorities, arrest, and successful prosecution. Their strong theological commitment to their cause must have been *necessary* for the Underground's members to attempt such dangerous and severe acts of destruction, yet it was not *sufficient* for their conspiracy to succeed.

What Motivates Terrorists? The Afterlife and Other Myths

Why do some religious terrorists succeed while others fail? Is it because some religious groups can motivate members by promising rewards in the afterlife? Are they particularly adept at "brainwashing" their followers? These are popular and romantic ideas. The pious Jihadist, programmed with an ideology of hate to be a human guided missile, or dreaming of virgins in heaven, makes for compelling news broadcasts and emotional sound bites,[7] but the concept does not stand up to scrutiny.

The research of Ariel Merari is particularly convincing in debunking myths about the religious motivation of terrorists. Merari is an Israeli psychologist who began studying the motivations of combatants after his own experience in battle during the Arab-Israeli war of 1973. He carefully interviewed families and friends of Palestinian suicide attackers, even interviewing suicide attackers themselves who failed to detonate their explosive belts and were captured in the attempt.

Merari's first conclusion is that suicide attackers do not fit the usual profile of suicidal individuals. They are not generally depressed, abusing drugs or alcohol, showing suicidal tendencies, or displaying other signs of mental illness. (In an exception that might prove the rule, Fatah attempted to exploit a mentally impaired West Bank youth to act as a suicide attacker during the second Intifada. When he was captured and disarmed, they were severely criticized by Palestinians for the cynical use of an innocent and have not repeated that mistake.)[8]

Is the primary motivation religion and its heavenly rewards, including the infamous seventy-two virgins? Even among suicide attackers from radical religious groups such as Hamas and the PIJ, the terrorists Merari interviewed did not generally mention religion as their main motivating factor. Moreover, many Palestinian suicide attackers come from secular organizations such as Fatah and the PFLP. This is consistent with what we know from other conflicts. The group responsible for the most suicide attacks in the late twentieth century was the LTTE (Liberation Tigers of Tamil Elam) in Sri Lanka, who perpetrated seventy-five attacks.[9] The LTTE are not only secular but neo-Marxist; members are (at least nominally) atheists. The PKK (Kurdish Worker's Party) in Turkey, another group that has carried out suicide attacks, is also neo-Marxist. Combining the religious radicals who don't mention heavenly rewards and the secular suicide attackers who are not counting on an afterlife, we must conclude that most suicide attackers are not motivated by rewards in the hereafter. Virgins in heaven make a colorful story, but that story is not consistent with most of the facts.

What about an ideology of hate? Here again, Merari's interviews reveal that hate, or even revenge, do *not* consistently form the primary motivation of a suicide attacker. The Palestinian assailants in Merari's sample frequently carry out their attacks within a few weeks after recruitment, scarcely long enough to be indoctrinated with an ideology of hate. Polls show that Palestinians are very angry in general, but only a few carry out suicide attacks. To be sure, throughout the world there is widespread animosity toward repressive governments, toward occupying powers in general, and toward the United States and Israel in particular, especially in the very places where terrorists recruit. That should cause concern and may be a *necessary* condition for terrorist attacks. Yet the evidence weighs against hatred, or an ideology of hate, being a *sufficient* motivation for suicide attacks.

If not theology, ideology, anger, or psychosis, what *is* the primary motivation of Palestinian suicide attackers? Merari does not claim to have a single simple answer. The suicide attackers he studied were typically not ignorant or economically deprived (relative to their neighbors), and had generally not suffered the loss of a close friend or family member. Although they defy simple characterization, if we were to look for a single answer, I think it must be that these individuals are altruists—at least with respect to their own communities. Merari's research suggests that the attackers truly believe that their courageous act will bring great benefit to some cause, and that their neighbors, community, or country will benefit.

An altruistic suicide attacker is an uncomfortable idea, so we should stop and consider his (or sometimes her) psychology for a moment. Altruism seems strange and even insulting to us when combined with a callous lack of empathy for the basic humanity of the victims. Unfortunately, such a lack of empathy is not unusual in an environment of violent conflict and certainly would not qualify as a psychosis in that setting. On the other hand, altruistic acts on behalf of a cause are quite common, especially if the cause is the safety of their family or community, or perhaps the liberation of their country. Firefighters ran up the stairs into the burning towers on September 11. They selflessly and regularly endanger their own lives. Bus drivers in Israel who suspect that a suicide bomber has boarded their bus have clear instructions: physically kick the suspect from the bus, and failing that, throw your body on top of the attacker to absorb the explosion. Soldiers throw their bodies on grenades to protect their comrades. The pilots who won the Battle of Britain faced a shockingly high risk of being shot down in order to defend their country. Perhaps terrorists see themselves as well-balanced altruists, and heroic at that?

Beyond altruism, a suicide attacker would seem to also require an exaggerated view of the importance of the attack. He must believe that the terrible price he has committed himself to paying is justified because the attack will truly make an appreciable difference to the outcome of the conflict. Otherwise why give up his or her life? Yet most acts of violence, however lethal, have very little effect on any given conflict, military or political. So an inflated view of the importance of one's act must generally be necessary for a terrorist. Yet that would be an easy criterion to satisfy; social scientists know that delusions of self-importance are hardly rare, especially among young men.

In short, attaching a psychological profile to a suicide attacker is not difficult: He lacks empathy for the victims, is altruistic toward his own cause or side, and is a little deluded about his importance in the grand scheme of things. Unfortunately that profile is not at all helpful in screening for possible suicide attackers—those three characteristics are simply too common in conflict-ridden areas of the world.

A large pool of psychologically healthy, basically altruistic, suicide attackers? That is a truly disturbing and frightening idea, which may be why we've been more comfortable thinking of them as psychotic or brainwashed, despite decades of evidence to the contrary, dating back to the secular terrorists of the 1970s. Yet understanding the phenomenon requires an unblinking look at Merari's findings. For one thing, the idea of psychologically healthy suicide attackers is disturbing because we would like to be able to draw an ethical distinction between acts of courage and altruism on our side and acts with the same motivation by our enemies. Firefighters, police officers, and soldiers who stare death in the eye when protecting and defending us are altruists. We think of them as heroes, and justifiably so. Altruism, we would like to believe, should be reserved for the "good guys." Like it or not, many people in conflict-ridden parts of the world feel the same way about suicide attackers who target civilians in the name of some higher cause. The ethical distinction between targeting civilians and targeting combatants is not compelling to many people, particularly in the Middle East. The key is how they judge terrorist acts, not how we do.

The profile of an altruistic suicide attacker is also frightening because it implies vulnerability for us, the potential targets. Imagine huge recruiting pools of very angry young altruists who would not hesitate to risk or even sacrifice their own lives to further their cause by attacking civilians. Indeed, there seem to be ample supplies of volunteers available for suicide terrorism, not only in Iraq and Palestine, but in much of the Middle East, Asia, and even in Europe. To make matters worse, explosives and other deadly weapons used by terrorists are extremely simple to devise or obtain, so that the pool of volunteers would not require a lot of equipment or training. That sense of vulnerability triggered the extreme reaction of Western countries to September 11, 2001, capturing our attention and driving a massive shift in government spending toward defending civilians against terrorism.

Terrorist Organizations—Why So Few?

Are we really that vulnerable? Two reassuring facts insulate our daily lives from the nightmare of a huge pool of suicide terrorists armed with truck bombs, explosive belts, and other simple, deadly weapons. First, terrorists almost never act alone. They are usually part of a coordinated network of operatives, which recruits, raises funds, motivates, arms, directs, covers tracks, takes credit, publicizes, and even compensates families. Timothy McVeigh, the lone terrorist of Oklahoma City, is an exception. True, he destroyed the Murrah Federal Building in April 1995 with a rental van full of homemade explosives and the help of only one other conspirator. Yet those cases are extremely rare. Terrorists are usually members of a single cell belonging to a larger organization with a political agenda. That's reassuring because of a second fact: very few militant groups in any given conflict actually succeed in carrying out coordinated violence. In fact, the U.S. State Department's list of foreign terrorist organizations has only forty-two entries for the entire world. Among those, most of the casualties are due to the eight deadliest organizations.[10]

Only forty-two entries for the entire world; why is the list so short? The technical requirements of terrorism are hardly onerous. The raw materials for explosive weapons are available almost anywhere and the technical details necessary to assemble conventional bombs—as opposed to nuclear or biological weapons—are fairly easy to download and understand. The supply of angry people with grievances (justified or not) is huge, be those disputes with their own government or with some occupying power. Considering the availability of recruits and technology, the number of truly dangerous organizations is tiny. Why are there so few successful militias and terrorist organizations? From what we know about people's grievances, it cannot be for lack of motivation or recruits. If volunteers for suicide attacks are many, it must be relatively easy to find willing operatives to take on lesser risks within terrorist organizations. Yet only forty-two organizations worldwide seem to be viable enough to pose a threat. Why?

If the supply of potential terrorists is large, and only a few terrorist organizations are viable, some terrorists must be failing, perhaps even before they get started. What makes some terrorist organizations viable while others fail? The economics we teach in business school, of all places, suggests an answer. Some organizations are more resilient than others. Much of this book will be about the *vulnerabilities* of terrorist organizations. I will argue that successful militias and terrorist organizations share one common characteristic. They have found a way to *control defection*, the Achilles' heel of coordinated violence. The more destructive terrorist organizations become, the more governments are willing to spend in order to buy information and bribe operatives into defection, and the more worried terrorist operatives must be about leaks and defection among their comrades.

The history of modern terrorism provides plenty of examples illustrating the vulnerability of these organizations to leaks and defection. For instance, the assassination of Abu Musab al-Zarqawi in June 2006 was reportedly made possible by information from an internal Al-Qaeda source. Former Al-Qaeda operative Jamal al-Fadl, a native of Sudan, defected in the mid-1990s after a dispute over finances. He informed on and incriminated his old comrades for a decade in exchange for a generous reward and witness protection in the United States.

In May 2008 Nelly Avila Moreno surrendered after twenty-four years as a senior leader of FARC, the Revolutionary Armed Forces of Colombia. Moreno, who the *Los Angeles Times* describes as a "fierce, resourceful and ruthless leader," is suspected of "orchestrating mass murders and summary executions." She faces charges of murder, terrorism, and drug trafficking. Her explanation for surrendering to undercover police and facing punishment, rather than fighting on, is very clear on the dangers of leaks and defection: "At a news conference in Medellin, Moreno said she surrendered because of increasing Colombian army pressure, the deterioration of rebel forces and her fear she might be killed by her own troops for the $900,000 bounty on her head. 'You may have a lot of fighters at your side, but you never have an idea of what they are really thinking,' Moreno told reporters at an army base."[11]

Considering the loyalty required of operatives in the face of such attractive incentives, it is easy to understand why so few terrorist organizations manage to function successfully for long. The vast majority of terrorist conspiracies go the way of the plotters who were exposed trying to make truck bombs in Toronto, also in June 2006. That group of seventeen men, who would gather to play soccer together, had been under surveillance for two years and was shut down by well-informed Canadian intelligence officers before anyone was harmed. The Canadian authorities could wait patiently for sufficient evidence to accumulate, without risk, because they had an informant.[12]

Internal Economies and Organizational Efficiency

The two facts just highlighted—that terrorists seldom act alone and that there are very few effective terrorist organizations—should put our fears in context, and should inform counterterrorist efforts. Rather than concentrating on the motivations of individuals, which would lead to rediscovering that there is no shortage of angry, capable, and very sane potential recruits,[13] security services should focus on the internal operation of the few *effective and resilient* terrorist organizations (i.e., those that continue to carry out high-casualty attacks despite intense counterterror efforts). Significantly, the deadliest among these organizations are radical religious groups. Al-Qaeda, Al-Qaeda Iraq, the Sri Lankan LTTE, Hamas, and Hezbollah together accounted for 5,880 of the 6,975 fatalities resulting from suicide attacks between 1983 and 2003. Of these five organizations, all but the LTTE are religious radicals. The four radical Islamic organizations were responsible for 4,917 of those fatalities, fully 70 percent of lives lost to suicide attacks over those two decades. We rejected theological motivations of *individuals* as an explanation for the lethality of religious radicals, which leads us to a more focused question: What makes radical religious *organizations* so deadly?

What we will see in the chapters that follow is that violent radical religious organizations survive, and even thrive, because they can limit leaks and defection. Why? The answer will be quite surprising. It has to do with a subtle relationship between defection and a very benign activity—mutual aid. Sociologists of religion have discovered a remarkable regularity: regardless of denomination or faith, radical religious groups typically share a common organizational design, which makes them magnificent providers of social services through mutual aid. By mutual aid I mean individual members providing goods and services through acts of charity within a community. Unpaid charitable work is common in many communities, religious and secular. It usually ranges from occasionally helping out, perhaps at a PTA bake sale, to volunteering regularly, maybe at a soup kitchen or hospital. Yet among religious *radicals* mutual aid is far more intense: an example familiar to Americans is a communal barn raising, where an entire Amish or Mennonite community turns out to donate labor for a day or two, working together to build a barn for a newlywed couple. Radical religious communities—Amish, Mennonites, Hutterites, and ultra-Orthodox Jews—also require that members demonstrate their commitment to the group through some costly or painful sacrifice, often giving time early in life to some religious cause. The theological explanation for that sacrifice differs across religious groups but the rules are the same; those who sacrifice gain acceptance as full members, while those who do not suffer marginalization, shunning, or even expulsion. This sacrifice and selection is divisive but crucially effective; it weeds out potential members who might cheat later in life, shirking their responsibilities in mutual aid. Weeding out shirkers—whom economists call "free riders"—is painful but critical, because shirking is the Achilles' heel of mutual aid organizations. Members who draw services when in need but do not volunteer to help when they are capable will leave barns half-raised, the bereaved unconsoled, soup kitchens unstaffed, and eventually bankrupt a mutual aid pool. Thus sacrifices early in life, while they are economically costly for individual members, are necessary to the economic survival of the mutual aid organization because sacrifice identifies shirkers and weeds them out. We will explore those benign forms of cooperative activity among religious radicals first, because of the insight they provide into violent cooperative activity such as rebellion and terrorism.

Militias and terrorist organizations face a very similar problem to that of a mutual aid organization. The cheaters they worry about are not shirkers, but informants and defectors—a far greater threat. A single shirker in a mutual aid organization can be disruptive and expensive, but a single defector can cause an entire cell to be exposed, probably leading to the arrest or assassination of all his fellow members.

Now here's the key point. Radical religious communities who turn to organized violence operate with a huge advantage over other militants. Having already weeded the cheaters and shirkers out of their mutual aid operations, they can be confident that the remaining members are loyal. Pressing that advantage, religious radicals can conduct deadly attacks against high-value targets with a low risk of leaks or defection, even against targets whose governments invest mightily in protection and counterintelligence.

At this point it will help to clarify what I mean by a "religious radical." Since September 11 the discussion of religion and violence has become so emotionally charged that even a neutral term such as *religious* or *Islamist* risks gratuitously insulting someone. All the more so for the expression "religious radical." Yet at the risk of seeming insensitive, careful analysis requires a foundation of well-defined terms. We need a term *for a member of a group whose religious practice is much more demanding—generally more time consuming—than is mainstream practice.* That is what I mean by a religious radical. I don't mean to suggest violence, extremism, or even political mobilization. Hutterites, Mennonites, Amish, Hassidim, Misnagdim, and members of the Muslim Brotherhood are all religious radicals, using the term as a sociologist (or an economist) would. Some of these groups are pacifists and distance themselves from politics. The vast majority of the communal activity that these radical religious communities perform is benign, if not downright noble. Two centuries ago Adam Smith used the term *sect* to describe these groups in his brilliant foundational text of economics, *The Wealth of Nations*. An economist or sociologist would use *sect* interchangeably with *religious radical*, although *sect* has taken on a more negative connotation in the two centuries since Adam Smith wrote. Other scholars prefer the term *fundamentalist*, which implies either literalism or reversion to some historical form of practice. That only adds confusion. Fundamentalism suggest reversion to the historical fundamentals of a religion, which is *not* what most religious radicals do. Denominations often labeled as religious fundamentalists, such as radical Islamists and ultra-Orthodox Jews, are anything but: compared with the historical practices of coreligionists, their current norms are far more stringent.

Having defined the term, let me restate more precisely the critical discovery of sociologists of religion: regardless of religious denomination and history, radical religious Christians and Jews offer mutual aid and other community services extremely effectively to members. One of my objectives in this book is to demonstrate that this finding applies to radical religious Muslims as well, providing insight into how radical Islamic communities function by viewing those communities through the lens of existing scholarship on Christian and Jewish religious radicals. I will then extend that approach to examine religious terrorism, and show that radical religious communities with strong mutual aid provision have the potential to be potent providers of coordinated violence, including terrorism, should they so choose.

This approach to religion will surprise many readers. It wasn't in your high school textbook because it hadn't been discovered yet. We have known only since the 1980s how important social service provision is to radical religious communities. An early hint came from studies by sociologist Rosabeth Moss Kanter, who demonstrated in the 1970s that nineteenth-century utopian communes were more successful if they demanded sacrifices of members.[14] By the 1980s Rodney Stark and William Bainbridge showed the same result for radical Christian communities.[15] In the early 1990s economist Laurence Iannaccone explained how religious sacrifices contribute to cohesive communities by improving social service provision, using analysis precise enough to allow his conjectures to be tested using survey data—and confirmed.[16] My own research on ultra-Orthodox Jews began in the mid 1990s. Luckily, Israeli data describing ultra-Orthodox Jews is much more extensive than what Iannaccone had available on radical Christians. With the additional data I had available, I managed to extend Iannaccone's analysis—which economists call the "club" model[17]—to explore the educational choices that religious radicals make for their children, and even how many children they choose to have. That research reinforced the evidence for Iannaccone's "club" approach.[18]

People of faith, even economists of faith, often object to this way of thinking about religion and religious radicals. First, it seems dismissive of faith and theology, emphasizing instead the social and economic aspects of life in religious communities. Second, it draws parallels between religious organizations whose ethics some readers might embrace on the one hand, and those that commit murderous terrorist acts on the other. As an individual, I empathize with those feelings.

Yet science requires putting our emotional biases aside for a moment in order to discover underlying patterns of human behavior. An objective examination of numerous successful communities of faith reveals that they often stand on two pillars. The first is their ability to meet the spiritual needs of their members, providing a sustaining theology. The second pillar is an ability to provide more tangible services, social and economic, generally through a system of cooperative charity (i.e., mutual aid). Distinguishing between those two functions is often difficult, but the distinction is critical. Regardless of the strength of a member's faith, and regardless of the salience of a theology, an organization that can *limit shirking* will be more successful at mutual aid. No matter what beliefs motivate a member's sacrifice, the act of sacrifice signals that the member will not shirk, creating the potential for productive mutual aid activity in that community. That potential is often realized, so that welfare services, education, healthcare, and other social services are provided to those religious communities. That's why social service provision and spiritual service provision so often appear together in communities, making it difficult to distinguish commitment to beliefs from commitment to community, for community members and outside observers alike.

To be sure, we should be disturbed by the ethical contradiction between a theology that holds human life to be sacred (as do all major religions) and an active policy of targeting innocent civilians. Yet that contradiction should not paralyze analysis. The organizational ability to carry out acts of terrorism stems not from theology but from the organizational strength of a mutual aid society, religious or secular. To illustrate that fact, I will examine some purely secular organizations quite adept at coordinated violence, though they lack theology altogether. What the Sicilian Mafia, street gangs, and the *Palmach* (the military force organized within the kibbutz movements of prestate Israel) have in common with frightening religious cults like the *Aum Shinrikyo* is a combination of coordinated provision of social services on the one hand, and sacrifices that indicate commitment on the other.

What's Coming?

This book will cover a lot of ground, collecting insights and data from scholars in many fields, several countries, and a number of centuries, so an overview of what's coming may be useful. I will start with the puzzle raised already: With so many angry people in the world, why there are so few resilient terrorist organizations? My discussion will draw on the history of the Taliban, Hamas, and Hezbollah to explain the sensitivity of terrorist groups to defection and information leaks, arguing that this is the central organizational problem that terrorists face. The discussion will be broad, touching on insurgencies in Malaysia and Iraq as well.

The next question is why, among the few resilient terrorist organizations, so many are made up of religious radicals. The answer requires a long detour through the world of nonviolent religious radicals, to understand what makes these communities so resilient. So we will take a break from violence and explore the benign provision of mutual aid within exotic radical religious communities, such as the Amish, Hutterites, Mennonites, and ultra-Orthodox Jews. These groups might be familiar to many readers through personal experience or from popular culture. The tension between the very restrictive lifestyles of religious radicals and the norms of mainstream American culture has provided some fertile material for scriptwriters. Actor Harrison Ford fell in love with an Amish widow at a barn raising in the 1985 movie *Witness*. Melanie Griffith (somehow) went undercover among Hassidim in New York in *A Stranger among Us* (1992), falling in love with a Talmudic scholar before solving the crime. Amish teenagers confronted the attractions of secular culture for a few seasons on the reality show *Amish in the City*, and the irrepressible Rabbi Shmuley critiqued secular parenting and relationship norms while offering advice to anyone who would listen on his reality show *Shalom in the Home.*

Most people are initially struck by the exotic beliefs of radical Christian and Jewish communities. Despite their disparate beliefs, we will see how similar radical religious communities of different faiths are to each other in their daily lives: they share generous mutual aid networks and religious norms that distance community members from mainstream culture and market economies. The very survival of these communities has puzzled economists for the same reason that *Amish in the City* drew viewers: Who can resist the attractions of modern technology and market economies? Why use mules rather than tractors, forbid the Internet—or even computers—in the home, and sometimes even refuse modern medical care for your children?

That puzzle was elegantly addressed by economist Laurence Iannaccone, who showed that those seemingly counterproductive social norms are in fact critical to the survival of a community based on mutual aid. I will explain Iannaccone's insight, examining the evidence and showing how it can explain the common social and economic structures of Christian and Jewish radical religious communities. I also use his approach, the "club" model mentioned above, to show how religiosity and lifestyles, including choices as intimate as a woman's fertility, are affected dramatically by government policy toward religious radicals. The club model is not the only way experts have approached the puzzling behavior of religious radicals. I'll also sketch and compare alternative theories drawn from the sociology and psychology of religion, letting the reader judge which does the best job of explaining the data.

Will club analysis help us understand radical Islam? It turns out that radical Islamic communities, although their religious practices are diverse and different from those of either radical religious Christians or radical religious Jews, share a common pattern of well-organized mutual aid within communities as well as norms that distance members from mainstream culture and markets. We will see how radical Islamic communities in Indonesia used mutual aid to mute the effects of an economic crisis in the late 1990s. As in the case of radical Christians and Jews, those mutual aid networks are sometimes observed directly but are often latent, observed only in the effects they have on fertility and educational choices. The tension between traditional and modern lifestyles is felt particularly by *women* in radical Islamic communities, who face strict norms governing how they may dress, whether they may work outside the home, how they may raise their children, and which schools the children may be sent to.

Studying radical Islamic communities is hard slogging. Dress codes and restrictions on work are easy to gather anecdotal evidence about but hard to measure systematically. On the other hand, fertility and school quality are readily observable in survey data. I'll describe research on several countries that checks whether Iannaccone's club model fits radical Islamists. The answer is positive; we observe distinctly club-like behavior among radical Islamists. Members of radical Islamic communities tend to have larger families than their Muslims neighbors. Not only that but, like ultra-Orthodox Jews, they tend to send their children to religious schools that provide poor training for employment after graduation, even though better public schools are usually available.[19] Why would mothers and fathers sacrifice their children's futures by choosing inferior schools for them? I will offer the same answer that explained the behavior of radical Christians and ultra-Orthodox Jews: sacrifice allows communities to weed out the cheaters who would undermine mutual aid.

Sacrifice is also the key to answering the central question of this book: *Why are religious radicals such effective terrorists?* I will look at radical religious organizations that turn to violence and explore what it is about religious communities who are adept at providing social services that makes them effective militias and terrorists, if they choose that path. The Taliban, Hamas, Hezbollah, and Sadr's Militia will be reexamined in some detail, examining their common social service provision base. I will also add to the mix a *failed* religious terrorist organization, the "Jewish Underground," which will illustrate that organizational structure rather than theology is critical to effectiveness.

Suicide attacks are the deadliest weapon in the terrorists' arsenal, and so suicide attacks by religious radicals will get special attention. Examining international data on suicide attacks since the early 1980s, we will first ask under what conditions terrorists choose suicide attacks over rocket attacks, roadside bombs, and other tactics of terrorism and insurgency. The answer, which comes from joint research with political scientist David Laitin of Stanford, is that the single best predictor of suicide attacks has surprisingly little to do with theology; it is the "hardness" of the target that matters—how difficult it is to destroy. As governments present terrorists with better and better defended (i.e., harder) targets, terrorists respond by switching to the tactic that is the most difficult to defend against: the suicide attack. Suicide attacks come at a high cost for the terrorist organization—the certain loss of the attacker—so terrorists almost always use less costly tactics when the chosen target can be destroyed without losing the attacker in a suicide attack.

This view of terrorists as thoughtfully choosing tactics may strike some readers as odd, given their media characterization as irrational. Yet recent scholarship paints a picture of thoughtful, instrumental, goal-oriented organizations. Political scientist Lindsay Heger, for instance, has shown that terrorists choose both tactics and targets in a way that reflects their goals and constraints. They are more likely to attack civilians in democracies—apparently because democratic governments are more sensitive to civilian casualties—and are less likely to attack civilians when they have a politically engaged affiliate, such as the Irish Republican Army had in Sinn Fein.[20] *What* the goals of terrorist organizations are is a separate question and beyond the scope of this book. Two points are worth noting, though. First, terrorist organizations have strong incentives to overstate their goals, in order to attract hopeful followers, so that their actual goals may not be knowable. Second, as far as the major terrorist organizations discussed in this book are concerned, they all seem to be using terrorism as an instrument to achieve some political objective.

If it is just a matter of tactics and targets, why then do radical religious terrorists use suicide attacks so often? The short answer will be: because they can. A conflict where targets are well enough defended to require suicide attacks is a harsh environment for rebels. Most rebel organizations will not survive there at all. Radical religious groups, with the benefit of their club structure, might be the only organizations potent enough to operate in an environment where targets are so hard that suicide attacks are the only feasible tactic.

What does all this imply about how to counter terrorism? One goal of this book is to make new research on religious radicals and terrorism accessible to interested readers. Another goal is to explain the tactics and strategies suggested by these new findings to practitioners of counterinsurgency and counterterrorism. Radical religious rebels currently challenge governments in the Middle East, Asia, and Africa; they also threaten civilians in much of the world. Knowing that radical religious terrorists draw their strength from organizations that provide social welfare services through mutual aid suggests that competing provision of particular social services will be an effective tool in the struggle against terrorist violence. That approach, which is inherently nonviolent, would undermine radical religious organizations without endangering civilians, disturbing freedom of religious practice, or dignifying violent Jihadist rhetoric with a debate. I contrast this approach with traditional development economics on the one hand, and traditional counterinsurgency on the other, and examine why recognizing these differences is critical to implementing effective policies. The proposed tools have worked well in places as diverse as Malaysia and Egypt and are a key component of modern counterinsurgency theory, as it is being developed on the fly in Iraq and Afghanistan.

The final challenge is the biggest, to put it all in context. Eight years after 9/11, is it possible to step back and view radical Islamic terrorism within a broad historical context? While terrorist acts can launch wars, forestall peace, and cause tremendous human suffering, I will argue that they are symptoms rather than causes of the underlying forces that shape human development. Radical religious traditions have a long history, and are also a symptom of deep societal change. Christian sects have survived at the fringes of European culture since the Protestant Reformation, despite persecution by the dominant denominations—persecution that was often violent. The Anabaptist tradition, which is today continued by the Amish, Hutterites, and Mennonites, dates back to sixteenth-century religious communities in Switzerland and the Rhineland that arose in a period of particular religious and political turmoil. Radical religious Jewish communities date back at least as far as the Essenes, who hid the Dead Sea Scrolls in the first century. They were a sect not unlike today's Amish—a functioning commune. The Essenes were one of many first-century sects that arose out of the deep societal change of the time—the collapse of the Israelite caste system. Drawing on the Essenes and early Anabaptists, we'll try to see what historical Jewish and Christian experiences with sects can teach us about where today's religious radicals fit in the broad sweep of history.

We know from Western history that market economies and functioning democracies have an empowering and liberating effect. Yet in celebrating that progress we often forget that empowerment and liberation are societal changes that threaten traditional societies. Imagine a traditional European or Middle Eastern town. When serfs, peasants, minorities, and women first had the opportunity to earn decent wages in the market, travel freely, and eventually even vote, they must have felt liberated as individuals. Yet their emancipation was a mixed blessing for communities: members with strong outside options were freed of their dependence on community-based institutions such as mutual aid networks for support and protection. But what about the community members left behind, who still depended on those institutions—now depleted by the defection of the most talented? In that sense, the arrival of markets and political upheavals of the nineteenth and twentieth centuries posed a challenge to traditional societies. Since many of the institutions of traditional communities are religious, markets and democracy challenge the religious order when they challenge the social order.

That challenge to the traditional structure of communities implies that a transition to markets, democracy, and secular governance requires particular attention to traditional structures threatened by the process. Historically, a key component of the European and American transition has been the eventual separation of church and state. The lack of that separation in younger nation-states is relevant today. Religious radicals seeking political power challenge governments from the Philippines to Algeria, and sometimes manage to take control. Understanding why these radical religious organizations succeed suggests a strategy that will not only undermine their potential for effective use of violence but can also limit the unique advantages that religious radicals have at political organization, leveling the political playing field. Comparing the approaches of different countries to religion and state, the analysis in the final chapter suggests some political ground rules that could limit the abuse of power by radical religious governments. Better yet, it would reduce the incentives for religious radicals to organize politically or seek power through violence in the first place. That argument explains why political-religious parties are largely absent in the most stable and economically successful countries of the world but thrive and seed political dysfunction in much of the Middle East and Asia, including Israel—an otherwise very Westernized country.

In closing, I will consider the analogy of that very Western history to political and economic development in the modern Muslim world. In the Middle East, attempts at Western-style governance have been largely unsuccessful, and the transition to modern market economies has been uneven. Many scholars argue that the rise of Islamist politics is a reaction to that failure.[21] Yet we shouldn't forget that in the West, where markets and democracy are today quite successful, the transition from feudalism, monarchies, and state religions was neither rapid nor bloodless. Europe experienced a long period in which nascent governments were poor providers of services and pockets of radical religious reaction flourished. As we will see, Anabaptist Christians in the sixteenth century and ultra-Orthodox Jews in the nineteenth century can be understood as a natural protective reaction by traditional societies to the threats posed by markets and political emancipation. In that sense, the rise of radical Islam looks like the twentieth-century version of a familiar story, a predictable reaction of traditional communities to the slow incursion of market economies and political emancipation into their lives. Keeping in mind the tremendous potential benefits of that process, for residents of those countries and for their neighbors and trading partners, the final chapter asks what our role in the West could or should be. How can Western governments and NGOs balance support for the natural incursion of markets, emancipation, and democracy into traditional societies, while dealing with the radical, sometimes violent, traditional backlash?

Taliban fighters, Amirabad, Afghanistan, November 2001 (AP Photo/Dusan Vranic).

2

The Defection Constraint

Four decades after the war ended Sam Popkin returned to Vietnam, retracing his steps and asking questions better left unasked on his initial visit. By this time Professor Popkin was an accomplished scholar of political science, an expert on polling, and a sometime consultant to American presidential campaigns. A big, friendly man in his sixties with a shock of white hair and a talent for getting people to talk to him, Sam returned to seek out the South Vietnamese villagers he had interviewed in the late 1960s. Then, as a graduate student, and again as a young assistant professor at Harvard, Sam had spent months walking around in villages, conducting interviews and gathering material for his research.[1]

This time around, it was safe to ask former Viet Cong rebels for answers to the questions he could only speculate about in the intervening years. Their answers provide a first, basic lesson about insurgencies:

Popkin: "If one of your members was killed, how long did it take for the organization to recover?"

Former Viet Cong rebel: "A few days."

Popkin: "And if a member defected?"

Former rebel: "Between a week and two months."[2]

A defection could shut down their insurgency for months. Why? A few more questions provided the answers. Drop points needed to be changed, members had to lie low to avoid arrest or capture, and plans possibly compromised would have to be revised. Otherwise, the leaked information might allow the Americans to ambush their comrades.

It may be a generation until we can calmly ask retired radical Islamists to reminisce, allowing us to replicate Popkin's findings from Vietnam.

Yet the lesson of sensitivity to defection is relevant today. It can help us understand why there are so few effective terrorist organizations world-wide, and what allows those few to be so lethally effective.

Origins of the Taliban

Hideous as we may consider them to be, it would be foolish not to rec-ognize the Taliban as some of the most accomplished rebels of modern times. Their success is a puzzle to students of warfare. The early Taliban were poorly educated villagers with little military experience. Their rein-forcements were Afghan madrassa (Islamic religious school)[3] students from the squalid refugee camps on the Pakistani side of the Afghan border. Yet the Taliban managed to conquer Afghanistan and then hold it for almost three years. They might still be governing Afghanistan today were it not for a single ill-fated decision: that of their leader, Mullah Omar, in October 2001, to protect Osama Bin Laden—the act that trig-gered their rapid ouster by local forces backed by Western air power.

To put the Taliban accomplishment in context, the Soviet military spent $45 billion in an unsuccessful attempt to hold Afghanistan in the 1980s. After the Soviets were finally expelled by a bloody mujahideen insurgency, the veteran mujahideen fighters could not successfully control the country either. At this writing, seven years after the ouster of the Taliban, coalition forces do not even attempt to control every corner of Afghanistan. Take a moment to mull over the photograph facing the opening page of this chapter of Taliban fighters crammed in the back of a pickup truck. To this day the Taliban remain irregular bands of young men, lacking uniforms and low on training. Yet this motley collection of madrassa graduate students with weak theological credentials, once managed to govern the entire country, and aspire to do so again. How did they do it?

The origins of the Taliban are rooted in a background of civil war, poverty, religious radicalization, economic chaos, and disrupted trade routes. Afghanistan is a famously ungovernable country. It has suffered civil war almost continuously for three decades, at an appalling cost of one and a half million lives. In 1978 a Marxist military coup over-threw the government of Muhammad Daud. Rural tribes responded by declaring a holy war against the new government. Meanwhile, a violent power struggle within the coup ended in the assassination of the new president. The Soviet Union, alarmed at the prospect of an unstable Islamist neighbor, invaded in December 1979 in support of the embattled Marxist generals. The Soviet invasion triggered widespread consternation in the West, leading to President Carter's boycott of the Moscow Olympics in 1980.

Over the next thirteen years the mujahideen, a loose tribe-based alliance of Islamists, mounted a successful guerrilla war, ambushing Soviet patrols and targeting their helicopters and aircraft with American shoulder-mounted missiles. Pakistan actively backed that insurgency, both out of a desire to influence Afghanistan and provide territorial depth in its conflict with India, and because of an ethnic affiliation with the Pashtun majority in southern Afghanistan. The mujahideen received about $10 billion in military support, mostly from the United States and Saudi Arabia, in an effort largely administered by the Pakistani Inter-Services Intelligence (ISI).[4] The mujahideen forced a Soviet retreat. The Afghan president was overthrown in 1992 when Kabul, the capital, fell to mujahideen from the northern Afghani Tajik and Uzbek tribes, the same "northern alliance" that would expel the Taliban from Kabul in the fall of 2001.

The mujahideen achieved the purpose of their Pakistani and American supporters in expelling the Soviets, but created a following for radical Islam in the process. Pakistani journalist Ahmed Rashid describes the effect of foreign support: "Prior to the war the Islamicists barely had a base in Afghan society, but with money and arms from the CIA pipeline and support from Pakistan, they built one and wielded tremendous clout."[5]

Yet the mujahideen could not control or govern Afghanistan. Their conquest set off a bloody internal battle between their alliance and a coalition of Pashtun tribes over control of Kabul, the Afghan capital, which had previously been under Pashtun control for three centuries. In 1994 General Dostum, leader of the northern Uzbeks, defected to join the Pashtun and their leader, Gulbuddin Hikmetyar. Despite that defection, Pakistani support, and a devastating campaign of shelling, Hikmetyar could not seize Kabul.

By the mid-1990s, the Pashtun south was in chaos. It was cursed with running battles between a patchwork of former mujahideen warlords in fiefdoms ranging in size from a few provinces to single villages. In the midst of that poorly governed space, the Taliban emerged in Kandahar, the largest city in the south. Rashid emphasizes the lawlessness contributing to their formation:

> International aid agencies were fearful of even working in Kandahar as the city itself was divided by warring groups. Their leaders sold off everything to Pakistani traders to make money, stripping down telephone wires and poles, cutting trees, selling off factories, machinery and even road rollers to scrap merchants. The warlords seized homes and farms, threw out their occupants and handed them over to their supporters. The commanders abused the population at will, kidnapping young girls and boys for their sexual pleasure, robbing merchants in the bazaars and fighting and brawling in the streets.[6]

Southern Afghanistan was in chaos; its meager economic base was being looted and extorted.

Banditry on the roads was an expensive obstacle for smugglers and traders—an important part of the Afghan economy. Truckers based in the Pakistani border city of Quetta had a long tradition of trading and smuggling goods through Afghanistan to Iran, Turkmenistan, and the rest of Central Asia. Their route from Quetta passed north through Kandahar and then west, skirting the mountainous central region of the country before heading north to the Afghan city of Herat, then controlled by the militia of Ismael Khan. In October 1994, Pakistani Prime Minister Benazir Bhutto met with Khan, and with Uzbek warlord General Dostum, to negotiate a secure route. The Pakistani government quickly forged ahead, backing an effort by the Pakistani ISI to reconstruct roads and create alliances along the Kandahar-Herat route.[7]

A quick look at the map illustrates what the Quetta truckers were thinking. Since at least the time of Marco Polo, Afghanistan has been a land bridge for trade between the Indian subcontinent to the East, and Iran, Turkmenistan, Turkey, the Middle East, and Europe to the West. The preferred route passes from the Pakistani capital, Islamabad, through the Khyber Pass, west to Kabul and north through Mazar e Sharif. Ongoing war rendered that route far too dangerous. Yet there were goods to be moved, including opium poppies, of which Afghanistan is the world's dominant producer. If someone could open a southern route

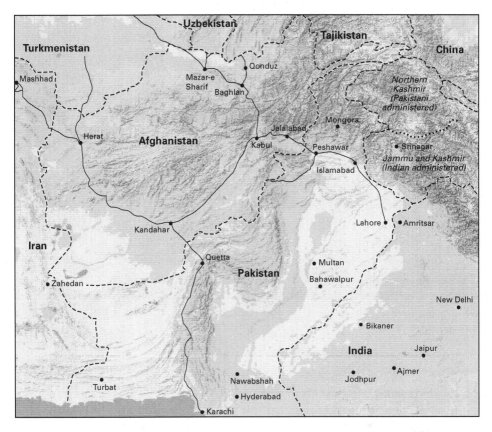

Figure 2.1
Trade routes in Afghanistan

through Kandahar and Herat, they could not only trade, they would enjoy a monopoly.

In October 1994, the ISI dispatched a trial convoy loaded with medicine north into Afghanistan from Quetta, bound for Ashkabad, in Turkmenistan. The convoy was immediately captured by warlords, south of Kandahar. To their surprise, a small, largely unknown group of radical Islamists, the Taliban, emerged to free the ISI's convoy. The Taliban were well armed, with rifles, mortars, ammunition, and vehicles they had ostensibly acquired by raiding an ammunition dump (somehow left unguarded) two weeks earlier on the Pakistani border. By December the

Taliban were operating a safe single-toll road through the Kandahar region from Quetta to Herat. They delivered to the ISI and the truckers precisely what the Kandahar warlords had previously failed to offer their new patrons. Convoys safely passed from Turkmenistan to Quetta and back for the first time in years. With alternate routes in northern Afghanistan blocked by heavy fighting, their route became a primary conduit for trade from Pakistan to Iran and Turkmenistan, and on into Turkey. Increased trade was so significant that the price of food began to fall. Smuggling increased so much that Pakistani customs complained of declining tariff revenue—smuggled goods were replacing legal imports.

The Taliban charged tolls, of course, for the use of their trade routes; they would go on to use those revenues to help finance their conquest of Afghanistan. Ahmed Rashid reports that in March 1995 the Taliban collected $150,000 in a single day from truckers, and about twice that much the next day.[8] They would capture Kabul in September 1996, and complete their campaign with the conquest of Mazar e Sharif in August 1998. The Taliban established an oppressive regime that subdued the country through ethnic massacres and brutal and misogynist repression. Their punishment for homosexuality was to drop a wall on the offenders. Women convicted of adultery suffered public execution.

The disastrous consequences of Taliban rule were enabled by their initial success at opening and guarding trade routes. How did they do it? In the aftermath of the Afghan insurgency against the Soviets the country was awash in automatic weapons, ammunition, and experienced mujahideen. How did the inexperienced Taliban succeed in monopolizing the trade-route business, rather than some veteran ex-mujahideen tribal warlord?

Trade Routes and Defection

Securing a trade route is a typical activity for a militia or insurgent organization interested in generating revenue. The Taliban would have had to use violence (or at least the threat of violence) in order to capture and then secure the trade route. Once successful, they could charge the truckers large tolls in exchange for keeping convoys safe as they rolled along the route.

A key aspect of securing a trade route is how sensitive the organization is to defection. Why? Imagine for a moment that the Taliban have already captured the route. Now they must secure it. So the Taliban would post armed members at checkpoints—crossroad passes where the convoy could be easily attacked, robbed, or stolen altogether in the absence of security. All this would apply to the main route connecting Pakistan to Turkmenistan on the Kandahar-Herat road, for instance. A convoy traveling that route would be quite valuable to bandits, especially as it neared the destination, where the contents could be sold at a handsome profit.

Now what's to stop the few Taliban members at a checkpoint from climbing into the cab, hijacking the convoy, and selling the contents at the eventual destination? The goods in that convoy could well be worth more than members would earn in a lifetime! In a country with well-enforced laws, employees stealing a few trucks full of goods from their employer could expect pursuit by the police, capture, prosecution, and punishment. Yet in the chaos of war-torn Afghanistan, an organization could not rely on the police. It would have to be self-policing.

Imagine two young Taliban sitting on some rocks with Kalashnikov assault rifles on their knees, at the last dusty checkpoint, weighing their options as the sun draws low in the sky over the Iranian border. If they defect and sell the loot, they can split the value of the convoy between them and live like kings. On the other hand, they would never be able to return to their homes, they will have betrayed their friends, and their families may suffer retaliation. If they remain loyal to the Taliban, they can return home to secure families, feel that they did their duty, and be paid some proportion of the revenues from tolls. So the young men do a quick calculation, as the convoy comes around the bend. Say that the convoy is worth $10,000 at the destination. This means they can share $5,000 each if they steal it. How much might they be paid if they remain loyal? Well, if the convoy is worth $2,000 at the origin and $10,000 at the destination, then the Taliban can charge $7,000 in tolls and leave $1,000 in profit for the trucker. The $7,000 in tolls might be divided among 100 members guarding the road to yield $70 each. So for a $10,000 convoy they could betray their friends, ruin the reputation of their families, and never return home in exchange for $5,000, less the

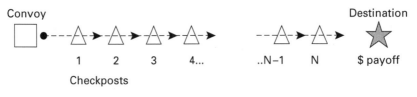

Figure 2.2
Trade route and checkposts

$70 they get for remaining loyal. The net return for defection is $4,930 ($5,000 –$70). Not enough, they think. They shrug their shoulders and lazily wave the convoy by.

Yet the incentives weigh against loyalty for more valuable convoys. Say that a convoy worth $100,000 shows up next at their checkpoint. A profit of $50,000 each should capture the young men's attention. They quickly calculate that it was worth about $20,000 at the origin, and that the Taliban will charge $70,000 in tolls to leave the trucker $10,000 in profit. The $70,000 in toll revenue split among a hundred members allows each to be paid $700 to ensure loyalty. That's a much better fee than they were making for the low-value convoy, but the attraction of defection is now much stronger: the two members manning the last checkpoint can steal the convoy and abscond with $50,000 each ($49,300 more than they would have otherwise earned)! The two Taliban guards stop the truck, jump into the cab, and head for Turkmenistan.

The math is clear. For low-value convoys the difference between half the value and 1/100th of the toll might be small and not worth a lifetime of regret in exile, but for high-value convoys the temptation to defect would be huge. When high-value convoys are at stake, it becomes crucially important to securing a trade route that members feel a very strong loyalty to the organization and to their families and friends back home. Otherwise, they will defect.

If the client and the Taliban middle management are paying attention, defection should not occur. Imagine the client. He owns the goods and is driving the lead truck around the bend approaching the checkpoint, sweating. When he was back in Quetta negotiating with the Taliban, he would have been imagining those two teenagers at the checkpoint, trying to predict their calculation. At the time he was sizing up the organization in advance, wondering how valuable a convoy he was willing to risk driving down the route. Perhaps he thought that a $10,000 convoy was safe but a $100,000 convoy invited too big a risk of defection—that is, of the two young Taliban guards jumping into the cab and holding him at gunpoint. He decided on a $20,000 convoy, and here he is trying his luck at the last checkpoint. The truck approaches the checkpoint. The driver smiles and waves nervously. The young men with the assault rifles look bored and wave him through. He sighs with relief. Maybe next time he will try a $30,000 convoy.

What the client is guessing at is what economists would call the *defection constraint*, the largest-value convoy that can be driven down the route without triggering defection and theft by members. Convoys with values below that constraint will always pass safely, because the guards' payoff from stealing is less than their benefit from remaining loyal (including their value of feeling loyal, combined with how much they care about being able to revisit friends and family). Convoys more valuable than the defection constraint will be stolen.

Now let's return to that negotiation in Quetta, before the convoy left Pakistan. If the client thinks that the defection constraint is very low, say a $1,000 convoy value, he will be willing to pay only a small toll to the Taliban to protect it, maybe $700. For $700 per convoy the Taliban may decide that conquering the trade route and protecting it is not worth the trouble. Only organizations with high defection constraints can aspire to profit from controlling trade routes.

To summarize, this story of the pair of Taliban guards illustrates two important points. First, securing trade routes in lawless places like Afghanistan is particularly sensitive to defection, since no contract with subordinates can be enforced through the legal system. Loyalty is critical, and is threatened by low defection constraints. Second, only an organization that can convince potential clients that its own members will remain loyal when the temptation to defect is high will be able to succeed at the business of controlling trade routes for profit. If not it shouldn't bother conquering those routes, because it won't be able to charge high enough tolls to justify the investment in conquest.

So far I've offered an explanation for why the existing warlords and militias in Afghanistan didn't manage to profit by securing and monopolizing trade routes. It requires a lot of loyalty among the guards to prevent them from defecting. I haven't explained how any organization might solve the defection problem. Let's look at some other examples of defection constraints first, before thinking through a solution.

Coordinated Assault

Another militia activity the Taliban had to master in conquering Afghanistan was the coordinated assault. For a group of inexperienced soldiers, they proved surprisingly successful at this essential component of ground warfare. The principle is simple and ancient. Soldiers (or units) attack the target by alternating between advancing and shooting cover fire. For instance, unit 1 might advance toward the top of a hill while the other units shoot at the defenders to distract them, drawing fire away from unit 1. Once unit 1 finds something solid to hide behind, it takes cover and starts shooting while another unit advances. The units continue this way, alternating between advance and fire as they progress up the hill. Eventually one of them gets close enough for the final assault, at which point they consolidate their forces and capture the hill from any remaining defenders.

As with the trade routes, this activity is extremely sensitive to defection. If a unit providing cover fire takes a break, it leaves the advancing unit exposed to fire from the target, causing the assault to fail.

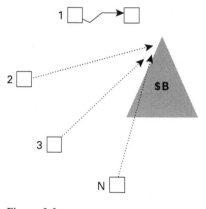

Figure 2.3
Capturing a hill

Why would a unit stop firing? Perhaps a cousin defending the hill called and offered a bribe. How big could that bribe be? As the advancing unit closed in on the top of the hill, the bribe to defect might approach whatever the defender had to offer, which would be the value of the hill to the defender (assuming that they could always surrender or flee—the bribe would be even greater if the defender wanted to avoid capture or punishment). This type of incentivized defection by allied units was not uncommon among Afghan fighters.[9]

Would a unit defect? It would depend on the size of the bribe, which would be approximately the value of the hill. A calculation will help illustrate the incentives of potential defectors. If the hill were worth $900 (it allows control of a minor road), then a single unit could extract a $900 payment from the defender in return for not firing. Should they remain loyal, they would have to split the value of the hill with all the other units. If there are three attacking units, a loyal unit would get $300 while a defecting unit would get $900. As in the trade route example, the $600 difference would have to be weighed against the penalty for defection, the shame of cheating your allies, and possible retribution against you and your family. So perhaps a $900 hill does not justify defection.

What if the hill were worth $90,000 (since it commands a major road)? In that case the same calculation leads the potential defectors to weigh a $60,000 (= $90,000 − $30,000) net payment against shame and possible retribution. Before attacking that hill a commander would be wise to look into the eyes of his allies and try to figure out how loyal they might be. He may have overreached his defection constraint, which in this case is measured in the value of hills. The more valuable the hill, the bigger the potential bribe to defectors and the bigger the gap between that bribe and the monetary value of remaining loyal—the gap that beckons to potential defectors.

In short, even though the potential profits from capturing hills and charging tolls to protect trade routes are potentially quite high, not just any organization is capable of capturing the profit opportunity. Profits come with an organizational curse, the *incentive to defect*, in an environment like Afghanistan where the legal system cannot enforce a promise by cadres to remain loyal. The higher the profits or the more valuable the hills, the harder it is to keep militia members from defecting, either by stealing the goods or by not covering the backs of their comrades in return for some bribe. The defection constraint limits the size of the project an organization can take on without triggering defection by members. It is calculated as the value of a project (hill, convoy) that, if offered as a bribe to a group of members, would cause them to defect. As long as an organization sticks to projects whose value does not exceed the defection constraint, it can thrive. Projects that exceed the defection constraint will bring on organizational failure: uncaptured hills, missing convoys, or worse—if the force defending the hill doesn't treat failed attackers gently.

This defection constraint should make it easier to understand why a country with rough terrain and valuable roads is so hard to conquer and hold. Yet the Taliban did just that, conquering Afghanistan and holding it from 1998 through 2001. How did the Taliban manage to relax the defection constraint when other mujahideen and warlords did not? That answer will have to wait until we know how religious radicals prevent defection in their benign activities. Before we get there, though, it's worth examining the insights defection constraints give us into the vulnerabilities of terrorists.

Terrorism and Defection—Hamas

The Taliban are not the only radical Islamist organization that has quickly outperformed rival, more experienced militants when it comes to coordinated violence. The Muslim Brotherhood in Palestine was a nonviolent group of clerics and community workers dedicated to an agenda of personal piety and local Islamist government until 1988. Then the Brotherhood created Hamas, and embarked on a violent nationalist struggle. At the time they had little or no experience at violence or terrorism, yet within months of that fateful decision they became the most potent rebels in the Israel-Palestine conflict. As we saw in the introduction, they carried out more attacks and caused more casualties per attack than their secular rival, Fatah (then led by Yasir Arafat) or than the more experienced Islamic Jihad.

To understand Hamas requires reviewing the origins of the Palestinian Muslim Brotherhood. Branches of the Egyptian Muslim Brotherhood, the first modern radical Islamists, began to appear in Palestine in the

1950s, when Gaza was governed by Egypt and the West Bank by Jordan. In 1971 Sheikh Ahmed Yassin founded an affiliated organization called Congress (*Mujamah*) in Gaza. Muslims in the West Bank and Gaza were relatively secular at the time, but Sheikh Yassin soon gained popular support for his movement by establishing a social service provision network including medical clinics, schools, charities, support for orphans, drug treatment centers, youth clubs, sports clubs, and mosques.[10] The "Congress" filled gaps in the limited safety net of social services provided by the occupying Israeli government, other Islamic charities, and international organizations, concentrating especially on supporting refugees. Yassin's organization drew its revenue from tithing (*zakat*) and from the support of Arabs abroad.[11]

Yassin's Congress shared the agenda of Hasan al-Banna, who had founded the Muslim Brotherhood in Egypt a generation earlier, in 1928. Their goals were personal ethical conduct, personal piety, and the eventual establishment of a local Islamic government. In contrast to their secular rival, Fatah (the dominant party within the Palestine Liberation Organization or PLO), the Brotherhood saw the liberation of Palestine as a long-term goal to be deferred until ethical conduct was widespread and local Islamic government was established. The Brotherhood was nonviolent, except for some skirmishes with Fatah supporters, which only increased their appeal to the Israeli authorities. They contributed to an increase in religious practice in the 1980s in the West Bank and Gaza: dress codes were more stringently observed and outward signs of piety increased, including the frequency of prayer. The increased stringency of practice was especially evident in Gaza, which is poorer, and where the Brotherhood has for many years had more support and stronger institutions.

Hamas was founded in 1987, as a result of the first Palestinian Intifada, a spontaneous revolt against Israeli occupation, led by neither Fatah nor the Brotherhood.[12] Angry demonstrations had broken out over a traffic accident. A truck driven by an Israeli in Gaza collided with a passenger car, killing four Palestinians. An angry crowd gathered and became violent, throwing stones at Israeli soldiers sent to restore order. The soldiers were hopelessly outnumbered. When they beat a retreat the demonstrators realized the power in their numbers, and stone-throwing demonstrations began to spread throughout Gaza, and then to the West Bank. Fatah harnessed the outburst of nationalism, gaining popular support among a new generation of local organizers. It was a shot in the arm for an organization whose leadership was in exile in Tunisia, after their ouster from Lebanon in 1982. Sheikh Yassin's local organizers in the Brotherhood urged him to endorse the revolt and start fighting, lest they lose popular support to the local leadership of Fatah. Yassin initially resisted, not wanting to endanger his carefully built network of mosques and charitable agencies. Yet he eventually agreed to establish an affiliated secret militia, Hamas, in late 1987, separating it from the Congress to protect the Brotherhood's social service institutions from reprisal.[13]

Hamas immediately began printing leaflets calling for violent opposition to the Israeli occupation. It underwent an ideological shift, adopting a nationalist position more extreme than that of Fatah, making the immediate conquest of all of Palestine (as opposed to just the West Bank and Gaza) a religious obligation. This was an expensive change in ideology. By taking a nationalist stand and leading violent demonstrations, Hamas provoked a campaign of arrest and suppression by the Israeli military, putting members at high risk of arrest. That ideological shift also provoked conflict with Fatah, and would eventually put Hamas members at risk of arrest once Fatah gained control of the police in Palestine following the Oslo peace accords of 1993.

Hamas soon became a singularly effective militia: hard to penetrate, disciplined, adequately funded, well trained, and committed. Members regularly risked arrest and endangered their lives by confronting soldiers, assassinating collaborators, and organizing and executing terrorist attacks. Their violence produced results. Hamas suicide bombings of buses in Israel in 1996 tipped a close Israeli election to the right-wing Likud party, crippling the Oslo peace process that might have delivered a secular Palestinian state to their Fatah rivals.

Hamas has proved effective at other forms of coordinated activity besides terrorism. They show discipline, managing to keep operatives quiet during truces. They conducted a well-organized campaign in the Palestinian elections of January 2006, surprising the more experienced Fatah to win a majority in the legislative council, partially by uniting behind a single candidate rather than allowing members to run against each other—as Fatah did. In June 2007, Hamas scored an impressive military victory over Fatah's Palestinian security forces, capturing Gaza in just three days. The Fatah-dominated security forces numbered in the tens of thousands, were trained and well equipped, yet they quickly folded in the face of Hamas assaults on their well-fortified positions.[14] The conquest of Gaza in 2007 may have been a political mistake—it forced Hamas to test their governing abilities in a narrow, besieged, overcrowded, and underresourced strip of land, while liberating the Fatah-run West Bank to receive donor aid held back by Hamas's participation in the elected government. (Hamas's rejection of Israel's right to exist and its refusal to renounce terrorism have disqualified it from receiving Western aid.) Political mistake or not, the rapid defeat of Fatah clearly demonstrated Hamas's military effectiveness. Hamas has subsequently translated a military defeat into a political victory following Israel's incursion into Gaza in December 2008, in response to rocket attacks from Gaza into southern Israel. It emerged with Gaza in ruins, but well positioned to negotiate a partnership with the secular Fatah in governing Palestine if it so chooses.

Against that background, consider the painful topic of suicide terrorism, but from the perpetrator's point of view. Hamas terrorists are subject to a defection constraint similar to that described above for the Taliban. Recall that in the introduction we saw that a lone terrorist is an anomaly. A group is almost always involved. Consider how a conspiracy might start. Operative 1 contacts operative 2, reporting that he has recruited a suicide attacker and asking him to bring the munitions. (Following the discussion in the introduction, assume that a motivated suicide attacker is available and will not defect.) Other operatives might be in charge of training, videotaping the attack, and reconnaissance of the target.

Operative 2 now has a decision to make. He could remain loyal and do his job as asked, in which case the attack may well succeed, perhaps at a horrendous cost in human life. Or, operative 2 could make a phone call to whoever is charged with protecting the targeted victims and offer information, perhaps to the Israeli security services, or in other settings to Iraqi intelligence or the CIA. If so, the attack will certainly fail. Operative 2 will collect a hefty payment from his grateful handler. Operative 1 and the other conspirators will be rounded up and arrested, or perhaps killed.

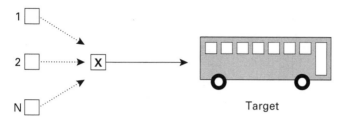

Conspirators

Figure 2.4
Terrorist attack

How large might the reward be for a defecting terrorist? We know from the media that governments of wealthy countries are willing to pay millions of dollars for information that leads to the capture of terrorists. That would be money well spent if it saved the lives of a bus full of schoolchildren, an airplane full of passengers, or a military patrol. So operative 2 can expect to be generously rewarded for his information, and the more valuable the target is to the victims, the greater the reward for snitching.

Imagine operative 2 as he considers his options. If he defects, picking up the phone and delivering information about the attack to the victims' government, he will receive a reward. On the other hand, if discovered, he faces execution for collaboration. Even if he avoids discovery, he could be forced to resettle in a location that is safe but far from friends and family. On top of that might be the shame of having betrayed the cause and sold out his comrades, and the pain of whatever retribution the other conspirators will carry out on his family. Alternatively, if he remains loyal he gets his share of the glory for successfully attacking the enemy, and perhaps promotion within the organization.

A key element of the potential defectors' calculation must be that the gain from a successful operation (the glory) is split with the other operatives, perhaps five or six of them. The gains from defection, on the other hand, go entirely to the informant, without sharing them with the other operatives. This calculation of costs and benefits should begin to sound familiar. It is analogous to the calculation that a potential defector would make in the context of trade routes or coordinated assaults. As the value of the project—in this case the target—increases, so does the reward for snitching, and with it the gap between the entire reward and his portion of the glory. If the targets of that terrorism are civilian citizens of a wealthy democracy, their intelligence services will pay handsomely for information that will avert an attack. To be sure, the gains from a successful operation also increase with the value of the target as well, yet the gains from defection increase faster because the defector's reward is not shared with the other conspirators. Therefore, the higher the value of the target, the more attractive is defection.

Does defection actually occur? Israeli intelligence does not provide details publicly but does report alerts daily on regions of the country at risk of attack, sometimes even describing the predicted method (a suicide attacker on the way to the coastal town of Netanya, for instance). In the latter stages of the second Intifada, from 2005 on, about nine-tenths of planned attacks were thwarted, according to Israeli media sources. Intelligence does leak out of terrorist organizations, and some of it is quite useful.

Knowing that leaks and defection are possible, what would operative 1 be thinking about when he contacts operative 2? He should be nervously calculating how valuable a target he can attempt to attack without risking defection by operative 2, or the others. Has he remained within the range safely allowed by the defection constraint, or is he inviting defection by other operatives? There is more to lose here than a convoy or a hill, since defection will almost certainly invite apprehension, or worse, by whoever is in charge of counterterrorism. With the defection constraint in mind, the quick ascendancy of Hamas to the status of the deadliest terrorist organization in the Israel-Palestine conflict is really quite remarkable. With no particular experience in coordinated violence, they managed to recruit operatives loyal enough to carry out high-value attacks successfully and all this shortly after launching their violent organization. How did they know that they could trust their operatives? Recall from the introduction that the answer does not seem to be religious fervor.[15] To understand trust and vulnerability to defection, it helps to consider a negative example: a terrorist organization that failed.

The Jewish Underground—Terrorists Who Overreached

What happens to terrorists who attempt projects beyond the limit implied by the defection constraint? The answer is illustrated by the Jewish Underground, a violent militia that operated on the West Bank in the 1980s. Their story is well documented by one of their own. Haggai Segal, a member, wrote a book about the Underground while in prison.[16] They recruited from the ranks of Gush Emunim, a messianic religious movement of Orthodox (though not ultra-Orthodox) Jews, which established settlements in the West Bank and Gaza beginning in the mid 1970s. Members of Gush Emunim believe that by settling the Holy Land they hasten a messianic redemption of the Jewish people.

Members of the Jewish Underground were military veterans and had some experience with civil violence as vigilantes. A survey conducted by David Weisburd in the early 1980s revealed that about a third of males in Gush Emunim settlements took part in some form of vigilante activity, which included threats, destruction of property, detention, and sometimes shooting.[17] Most Gush Emunim settlers approved of aggressive, though nonlethal, vigilante activities against the local Palestinian Arab population, as a means of reducing stoning of their vehicles and other attacks. The settlers considered vigilante activity legitimate, since in their view the government had failed to provide adequate protection for their settlements against attacks by Palestinians. Opponents of the settlers saw these actions as an attempt to provoke local Arabs and to pressure the Israeli military into suppressing the Palestinian stone throwers. Nevertheless, Gush Emunim settlers clearly felt that vigilante militias provided a valuable public service by enhancing their personal safety. With a high level of tacit support among the settlers, Israeli investigators could seldom successfully prosecute vigilante crime, largely because they were unable to find witnesses who would offer incriminating evidence.[18]

In the aftermath of Anwar Sadat's visit to Jerusalem in November 1977, Gush Emunim settlers were deeply troubled about the future. The prospect of Israel surrendering control of the West Bank and Gaza as part of a peace treaty threatened their messianic aspirations. In desperation, about a dozen settlers organized a conspiracy in 1978 to carry out an incredible plot to detonate explosives in the Muslim holy sites on the

Temple Mount in Jerusalem, the *Haram al-Sharif*. The Temple Mount is considered the third holiest religious site in Islam. According to tradition, the prophet Mohammad ascended to heaven on a horse from the Mount, leaving a hoof print in the stone. The distressed conspirators believed that their attack on the Muslim holy sites would trigger redemption, or at least halt the peace process, by either clearing the way for a Jewish temple to be built on the site of the ancient temple, or perhaps by triggering an Armageddon-like conflict with Islam, which would force messianic intervention. Though the conspirators made careful operational plans, they could not find a rabbi who would approve their project; all denominations of Judaism forbid acts meant to blackmail the Almighty into dispatching the Messiah. The conspirators abandoned their extreme plot by 1982, for lack of authorization.

The conspirators found themselves a different cause. Following the murder by the Palestinian Fatah of six yeshiva (Jewish seminary) students in Hebron in 1980, leaders of the Jewish settlement in Hebron sought individuals "of deep commitment and dedication" to carry out a reprisal, and turned to Menachem Livni, a leader of the Temple Mount conspiracy.[19] The Jewish Underground planted explosives around the vehicles of three Palestinian mayors, maiming two (Bassam Shaka'a and Karim Khalef) and blinding an Israeli demolitions expert sent to dismantle their explosive device. They also planted bombs in a mosque and at a local soccer field. Subsequently, to avenge the murder of a yeshiva student by Palestinians, the Jewish Underground murdered three civilian students in the Islamic College in Hebron in 1983.

The Islamic College killings were their first and last. The Israeli General Security Service (GSS) had already obtained the identities of conspirators from a settler who the Underground had attempted to recruit. Unfortunately for Livni and the other operatives, sometime after the settler rebuffed them he applied to work at the GSS! In his entrance interview, according to the GSS telling of the story, the settler's answer to a standard question about connection to dangerous groups set off a jump in the polygraph needle. The settler was then tricked into revealing information about the conspiracy through a clever ruse. The interrogators downplayed the polygraph result, but asked him to write down on a piece of paper, which he could keep, the information that was triggering the polygraph needle. Then, they told him, they could get on with his interview. He kept the paper, and after leaving the office tore it into pieces and threw the pieces in the trash. The GSS interrogators confronted the settler with his torn pieces of paper the next day, all taped together. Based on this information the GSS applied surveillance to members of the Underground (and perhaps also used an informant). One night in 1984 in East Jerusalem, they caught the conspirators red-handed, planting bombs on four Arab buses, which were to be carrying civilians the next day. The Underground did not survive the subsequent interrogation, either because the arrested conspirators squealed, or because the original informant was a rich source of information. The subsequent sweep rounded up essentially the entire membership, resulting in twenty-eight convictions involving several terrorist plots.

Like the Viet Cong in Sam Popkin's interviews, the Jewish Underground was tremendously vulnerable to leaks. It was an organization that overreached its grasp, attempting a high-value attack that exceeded the defection constraint of the settler they attempted to recruit. Targeting civilian Palestinians was too destructive an act for their constituency to support, which set the stage for an informant to defect. Their recruiting base, the settler population, was generally supportive of vigilante violence, but it balked at murdering innocent civilians. Settlers could be induced to report (or be tricked into reporting) those activities to the authorities. The episode led to a split in the leadership of Gush Emunim, with the mainstream denouncing and repudiating the Underground. Even among settlers the Underground fiasco contributed to the political marginalization of Gush Emunim.

The demise of the Jewish Underground was not caused by a lack of ideological commitment, extensive training, or access to munitions. Gush Emunim's ideology dictates that surrendering any part of the Holy Land constitutes a theological catastrophe, which they must avoid at all costs. Nor did they fail for lack of *individuals* in their settler constituency who had a theologically motivated inclination toward violence. Acting alone, Baruch Goldstein massacred twenty-nine civilians at prayer in 1994. Yigal Amir, apparently in conspiracy with only his brother, assassinated Israeli Prime Minister Yitzhak Rabin in 1995. They did not lack training or access to weapons and munitions, being veterans of the Israeli military and most likely of settler vigilante groups. The Underground failed because they could not consistently induce loyalty among members and potential members privy to their secrets. Projects with high stakes, such as the September 11 attacks, the Temple Mount assault, or securing trade routes in Afghanistan, apparently require not only motivated individuals but also the coordinated actions of a militia, in which members are convinced that their comrades will not defect.

The fate of the Jewish Underground is not unusual. The failed plot mentioned in the introduction, in which an informant in Toronto frustrated the truck bombers, is common. It is echoed in other terrorist failures, such as the conspiracies to attack Kennedy Airport in New York and Fort Dix in New Jersey in 2007.

The Fort Dix terrorists were amateurs, but even established terrorist organizations are extremely vulnerable to leaks. In 1999, an alert U.S. Customs agent in Port Angeles, Washington, stopped a suspicious-looking Chevrolet driving off the ferry from British Columbia. The agent captured Ahmed Ressam, with a load of explosives. Ressam was en route to Los Angeles to plant a "millennium" bomb at the Los Angeles airport. According to court documents, Ressam subsequently provided information that incriminated 100 suspected terrorists and that led to the shutdown of several Al Qaeda cells. Ressam's defense lawyers claim that he saved the lives of FBI agents by tipping them off to the possibility that Al Qaeda operative Robert Reid's sneakers had a well-concealed explosive in them.[20] In 1996, Sudanese Al Qaeda operative Jamal Ahmed al-Fadl walked into the U.S. Embassy in Eritrea, offering information about his work for Osama bin Laden in Afghanistan and Sudan. Al-Fadl subsequently became the single best source of information on the inner workings of Al Qaeda, leading to the conviction of four Al Qaeda members involved in the 1998 bombings of U.S. embassies in Kenya and Tanzania, which claimed 224 lives. As it turned out, interrogators eventually learned that al-Fadl's defection was due to an earlier disloyalty: he had stolen a six-figure sum from Al Qaeda and was afraid of the consequences.[21] A single midlevel Al Qaeda operative in American custody in Iraq, in June 2006, began leaking information about the staff of Abu Musab al-Zarqawi, the commander of Al Qaeda in Iraq. Soon Al Qaeda members were being captured or killed. The defector's tips eventually identified an operative, who was tailed by a drone as he drove to a safe house north of Baghdad. Shortly after the car pulled up, the U.S. Air Force dropped two 500-pound bombs on the building, killing the other occupants instantly and mortally wounding Zarqawi.[22]

Some terrorist organizations initially manage to carry out attacks successfully, but seem to eventually face a defection constraint once intelligence services start monitoring carefully. This may be why the wave of urban terrorist organizations of the 1960s and 1970s eventually receded in the face of counterterrorism efforts. The FLQ, Red Brigades, and Baader-Meinhoff could not sustain active cells that were not eventually compromised. This should not be surprising. Considering what's at stake, once intelligence services launch active surveillance and begin paying for information, the incentives to defect create internal pressures that are too great for all but the tightest organizations.

Yet the landscape of terrorism in the early twentieth century is more challenging. It contains a number of resilient terrorist organizations that pose an ongoing threat. Like Hamas and the Taliban, Hezbollah and Al Qaeda have managed to consistently attack targets in their own countries and abroad.

Hezbollah and Suicide Attacks

The modern, high-casualty suicide attack, which has changed our lives irreversibly, was invented by Hezbollah in Lebanon in 1982. The very year Hezbollah was founded it became the most lethal terrorist organization in Lebanon. The first major attack came quickly, in November. A suicide attacker drove a vehicle full of explosives into the local Israeli military headquarters in the Lebanese coastal town of Tyre. The explosion demolished the building, killing ninety Israeli soldiers and a number of Lebanese and Palestinian prisoners. Though Fatah had been active in Lebanon since 1971, and Abu Nidal since 1981, neither had ever managed to spill so much blood in a single incident.

Hezbollah did not take responsibility for the attacks that followed, though the method was similar and most commentators hold them responsible. The first of these was a suicide attack on the U.S. Embassy in Beirut in April 1983, which killed 60 people. The most painful were twin attacks in Beirut in October 1983, one on the U.S. Marine barracks and the second on the barracks of French peacekeepers. The first attack killed 241 people; the second killed 59. Both suicide attackers used the same method: a vehicle full of explosives driven into the building, an extremely difficult tactic to defend against. Suddenly American and allied forces were vulnerable, despite their motivation, training, technological dominance, and immense resources. The balance of power had shifted in favor of a small, dedicated organization using a very low technology weapon—a suicide bomber driving a truck packed full of explosives.[23]

How did that threat emerge? In 1982, Ayatollah Khomeini, the leader of the Iranian revolution, dispatched a delegation of Iranian Revolutionary Guards to Lebanon to train and equip Hezbollah, a nascent terrorist organization. Their trip was preceded by two significant events that foreshadowed future alliances. Khomeini had personally approved a manifesto that established Hezbollah as a Shiite political Islamist organization whose goals included resisting the recent Israeli invasion. Syrian President Hafez Assad had also agreed to let Iran establish a proxy militia in Lebanon, a Syrian area of control.[24]

The young Hezbollah trainees shared a common background with the Iranian Revolutionary Guards, because Hezbollah's leadership was composed almost entirely of clerics in their thirties who had studied in the Shiite holy cities of Najaf in Iraq and Qom in Iran.[25] The Iranian trainers were probably not strangers to Lebanon either. Revolutionary Guards trained in the Bekaa valley with the Lebanese Shiite Amal militia before helping Khomeini take charge of the Iranian revolution and take the American embassy staff hostage in Tehran in 1979.

Yet Hezbollah is not just an Iranian proxy. It has roots in earlier, homegrown Islamist militias and charities. Sheikh Naim Qassem, a founder and currently Deputy Secretary of Hezbollah, lists three primary sources of early leadership.[26] The first two are Ayatollah Shamseddine, who chaired the Cultural and Charity Association in the southern suburbs of Beirut, and Ayatollah Fadlallah, who founded the Association of Philanthropic Organizations, also in southern Beirut. Their charities included mosques, schools, clinics, orphanages, youth clubs, and the Islamic Institution of the Arts. The third and most significant source of

Hezbollah leadership is the Imam Mussa al-Sadr. He established the Charity and Philanthropy Association in the 1960s in Tyre and later the Movement of the Oppressed, which had the stated aim of alleviating poverty among Shiites in southern Lebanon, the Bekaa valley to the east of Beirut, and the squalid suburbs that were then spreading around Beirut. In 1974 al-Sadr founded the Shiite militia/political party, Amal. He headed Amal for four years, until he made the mistake of accepting an invitation to visit Muammar al-Qaddafi in Libya, where he disappeared forever in September 1978, reportedly assassinated. Al-Sadr's successor as Amal leader was the more secular Nabih Berri, a lawyer who enjoyed Libyan support. At this writing, three decades later, Berri continues to lead Amal and is currently speaker of the Lebanese Parliament, a position traditionally held by a Shiite in the Lebanese ethno-religious power-sharing arrangement. Berri made the mistake of briefly allying himself in 1982 with Bashir Gemayal, leader of a Maronite Christian faction that enjoyed Israeli support. The Ayatollah Khomeini reacted by sponsoring an alternative to Amal, a Shiite political-Islamist militia made up of the factions outside Amal, which banded together to form Hezbollah.

One of the early Hezbollah leaders was Hussein Moussawi, Berri's former deputy. Moussawi broke with Amal in 1982 in a dispute over an operation apparently conducted at the behest of the Iranians, the kidnapping of a priest in retaliation for the abduction of an Iranian representative in Lebanon. Moussawi's former seminary student in Najaf, Hassan Nassralah, left Amal to join Hezbollah the same year. Nassralah would later succeed Moussawi as the leader of Hezbollah, after his teacher was assassinated by an Israeli missile.

Understanding Hezbollah's ties to Iran requires a historical digression. The Lebanese Shiite community has a strong connection to the Shiite population centers in Iran and southern Iraq. The Shiite tradition within Islam split from the Sunni in the years following the death of the Prophet Mohammad in 632. Shiite Muslims believe that the designated successor as leader and interpreter of the Koran was Ali, the Prophet's son-in-law and cousin. Sunni Muslims disagree, believing that the legitimate successor was Abu Bakr, the Prophet's father-in-law, who became caliph of the young Islamic empire. In the power struggle that followed the Sunni stream prevailed. Ali was assassinated in 661 and eventually his sons Hasan and Husayn suffered the same fate. The Shiite retreated to southern Iraq and Iran, which they controlled by the tenth century.

The large Shiite population in Lebanon dates back to the tenth century when a Shiite dynasty, the Fatimids, gained control of Egypt, North Africa, and Syria. When the Mamluks—Sunni Muslims from Turkey—conquered Syria and Lebanon in the twelfth and thirteenth centuries, they expelled the Shiite population from the prosperous coastal cities and strategic mountains. Shiite refugees fled into the scenic but poor rural areas of southern Lebanon and the Bekaa valley. The Ottoman Empire, which succeeded the Mamluks in the fourteenth century, was Sunni, and was often suspicious of Shiite ties with Iran. The Ottomans discriminated against the Lebanese Shiites in favor of Sunni Muslims and even in favor of Christians and Druze. The National Pact, which established Lebanon's current political structure in 1943, favored the two largest groups, Maronite Christians and Sunni Muslims. Shiites were relegated to the least influential positions in government. Government service provision to Shiite areas of the country has been a low priority both before and since. That, and economic pressure, has prompted Lebanese Shiites to migrate from the rural south to the overcrowded southern suburbs of Beirut.

When Khomeini's financial and military support began flowing to Hezbollah in 1982, he invigorated the connection of Lebanese Shiites to Iran and Iraq, a connection nurtured by a flow of religious scholars between Lebanon and the Shiite holy cities over the centuries. With Iranian sponsorship, reported to total $100 million annually, Hezbollah established a viable militia and began providing social services in the Shiite areas of Lebanon. It challenged Amal's control, first in the border areas and the Bekaa, and eventually in the southern suburbs of Beirut, which they seized in 1989 after a violent struggle with Amal that included the use of heavy weapons.[27] Visible signs of religiosity increased. Women adopted Islamist customs of modest dress. The sale of alcohol was banned.[28]

Hezbollah became the deadliest terrorists in the Middle East with remarkable speed. The horrendous suicide attacks of 1982 and 1983 have been described already. Hezbollah mastered other tactics as well. Swedish terrorism expert Magnus Ranstorp concludes that Hezbollah was responsible for several other actions against Western targets in Beirut in the 1980s (for which they did not claim responsibility). Those include the abduction of Terry Waite, the representative of the Archbishop of Canterbury; the disappearance of David Dodge, acting president of the American University in Beirut; the assassination of William Buckley, Beirut CIA chief; and the torture and murder of Marine Lieutenant Colonel William Higgins. Hezbollah's role in the hijacking of TWA flight 847 and the murder of a U.S. Navy diver on board was established by the indictment of three Hezbollah terrorists in the case by an American court.

Hezbollah claimed responsibility for suicide attacks from October 1983 onward, including a subsequent suicide car bomb attack on an Israeli command post in Tyre, which killed twenty-eight Israeli soldiers and thirty-two Lebanese prisoners. They used suicide attacks effectively against Israeli armored convoys. Hezbollah has also used kidnapping, roadside bombs, frontal attacks, ambushes, and rocket attacks to conduct guerilla warfare and urban terrorism against its enemies. Their targets have mostly been Israeli forces and members of rival Lebanese militias, but have also included UN peacekeepers, foreign diplomats, and foreign journalists. The Memorial Institute for the Prevention of Terrorism records 179 Hezbollah attacks through June 2007 in Lebanon, accounting for 836 fatalities.

Hezbollah has also demonstrated an ability to operate beyond Lebanon. Argentine prosecutors have accused Hezbollah of carrying out, with Iranian assistance, the 1994 destruction of a Jewish cultural center in Buenos Aires, which claimed eighty-five civilian lives.[29] The U.S. State Department believes that Hezbollah is responsible for that attack and an attack two years earlier on the Israeli Embassy in Argentina, which killed twenty-nine civilians.

Hezbollah's violence has furthered several of the organization's objectives: President Reagan's withdrawal of American peacekeeping forces from Lebanon; Hezbollah control over the Baalbek region and the Shiite suburbs of southern Beirut; the collapse of the Southern Lebanese Army; and the subsequent withdrawal of Israeli forces from southern Lebanon in 2000. In the summer of 2006, Hezbollah set off a small war by kidnapping three Israeli soldiers on the Israeli side of the Lebanese border. In the ensuing month of warfare it survived daily shelling and aerial assaults, managing daily rocket attacks on northern Israel that severely disrupted the lives of half a million civilians. Hezbollah continues to threaten to topple the Lebanese government, with the support of Syrian and Iranian interests.

In the 1980s and 1990s so many militias and terrorist organizations seemed to act with impunity in Lebanon that one might wonder if defection was really a threat to Hezbollah. Perhaps there was no opponent with the resources and the willingness to bribe their members into defection? Or perhaps no opponent was capable of acting on the information that defectors revealed? Yet Naim Qassem, Deputy Secretary General of Hezbollah, in his insider's history of the organization, writes that Hezbollah was extremely sensitive to leaks and defection:

Secrecy was the key to success on the *jihad* battlefield. Surprising the enemy achieved the best results with the fewest possible losses. The enemy worked through spies and agents to uncover targets and operations. . . . As such, secrecy was important for rendering such surveillance and investigation futile. A limited circle of individuals was aware of resistance operations. Only those directly involved with planning and execution . . . formed part of this circle. Taken together, these are the reasons behind the enemy's inability to discover any operation before its execution or during its preparation.[30]

In Qassem's telling, secrecy creates a need for careful recruitment:

The individual's personality is the core of resistance configuration. For this reason, the applicant's file is studied in depth prior to granting approval for membership in the Resistance. Under focus is the individual's belief in Hizbullah, his preparedness for further developing this belief, his cultural and military capabilities, and the non-existence of any security of questionable doubts around him. The individual is closely followed up and appraised throughout his functional training and development in order to determine the benefit that he could bring to the Party.[31]

Qassem's internal evaluation of Hezbollah's track record at recruiting loyal operatives might exaggerate their success, yet his pride in the loyalty of members is worth paying attention to: "No field desertion has ever been recorded in resistance ranks, and no objection to the battle's extension was voiced."[32]

According to Qassem, Hezbollah became the most effective terrorist organization in Lebanon, carrying out massively destructive operations without ever violating the defection constraint.

The Mahdi Army in Iraq

Muqtada al-Sadr's militia in Baghdad, the so-called Mahdi Army, provides an additional example of an Islamist militia suddenly emerging from a civilian social-religious organization with remarkable tactical ability, like Hamas and Hezbollah. Al-Sadr's emergence created a serious obstacle to the post-invasion stabilization of Iraq, both militarily and politically.

Al-Sadr's family has strong credentials among Shiite Iraqis. His father's cousin, Mohammed Baqer al-Sadr was an important Shiite cleric in Najaf, a radical Islamist in the tradition of Hasan al-Banna in Egypt, and the Ayatollah Khomeini in Iran. He argued for a politically active clergy, in contrast to the conservative Shiite tradition of self-imposed separation of mosque and state. Following the successful revolution by like-minded Islamists across the border in Iran, Saddam Hussein felt threatened domestically. He launched a brutal campaign, killing or expelling Shiite leaders and Iranians in Iraq. He had Baqer al-Sadr assassinated. Twelve years later, following Saddam's defeat in the first Gulf War and the suppression of a Shiite uprising, Saddam Hussein was looking for an accommodating Shiite cleric he could deal with. Hussein chose the relatively unknown Mohammad Sadeq al-Sadr, a cousin and former student of Baqer al-Sadr's. With the benefit of state support, Sadeq al-Sadr gained control of Shiite schools, social work network, and courts.[33] He used his position to expand the welfare provision network in the poor Shiite neighborhoods of Baghdad and Najaf during the 1990s. Yet al-Sadr overstepped the boundaries of authority that Saddam had circumscribed for him, calling for political involvement of the clergy, claiming political and religious authority himself, and even calling on Saddam Hussein to repent. In 1999 gunmen ambushed Sadeq al-Sadr and his two oldest sons as they drove through Najaf, killing all three. The assassination was presumably carried out on Saddam's orders.

Sadeq's younger son, Muqtada al-Sadr, was left to inherit the network of charities.[34]

Despite his lineage, Muqtada al-Sadr is an unlikely religious leader. Middle East expert Vali Nasr reports that Muqtada never completed his seminary education, earning instead the nickname "Mullah Atari," since rather than study he preferred Atari video games.[35] Yet after the conquest of Baghdad by coalition forces in 2003, Muqtada al-Sadr built out of his father's network a surprisingly effective militia. He named it the Mahdi Army, an allusion to the messianic twelfth Imam. Sadrists quickly took control of mosques, schools, welfare centers, and hospitals in areas where Mohammad Sadeq al-Sadr had established his network. Those included parts of southern Iraq, but mostly the poorest Shiite neighborhoods of Baghdad and Najaf, most notably the former Saddam City, renamed Sadr City, after his father. In areas under his control, al-Sadr's militia provided law and order and attempted to impose Islamic law. His newspaper published the names of reputed collaborators, inviting violence against them. The murder of moderate Shiite religious leader Ayatollah Majid al-Khoei, outside the holy shrine of Imam Ali in Najaf in April 2003, is attributed to al-Sadr's men.[36] The Mahdi Army and its affiliates, the Divine Wrath Brigades and the Brigades for the Defense of the Holy Shrines, have been implicated in a number of bombings, kidnappings, and attacks on coalition and Iraqi forces.

In March 2004, Muqtada goaded coalition forces, attacking them in the south and calling the 9/11 attacks "a miracle and a blessing from God."[37] In the summer of 2004, al-Sadr broke a truce agreement, occupying a holy shrine in Najaf and triggering battles with U.S. Marines. Though that effort failed, by early 2005 al-Sadr had forced the Shiite political establishment, Shiite religious elites (such as Grand Ayatollah Ali al-Sistani), and coalition forces to negotiate an accommodation with him. Afterward he attempted to expand his range in southern Iraq, fighting over control of territory against the Badr Brigades, the militia of the more popular SCIRI (the Supreme Council for the Islamic Revolution in Iraq), a Shiite political party more closely aligned with Iran. Al-Sadr translated influence in neighborhoods into political power, effectively controlling a party with thirty-two seats in the Iraqi parliament, and positioning himself as the kingmaker in Shiite coalition politics. Through control over three government ministries, he provided patronage jobs to members and security contracts to his militia. The Mahdi Army has contested control of territory in much of southern Iraq, including even Basra, where his father's support was weak. Despite his organization's ongoing sectarian attacks and turf wars with other Shiite militias, Muqtada al-Sadr seemed to be generally immune to Iraqi government and coalition counterterrorism efforts.

Does the defection constraint help us understand al-Sadr's success? It is hard to know from published sources to what extent al-Sadr's forces are sensitive to defection. His prowess at evading capture during six months of active confrontation with coalition forces in 2004 suggests that his forces are fairly defection-proof. The coalition was motivated to find him, knew who his constituency was, and had plenty of resources to spend on the effort. The frustrated American administrator of Iraq at the time, Paul Bremer, in recalling the episode, described the Mahdi Army as "a small, *fanatically loyal* gang of armed followers."[38]

To recap, Hamas, the Taliban, al-Sadr's Mahdi Army, and Hezbollah share some surprising characteristics. They all share a history of social service provision. Considering their initial lack of military experience and training, they have all been remarkably effective at coordinated violence in general and terrorism in particular.[39] While Al Qaeda threatens the safety of citizens in the United States and the West, it does not threaten the stability of our governments. In contrast, these four organizations are a very real threat to governments allied with the West in Lebanon, Afghanistan, Iraq, and Palestine. Hamas has already taken control of part of Palestine, in Gaza, and threatens to control the rest. The Taliban is a resurgent threat in Afghanistan, carrying out attacks even in Kabul. The Pakistani Taliban forced the Pakistani government to sign a truce in February 2009, granting them effective sovereignty in the North-West Frontier Province, then advanced toward Islamabad in the spring.

So far I've argued that a necessary attribute of effective terrorist or rebel organizations is resistance to defection, which allows them to take on high-value targets without being compromised. That resistance to defection distinguishes these four organizations from failed terrorist organizations such as the Jewish Underground. What makes these groups resistant to defection? One obvious parallel between these groups is radical Islam. Yet we saw at the outset that theology was not the main motivating force for suicide attackers, even among Islamic radicals. So what *is* special about radical Islamic organizations that makes them such deadly effective terrorists, when they choose violence? To answer that question we need to understand how radical religious communities work, which is the subject of the next chapter.

Dress codes among religious radicals: (clockwise from top left) Amish men at an auction in Mt. Hope Ohio, 2004; Hassidic boys waiting to view Rabbi Moshe Teitelbaum's convoy, Jerusalem, 1994; Bangladeshi madrassa students in Dhaka, December 2005. (AP Photo Tony Dejak; Menahem Kahana/AFP/Getty Images; Farjana K. Godhuly/AFP/Getty Images).

3

Sects, Prohibitions, and Mutual Aid: The Organizational Secrets of Religious Radicals

It gives to all members of the same faith, i.e., to all believers in the Unity of God, a common bodily sign, so that it is impossible for any one that is a stranger, to say that he belongs to them. *For sometimes people say so for the purpose of obtaining some advantage....* It is also a fact that there is much *mutual love and assistance* among people that are united by the same sign when they consider it as [the symbol of] a covenant.

—Twelfth-century Philosopher Moses Maimonides explaining the Jewish custom of circumcision, in *The Guide for the Perplexed* (emphasis added)

Larry Iannaccone just wouldn't listen. According to rumor, years after he graduated from the elite University of Chicago economics program he was held out as an example of *how not to write a doctoral dissertation.* A polite young man, he wore slacks and button-down shirts and generally insisted on holding his ground in discussions. Yet what he was proposing was just too much for his dissertation advisors. He wanted to revive an ancient and forgotten academic field, the economics of religion.

To be sure, University of Chicago economists are hardly a bunch that shy away from controversial ideas. On the contrary, they embrace iconoclasts who insist that there's an economic approach to just about everything. Chicago economist Gary Becker won the scorn and ridicule of other social scientists early in his career by insisting that education is best thought of as an investment, rather than a noble intellectual and moral adventure, labeling it "human capital." By the time Iannaccone sat in Becker's lectures in the 1980s, though, human capital had gone mainstream. Becker was on his way to winning a Nobel Prize for introducing another initially controversial idea, the "demand for children," into mainstream demography. Becker's graduate students were busy in those days analyzing crime, immigration, marriage, and divorce, among other topics, as decisions that practical, rational individuals made in cost-benefit terms. Yet, when Iannaccone proposed applying those tools to *religion*, even Gary Becker hesitated.

Most people, even most economists, don't think that economics and religion mix well. Religion is at its core, after all, about spirituality and faith. Religions make bold statements that are inherently metaphysical, unverifiable, and irrefutable—about the immortality of the spirit, the existence of heaven, the goodness of man. Economics, on the other hand, is composed of much more mundane stuff: the demand for gasoline, how to invest your retirement savings, and why government should regulate banking. Furthermore, economics is an empirical science, drawing strength from its ability to refute or support those relatively mundane claims with data. What could economics possibly have to say about spirituality, faith, and irrefutable propositions?

Yet Adam Smith, the founder of modern economics, had disagreed. Smith saw religion as fair game for economic analysis. In his brilliant text, *The Wealth of Nations* (published in 1776), he wrote a half chapter on religion. Smith, himself a religious man, made the bold claim that the patterns of human behavior familiar to economists apply to clergy and religious institutions as well.[1] He argued that clergy are motivated by self-interest; that demand for religious services limits churches just as it limits secular firms; that competition among congregations and denominations improves the quality of the religious services they provide; and that monopolies and other symptoms of excessive government regulation harm our religious lives, by reducing the quality of spiritual services and promoting intolerance and violence between denominations. Smith sketched a theory of denominationalism (which he called sectarianism) to explain why groups of religious radicals arise and split off from mainstream denominations. Two of his contributions remain remarkably relevant today: a theory of religious violence and civility, and a general theory of denominations, church, and state.[2] Smith looked back at the Thirty Years' War, in which some 15 to 20 percent of Germans died, and saw a conflict over political power between competing groups of clergy aligned with mercenaries and princes—a description disturbingly familiar to observers of Iraq or Afghanistan today. Smith even offered a solution, based on economic logic—which I will return to when we explore new ideas for dealing with religious radicalism. The main point for now is this: Smith did not see his economic approach as a inconsistent with spirituality or faith. When clergy and members of religious communities wander away from the spiritual—sanctuaries, prayer, and faith—and into the practical—markets, organizations, and politics—Adam Smith was convinced that the usual rules of economics apply.

Iannaccone embraced Adam Smith's approach. His undergraduate degree was in mathematics, but as a doctoral student he had already decided that he wanted to study a field with a more human face. Like many students with strong mathematical training, he discovered that economics was surprisingly stimulating. George Stigler (already a Nobel laureate) and Gary Becker (the true founding fathers of Freakonomics) were applying the principles of economic reasoning to such interesting topics in human behavior. Why not apply the same principles to religion, and see what happens? Economic analysis was a tool he might use to understand a real and compelling part of people's lives, including those of his own family and friends.[3]

So he tried. Despite the concerns of his faculty advisors, Iannaccone wrote the first dissertation on the economics of religion that anyone at Chicago could remember.[4] One reason that he may have spotted a vein of intellectual gold that his advisors did not is that he probably knew a lot more about religion than they did. His paternal grandfather was Catholic, an immigrant from Italy. One day, not long after arriving in New York, the elder Iannaccone was invited to a Bible study class in a Protestant church. He accepted the invitation and remained, participating actively. His family and friends were horrified, but he was unfazed. It was not that he had abandoned the faith, or had experienced an epiphany about Martin Luther's teaching. The Protestants offered him something else of great value, which the church he grew up in had not. The Protestants were teaching him *to read* so that he could understand the Bible. Larry's grandfather embraced his new congregation and the family history gained a parable about the benefits of competition between churches—which Adam Smith might have enjoyed. His son became a minister, and his grandson Larry, a minister's son, absorbed a lot of insights about faith and the inner workings of religious communities growing up.

Iannaccone's professors at Chicago were right about one thing: the academic world was truly not ready for a groundbreaking young professor specializing in the economics of religion. His mentors struggled to get him job interviews at top universities. Eventually, Iannaccone managed to obtain a placement at Santa Clara University, a good teaching college with lovely Spanish arches and red tile roofs, just north of Silicon Valley. It was a good job but not as prestigious or as supportive of research as the positions offered to his peers at the top of the class in Chicago's world-class economics program. Still, he was happy to have an academic job where he could chip away at his personal research agenda, stubbornly applying economic thinking to vast, rich, literatures in theology and the sociology of religion. Economists regarded him with curiosity. Sociologists were alarmed. Yet with time and effort, he set about changing those views to respectful curiosity and respectful alarm.

While at Santa Clara Iannaccone took on a puzzle of human behavior that even Adam Smith and Gary Becker had never attempted: Why would anyone volunteer to join a group that required prohibitions and sacrifices?

Prohibitions and Sacrifices—the Benign Puzzles

Violent radical Islamists, such as the Taliban, Hamas, Hezbollah, and Muqtada al-Sadr's followers, practice a conservative, highly ritualistic form of Islam, which gathered a growing following over the twentieth century, beginning with the Muslim Brotherhood in Egypt and the Jamaat-e-Islami in British India. The vast majority of these radical Islamists are nonviolent, and not as exotic as one might think. If we ignore the theological differences and concentrate on observable, day-to-day behavior within communities, radical Islamists are actually quite similar to religious radicals among Christians and Jews. Religious radicals in all three of those religions share a common approach to mainstream culture: they fear it threatens their traditional values and dedicate themselves to an unrelenting effort to differentiate themselves from its insidious lifestyle.

The photographs that introduce this chapter illustrate similarities among religious radicals across religions. The boys in the top-right corner are ultra-Orthodox Jews in Jerusalem. They could be anywhere in the world, though, because ultra-Orthodox dress codes ignore practical considerations that vary across countries—such as heat and humidity—so that, for example, men are required to wear black suit jackets through both the Brooklyn winter and the hot Israeli summer. The men gathered in the upper left picture are Amish. These radical Christians also have strict rules of acceptable dress, which, like those of ultra-Orthodox Jews, include head coverings, prohibitions on shaving. Their dark suits recall the fashion of European nobles in the period when these denominations were founded. The lower picture is of radical Islamists in India. Among radical Muslims throughout the world modest appearance requires being almost completely covered—as it is among radical Christians and Jews. Like radical Christians and Jews, radical Islamists have a uniform dress code (within subdenominations), wear head coverings, and adhere to restrictions on shaving.

Outward appearance is important because it distinguishes members from the general public. Yet appearances only hint at the broad similarities that religious radicals share across religions in their lifestyle restrictions. Radical Muslims and radical Jews both observe strict dietary restrictions. Radical Muslims, Christians, and Jews strictly limit what one can do on the Sabbath. Sexual practices are restrictive in the type, timing, and gender of partners. Infidelities are severely punished. Beyond the restrictions common to radicals of all three of these religions, there are long lists of prohibited activities that some groups observe but others do not. Most have some sort of rules about shaving, generally prohibiting shaving beards. Krishna men shave their heads rather than not shaving their beards, while Amish men must have beards but not mustaches. Seventh Day Adventists eat no meat. Many Jehovah's Witnesses refuse vaccines, organ transplants, and blood transfusions, endangering their lives and those of their children. Amish prohibit the use of electricity and automobiles, not just on the Sabbath but always, and do not accept Social Security payments. They forbid wearing jewelry and even wristwatches, as do some Islamist seminaries. Like Muslims, Mormons prohibit alcohol consumption. The list could go on and on, yet the basic point should be clear: religious radicals prohibit numerous activities that most people find useful and pleasant, and therefore experience very different lifestyles than their mainstream coreligionists do.

Sociologist James Hurd of Bethel University studies Anabaptist communities in the United States. He describes the Hutterites, Amish, and Wenger Mennonites (often called "horse-and-buggy" Mennonites) like this:

> [They] all wear distinctive clothing and shun certain types of technology. Just as their forebears did, most persevere in a rural, sectarian way of life where their cultural practices separate them from mainstream U.S. society. Their children attend school only through the eighth grade, since they consider higher education prideful, and a danger to their simple way of life. They refuse to baptize infants, teaching that only believing adults should be baptized. They put great importance on the local church, believing that God guides through the congregation, and that each church member should adhere to the group's decisions about lifestyle practices.[5]

Another shared feature of radical religious groups is sacrifices—doing something that will be expensive or impossible to reverse later on. The ritual male circumcision that Maimonides puzzled over is a good example. What's so important about a circumcision? Today for most Jews and Muslims it is merely an awkward ceremony that we've become accustomed to. Off comes a foreskin. The crowd winces, and then everyone celebrates their relief with a bite to eat. Yet for a vulnerable minority in a hostile environment, a circumcision could have deadly consequences. Among my grandmother's ancestors in the Ukraine, if a boy was circumcised and a pogrom of Cossacks arrived one night, the child was marked, perhaps for death. Uncircumcised, perhaps the boy could have been hidden among the Christian neighbors as one of theirs. Why would parents endanger their own child with such a mark? Yet even secularized Muslims and Jews are unwilling to abandon the practice of circumcision, often for reasons they struggle to explain.

These prohibitions and sacrifices all have theological explanations, and many have practical rationalizations as well. Dietary restrictions are interesting because the rationalizations for them differ across religions. (For example, Jews and Muslims might tell you that they eat cows but not pigs, because pigs spread disease. So why do practicing Hindus eat pigs but not cows?) Taken together, it is striking that dietary restrictions acquire such an important role in different religions: Jews separate dairy products from meat (out of empathy with the mother sheep), while Catholics avoid eating meat on Friday (as penance to mark the weekday of the crucifixion). The fact that similar dietary restrictions appear consistently among many religions suggests that we should not be satisfied with religion-specific theological explanations and look for some common explanation instead.

All prohibitions and sacrifices, even those in more mainstream denominations, are a puzzle. (By denomination I mean a group or form of practice within a religion, such as Baptists among Protestant Christians.) Some degree of prohibition is common in all denominations, though it is much more subtle among Methodists, say, than among Seventh Day Adventists. If we all ignored our upbringing and theology for a moment, doesn't it seem strange that anyone would volunteer to join a denomination that prohibits enjoyable activities? Religious radicals tend to impose more extreme versions of these prohibitions, insisting on stricter dietary standards, more stringent Sabbath observance rules, more restrictive dress codes, and more time spent in prayer, for example. If prohibitions are puzzling, the more extreme prohibitions that religious radicals impose on themselves are doubly puzzling.

Here's a related riddle. The modern world is full of two-career couples, all hurrying about, struggling to manage careers and raise children, trying to economize on their increasingly valuable time. Meanwhile, the buying power of their earnings has been rising for generations in the secular marketplace, further increasing the value of time spent working.[6] With time at a premium, how do time-consuming religious practices, such as prayer, retain their appeal? Why aren't religions in general, and religious radicals in particular, disappearing? Mainstream religions *are* in decline in Europe, where church attendance rates have been falling for decades.[7] The United States is an exception, though, with high and fairly stable church attendance from the early twentieth century to the present. Remarkably, the fastest growing religious denominations in the United States are the most time consuming: evangelical Christians, Mormons, and ultra-Orthodox Jews, for instance, are experiencing rapid growth. In Central and South America evangelical Christianity is expanding quickly, at the expense of (less demanding) Catholicism. Anecdotally, radical Islam seems to be gaining an increasing following among Muslims, though denominational data on Muslims in most countries is generally unavailable. (We will see some evidence below.) Taken as a whole, not only are religious prohibitions and sacrifices a puzzle, they are a world-wide puzzle that applies both to ancient practices and to modern times.

Iannaccone could not have known what he was getting into in the 1980s when he began asking these questions. He recognized that religious prohibitions and sacrifices posed a true challenge for the usual logic of economics, which implies that people will not volunteer to have their choices restricted—they might miss out on a choice they prefer. Yet the Christian version of that challenge, which he was most intimately familiar with, was only part of the story. Religious radicalism among Muslims would prove to be a major force in twenty-first-century history.

Where Are the Dads?

Before examining Iannaccone's explanation, it helps to examine another dramatic instance of sacrifices and prohibitions, as they express themselves among ultra-Orthodox Jews. In truth, I knew even less about what I was getting into than Iannaccone did, when, without meaning to, I stumbled onto the mystery of the missing dads. I was spending a summer in Israel, between graduate school and my first academic job, when an old friend and teacher, Professor Ruth Klinov of the Hebrew University, asked me a seemingly unrelated question: Why were so many Israeli men not participating in the labor force (i.e., not working or looking for work)? A full 12 percent of Israeli men of prime working age (age twenty-five to fifty-four) were nonparticipants in the early 1990s. That seemed very high. Nonparticipants are usually disabled, have retired early, or have given up looking for work for other reasons, but how many people like that could there be? The U.S. nonparticipation rate is typical of developed economies, at about six percent, which is what the Israeli rate had been in 1970, but since then Israeli nonparticipation had been increasing steadily, reaching twelve percent of the labor force by the early 1990s.

Curious, we did the first natural thing: we asked around. Over lunch and in the halls of the Hebrew University's economics department we heard lots of suggestions from knowledgeable scholars. Maybe the missing males were traveling abroad, or serving in military reserves, or really working but somehow not recorded in the official statistics? Nobody had a convincing answer, so we assembled data and started poking at it. The data in this case was easy enough to obtain. Like most countries, Israel runs monthly household surveys to keep track of the unemployment rate, wages, and other labor-market information. The raw data from those surveys is available to researchers (with enough information erased to keep personal information confidential). Unlike most countries, though, the Israeli version of the labor-force survey (roughly) identifies religious radicals when they answer "yeshiva" to a question about the last school a respondent attended. What we found was shocking: *Among ultra-Orthodox men in Israel, 60 percent of those of prime working age were not participating in the labor force—not working and not looking for work.*

The ultra-Orthodox accounted for about five percent of the Israeli population in the early 1990s when we first looked at these data, but they made up about a third of the male nonparticipants! If they weren't

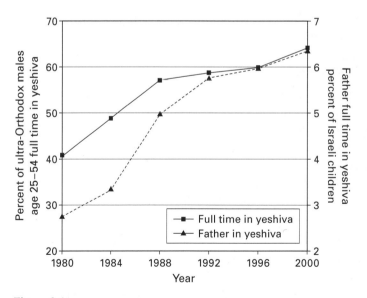

Figure 3.1
Yeshiva students and their children

working, what were all those prime-aged ultra-Orthodox men doing? The survey data had an answer to that as well: nonparticipant ultra-Orthodox males were almost all full-time students in yeshivas—religious seminaries devoted to the study of holy texts.

The upper line in figure 3.1 illustrates increased labor-force non-participation (i.e., decreased labor-force participation) among ultra-Orthodox men because of yeshiva attendance. Reading off the left vertical axis, the proportion of prime-age ultra-Orthodox men (age twenty-five to fifty-four) not working because they were studying full time in seminaries rose from 41 percent in 1980 to 60 percent by 1996 and did not level off until around 2000.[8] These rates of yeshiva attendance are *unprecedented* among Jews. They far exceed yeshiva attendance in ultra-Orthodox communities in the United States or elsewhere outside of Israel, where young men rarely study in yeshiva past age twenty-five, unless they are planning careers as rabbis and teachers—which clearly two-thirds of yeshiva students cannot aspire to.[9]

The combination of increased yeshiva attendance and rapid population growth among the ultra-Orthodox has caused serious problem for ultra-Orthodox families. The lower line in the figure reports the proportion of Israeli children not supported by a working father because he is studying in yeshiva. That proportion more than doubled between 1980 and 1996, from 2.7 to 5.9 percent, reaching 6.3 percent by the year 2000. Who *does* support these families? Returning to the data, Ruth Klinov and I discovered two disturbing facts. First, the average family with a father in yeshiva was large and very poor, with four or five children (so far), and was living in poverty according to official Israeli standards. Second, these families were extremely dependent on government support. Only a fifth of their income came from the mother's earnings. Most of the remainder, about 70 percent, came from a government stipend the father received while studying in yeshiva and from Israel's generous child allowance program.

There I was, a fresh young PhD in economics staring in wonder at graphs stranger than anything I'd been taught in graduate school, showing a 19 percentage point decline in labor supply. I felt like a budding zoologist might, if on vacation he spotted a member of some endangered species, maybe a Tasmanian devil, in the motel parking lot. To this day

I don't know of a comparable decline in the labor supply of any sub-population anywhere.

My first reaction was to doubt our calculations. I'd lived in Jerusalem, a city with a large ultra-Orthodox population—the bus to the university rides right through ultra-Orthodox neighborhoods. How could it be that 60 percent of the men in that community (67 percent if you counted the unemployed) were not working, and I somehow had not noticed? We started collecting anecdotes. Israel is a diverse country but it's also a small country with large families. It didn't take long to find friends with ultra-Orthodox brothers, sisters, and cousins, and to track down some old friends who had become ultra-Orthodox themselves. Soon I'd visited a yeshiva and chatted with the students, keeping track of their ages and listening carefully to their career plans. What I found was surprising to me but consistent with the statistics: men in their forties, fathers to large families, who proudly told me that they were studying full time in yeshiva!

Eventually some friends guided me to Menachem Friedman, a sociologist at Bar Ilan University, an Orthodox (as opposed to ultra-Orthodox) institution in the suburbs of Tel Aviv. Friedman is the dean of scholars of ultra-Orthodoxy, having devoted most of his professional life to studying religious radicals, Jewish and otherwise. With an Orthodox education himself, Friedman puts community members at ease. He conducts interviews in Yiddish and can mingle unobtrusively when he walks through ultra-Orthodox communities, reading the notices pasted on the walls, chatting with members, and trading gossip and insights. A few times, at Friedman's invitation, I wore a white shirt myself and accompanied him on these walking tours, jotting down explanations, learning details, and trying to follow the conversation. Like most social scientists, I had very little intuition about how radical religious communities look from the inside. Like me, most Israeli social scientists had a blind spot where the ultra-Orthodox were concerned, because the two communities had so little contact with each other. The decline in ultra-Orthodox employment, which everyone had missed and I had doubted, was very real. That decline, and the economic pressure it put on families, was familiar to Friedman and to the ultra-Orthodox community, though they could not estimate its magnitude.

My casual sampling had another effect as well. It increased my own empathy for the young men I met and for their families, whose economic situation was truly dire. Eventually that empathy would influence our efforts to change the policies that had sunk the ultra-Orthodox into such dire economic straits.

We had stumbled onto a very real example of modern religious sacrifice. Why would anyone choose to study in yeshiva over working when they had a family to support? Our calculations showed that at age thirty-five a yeshiva student could earn more than twice his monthly stipend by working, and would be eligible for child allowances regardless of yeshiva attendance. By age forty-five, he would be earning two and a half times the stipend with a decade of work experience. Yet supporting *children* is just the beginning. Starting in their late thirties, a typical ultra-Orthodox couple would have children getting married. In this community—since the groom will certainly be in yeshiva—the young couple will be too poor to pay the rent. The solution is for the parents and in-laws, beginning in their late thirties, to guarantee minimal financial security by purchasing an apartment for the young couple. By their forties, these typical parents will have seven or eight children to support, including buying apartments for them, in order to support the next generation and all the *grandchildren*—a daunting challenge in Israel, where apartments in the larger cities are not much less expensive per square foot than the U.S. average. So why choose yeshiva over work?

We tried every explanation we could think of. Maybe it was purely a matter of religious belief, with a love of sacred learning inculcated into ultra-Orthodox boys from an early age? After all, when I asked the yeshiva students themselves that's what they told me, with a twinkle in the eye and a stroke of the beard, humoring the naive young professor who was clearly out of his element. Yet it was hard to square that with what I knew about members of ultra-Orthodox communities in the United States and Canada. North American yeshiva students, who appear to be equally devout—and are often followers of the very same rebbe (religious leader)—seldom remain in yeshiva past the age of twenty-five, and bear no cultural penalty for leaving in their twenties.[10] Besides, an explanation based on religious belief alone would need to somehow explain why beliefs changed so quickly in the 1980s. Men were suddenly spending a decade more of their lives in yeshiva in the mid-1990s than they were in the early 1980s, and even that was unprecedented in the history of ultra-Orthodoxy.

Perhaps yeshiva students were compensated for their years of study with high-paying jobs later in life that we simply didn't know about, so that their lack of a secular education was not a handicap? Klinov and I returned to our computers, examined the earnings of yeshiva students after graduation (typically when they were in their forties), and compared them to the earnings of graduates of secular Israeli high schools and universities. Economists find it useful to calculate the economic "return" on a year of education, which is the average amount that each year of education adds to annual earnings after graduation, measured in percentages. Israeli secular education in the 1990s had a return of 9.4 percent, a pretty good investment (a little higher than the U.S. return). Ultra-Orthodox education, on the other hand, was a terrible investment, at 1.8 percent. In other words, for every year in yeshiva a student was forgoing a permanent raise of about 7.6 percent, which they could have realized by spending that same year in a secular school. As puzzles go, the Tasmanian devil roaming the parking lot was only getting bigger and stranger.

Finally, there was the explanation for prolonged yeshiva attendance that upsets Israelis most: draft deferrals. Israeli males face three years of compulsory military service—often dangerous. Yet full-time yeshiva students have their service deferred. That seems unlikely to foreigners, given how seriously Israelis take their security, but it's true. The draft-deferral arrangement dates back to a historic agreement between the first Israeli government and the ultra-Orthodox leadership. It was a gesture of support from Prime Minister David Ben Gurion's secular government to a small minority of religious radicals, mostly refugees from Europe, who had survived the Holocaust and were desperate to preserve the culture of European yeshiva study. Yeshiva students could thus avoid military service as long as they studied, which would explain why so many ultra-Orthodox men were not working.

Ben Gurion's original arrangement had imposed a cap on the number of deferrals. Prime Minister Menachem Begin lifted the cap in 1977 as part of an agreement to include an ultra-Orthodox political party in his coalition government—which he needed to ensure a majority in the Israeli Knesset. Other Israeli Jews were outraged at the waiving of the cap. Begin probably did not understand the long-term implications of lifting the cap. Since then, the number of draft deferrals has increased steadily. By the mid-1990s about 7.5 percent of males newly eligible for the draft were taking a yeshiva study deferment instead. Popular resentment of the ultra-Orthodox also increased. In Israel's 2003 parliamentary elections a radically anti-ultra-Orthodox political party, Shinui, became the third largest party by campaigning against what they perceived as religious coercion by the ultra-Orthodox.

Yet draft deferrals cannot explain prolonged yeshiva attendance either. The yeshiva draft-deferral rules by the 1980s worked like this: yeshiva students received a deferral of regular service (the first three years) and reserve duty (about thirty days annually during the period we studied) as long as they studied in the yeshiva. The deferral would eventually convert to an exemption if they remained in yeshiva until age forty-one, or until age thirty-five for men with at least five children—the usual draft-exemption rules for Israeli males. If it was really the prospect of military service that was keeping ultra-Orthodox Jews in yeshiva, then we should have seen them leaving yeshiva in droves when they became draft exempt, at age forty-one (or at age thirty-five with five children, which often applied).[11]

That implication is testable, and clearly refuted: among ultra-Orthodox men with at least five children 66 percent were still in yeshiva between the ages of thirty-five and forty, despite the fact that they were already draft exempt, in yeshiva or not. Among ultra-Orthodox men aged forty-one to forty-four, all of whom were draft exempt because of their age, 46 percent were studying in yeshiva. It was not draft avoidance that kept students in yeshiva until their forties.

So if it isn't the draft deferral, or the economic returns, or the religious beliefs, or the lack of an alternative, then why was Israeli yeshiva attendance so high? That's what Iannaccone had figured out, when he was thinking about churches, prohibitions, and sacrifices.

Mutual Aid

The first key to Iannaccone's explanation of why religious radicals behave as they do is to realize how much collective activity—material as well as spiritual—goes on within radical religious communities. Anyone who has attended a prayer service knows that the spiritual experience is collective—it's a lot more satisfying if the other participants show warmth, enthusiasm, dedication (and hopefully some ability to sing in harmony).

What outside observers often miss are the *nonspiritual* services that radical religious communities collectively provide, in addition to the spiritual services. For example, Amish and Mennonite communities are famous for barn raisings. All able-bodied adults in the community cooperate to build a new barn for a newlywed couple, dropping everything else for a day to do so. A barn raising is a wonderful example of mutual aid within communities. Individuals donate work time to the community in response to the needs of a young couple. In return, volunteers can expect that they (or perhaps their children) will benefit from mutual aid at some later date. Yet mutual aid does not rely on goodwill alone. While the builders are volunteers, a barn raising does have an element of a draft to it, in the sense that members not volunteering are liable to be censured by the community.

Mutual aid is so developed among the Old Order Amish that Temple University sociologist Julia Ericksen (writing with three colleagues) describes the Old Order Amish community of Lancaster, Pennsylvania, as a single economic entity: "There is a great deal of mutual aid and advice within Amish extended families and between Amish families. In a way, the Amish society in Lancaster County can be likened to a very successful agricultural corporation."[12]

Mutual aid of this type is common among religious radicals, be they Christians, Muslims, or Jews. Communities tend to use volunteer labor to create and maintain extremely tight social service provision networks, providing members with education, healthcare, soup kitchens, and even safe streets.

The degree of mutual aid currently practiced by ultra-Orthodox Jews is unprecedented in Jewish history, according to Friedman.[13] No sick member is without visitors; no child lacks food and clothing. No single member is without an arranged match—if they don't adamantly refuse, that is. Cooperative stores provide essential food and household items at reduced prices. Israeli journalist David Landau, in his book *Piety and Power*, reports on dozens of goods available on loan, for free, advertised in flyers by neighborhood rabbis in the *Bayit Vegan* neighborhood of Jerusalem, ranging from Torah scrolls to wedding gowns to playpens.[14] Free services are also available, including visits to the sick, support and advice for mourners, and frozen meal service for the elderly, for the sick, and for mothers after childbirth. The flyers include a request to donate time and money, but also to identify anyone needing help. Most recipients and all volunteers and contributors are ultra-Orthodox.

Landau also describes a well-organized system of fundraising among the ultra-Orthodox for emergency medical expenses not covered by regular medical insurance, as well as a decentralized system of voluntary donation and solicitation for individual hardship cases. All these charities, including individual cases, are endorsed by a leading rabbi; "the Rabbis' signatures attest to the veracity of the information."[15]

Charity is ubiquitous and interest-free loans abound, both in money and in kind:

Just as "Torah" is not a select or elitist pursuit, but embraces the entire community, so too "Charity" does not merely, or even mainly, follow the classical pattern of rich-to-poor assistance. Almost everyone in the Israeli *haredi* [ultra-Orthodox] world is a recipient of charity, in one form or another. Yet at the same time the *haredim* give charity too, participating in cash or kindness in the cost of this universal Torah-learning. . . .[16]

But the most important money-saver for the *haredim* is money itself: the availability of countless free-loan [funds] . . . where one can borrow hundreds, and in some cases thousands of dollars without interest . . . the administrators are all volunteers; there are no office expenses since there are no offices; and hence the only overheads are bad debts—of which there are remarkably few.[17]

Mutual aid among religious radicals has an ancient history, as recorded by the historian Josephus. He writes about the Jewish Essenes, two millennia ago in Israel:

Riches they despise, and their community of goods is truly admirable; you will not find one among them distinguished by greater opulence than another. They have a law that new members on admission to the sect shall confiscate their property to the order, with the result that you will nowhere see either abject poverty or inordinate wealth; the individual's possessions join the common stock and all, like brothers, enjoy a single patrimony.[18]

Communal sharing by a commune called the Damascus Covenant is described in a fascinating relic, one of the 2,000-year-old "Dead Sea" scrolls found in a cave near the excavated site at Qumran, on the north-western shore of the Dead Sea. The Damascus Covenant was a radical religious community related to the Qumran sect, whose members worked outside, in the larger economy. Members of the Covenant were required to contribute to a mutual-aid pool: "They shall place the earnings of at least two days out of every month into the hands of the Guardian and the Judges, and from it they shall give to the fatherless, and from it they shall succour the poor and the needy, the near kin, and the ma[id for] whom no man cares."[19] Members were forbidden from buying and selling with each other, but rather were expected to provide for each other free of charge, as a nuclear family would.[20]

While modern scholars now know a fair amount about communal activity among Christian and Jewish religious radicals, there is less good sociological or anthropological evidence about radical Islamic communities. We certainly know that charity is a pillar of mainstream Islam and that radical Islamist groups like the Muslim Brotherhood are famous for running religious schools, orphanages, soup kitchens, clinics, hospitals, and even youth centers and soccer clubs, all operated as charities. We lack direct evidence on how much that activity depends on volunteer work and to what extent access is limited to members, as we know it is among radical religious Christians and Jews.

One exception to our general lack of knowledge about the mechanics of charity among radical Islamists is the research that economist Daniel Chen did as an MIT graduate student on mutual-aid funds in rural Indonesia.[21] Chen studied an explicit mutual-aid arrangement associated with Koran study groups, *Pengajian*. Community members gather for study and religious instruction, but at the same time donate to a common fund. In times of need members can draw on the fund. Their credit is greater the more they contribute relative to their own income. That is, if a poor member made the same absolute contribution as a wealthier member to the fund, the poor member would have greater drawing rights. In that sense, the fund provides both insurance and support for the poor.

Chen was interested in the effect of economic conditions on religiosity in Indonesia. In 1997–1998 Indonesia suffered a currency crisis, driving up the prices of imports and exportable goods, such as rice. During the crisis, as food prices soared by 150 percent, rural families increased their attendance at Pengajian and sent their children more often to madrassas for schooling. Those increases in religious behavior did not occur for rice farmers, who benefited from the high cost of food, indicating that financial distress caused increased religiosity. Chen also found that the increase in Pengajian attendance caused by declining income was muted in villages that had alternative sources of credit. This last result suggests that these Muslim religious institutions play an especially important role in buffering community members against economic shocks when alternative forms of insurance are unavailable.

Prohibitions and Clubs

Mutual aid sounds lovely, but it is a bit of a concern to economists. (This is the last puzzle on my list—before we turn to Iannaccone's clever solution.) We are, after all, the designated worriers about whether members of an organization have the right incentives to do their jobs. Mutual-aid contracts are informal and implicit, so how would you ever enforce them?

Here's an example of what worries economists: I might propose to my neighbor, "How about we agree to help each other out? If your roof leaks in the middle of the night, or you need help bringing the crop in, I'll be there for you." "Sure," he replies, "sounds great." Then I would watch his eyes carefully while reiterating the conditions. "I'll help you in time of need but you have to do the same for me, okay? When I need someone to watch the children while I take the baby to the doctor, say, I'm going to count on you, right?"

How do I know that I can trust my neighbor to be supportive in time of need? When I do ask him to watch my children, he might tell me that he's too tired, or that he has a date that night, or perhaps a business trip the next morning. How can I tell that he is going to remain committed to our deal, rather than just shirk?

avoid

This shirking problem is familiar to any manager (or parent) and rears its ugly head in the collective production that occurs in most workplaces. In my job, at a research university, collective production is critical in research seminars and classes, whenever challenging material gets presented. Everyone benefits from the wisdom of good citizens. They're the ones who come prepared, pay attention, and ask good questions, making learning easier and more enjoyable for everyone else in the room. They provide appropriate encouragement, constructive criticism, good answers, and new ideas. Presenting to a seminar full of colleagues and graduate students who behave like good citizens is a satisfying, fulfilling, collective-learning experience. It has a warmth and a unity of purpose to it—a little like praying in a dedicated congregation.

Consider the problem of shirking in seminars. What incentive do my graduate students and colleagues have to be good citizens? What's to keep them from partying all night, arriving unprepared, and dozing off when I present? What we teach budding economists in Econ 101 is that to fix such "collective action" (i.e., shirking) problems you provide incentives, like giving someone a dollar for each good question or clever suggestion, or maybe fining them for falling asleep in seminars. (I've actually tried this and can report that it doesn't work very well. It's considered crude and colleagues find it mildly insulting.) Moreover, it's too late to induce people to *prepare* for the seminar—which we wanted them to do the night before. Shirking isn't just my seminar's problem either. The members of any sports team, the partners at any law firm, the surgical staff at any hospital, anyone who has run a business meeting, or the members of any fraternity will have a story about the shirking problem.

Here's a solution. Imagine for a minute that we could impose some rules on what the graduate students, colleagues, teammates, partners, fellow surgeons, officemates or fellow fraternity members could have done the night before. We might choose rules like:

• Avoid alcohol consumption with anyone not in our group.

• Do not travel by car.

• Avoid beaches, coffee shops, and movies.

• Do not watch television or use the Internet.

• Do not read books other than the texts of our profession.

• Follow our own very unusual dress code.
• Eat only according to the strict rules of our membership.
• Speak only our fairly arcane language.
• Adhere to rules about how, when, and with whom you can have sexual relations.

Those rules would pretty much destroy dating options and most other social activities with outsiders. If we could impose all of them, though, we should be able to guarantee a high-quality seminar (or other collective product) the next day, simply because nobody will have had anything better to do with their time than get a good night's sleep and prepare for the seminar!

How might we enforce those severe rules? Well, if the seminar becomes exciting and productive enough—thanks to all those good citizens—the threat of being excluded might be enough. In that case, enforcement is simple: if we catch you breaking the rules, perhaps by being out of uniform, or in the wrong restaurant, we expel you from seminars. My own seminars and classes may not be scintillating enough to make the threat of expulsion sufficiently frightening to enforce all those prohibitions, but hopefully the reader can imagine some cooperative activity that is worth the pain of living with restrictive prohibitions. (Actually, if you make this argument to economists, the graduate students will giggle when you mention the academic economists' schlumpy dress code and arcane language—the closest thing we have to prohibitions.)

What do exciting seminars have to do with religious radicals? The nine rules on my wish list for ensuring good citizenship in a seminar have direct parallels in the religious prohibitions imposed by religious radicals, the communities Iannaccone was puzzling over. Dietary codes, dress codes, Sabbath restrictions, and the like all limit social and market activities with members of outside society. Those religious prohibitions have the effect of distancing members from outsiders, which keeps members closer to the community.

The community benefits by distancing members from outsiders, since the less time members spend on dates, restaurants, beaches, and shopping, the more time they have available for mutual aid, volunteer work, church attendance and other community activity. Moreover, if a member isn't going to wear the fancy clothes, eat in the restaurants, or drive to the beach on the Sabbath, why work so hard to buy clothes, food, and a car? As consumption opportunities are limited, work for pay becomes less appealing, freeing up even more time for community activities.

That was Iannaccone's first remarkable insight about religious radicals. He had wondered why people would submit to religious prohibitions and how groups that required them could survive. The answer he discovered is that *religious prohibitions are productive* for the community because they increase the availability of members for collective activity such as mutual aid, an essential part of what makes radical religious communities cohesive. His approach is called the "club" theory of religious radicals, a term suggesting that these communities are organized around a collective activity (such as mutual aid) from which members benefit, but that nonmembers can be denied—the way a golf club might exclude nonmembers from the greens. Prohibitions distance club members from outside activities (just as my wish list of prohibitions would distance graduate students from distractions), which makes members more available to help the community with its collective activities.

Evidence

Iannaconne's rationalization of religious prohibitions is clever, but that alone would not convince an empirical scientist, not without some proof. At least since Galileo Galilei was reputedly dropping balls from the Leaning Tower of Pisa (to test Aristotle's conjecture that heavier things fall faster), we've required that theories be subjected to possible falsification before we embrace them. Iannaccone's club model needed to be tested with some fresh data. His approach generated a number of novel predictions about religious radicals, that lent themselves to testing. Radical religious communities will be tighter socially than other groups, minimize outside contacts, have smaller congregations and higher attendance at services (making enforcement easier), have less education and earn less (increasing their demand for mutual aid), but donate a greater proportion of their income to charity because they are more committed.

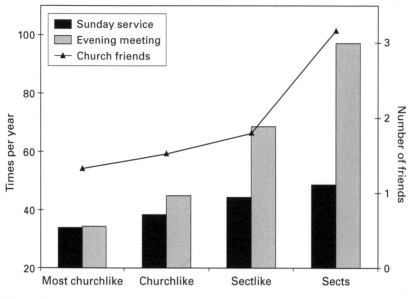

Figure 3.2
Denominations, attendance, and community

All those predictions were validated in data from two surveys: one on members of Protestant congregations from Northern California in the 1960s, and another using national data in the 1980s. Sociologists of religion have developed a classification scheme for denominations, based on the clustering of behaviors and beliefs. That scheme designates denominations as "sects," "sectlike," "churchlike," or "most church-like." Figure 3.2 illustrates the classifications. (Iannaccone used the term *sects*, following Adam Smith, so let's use that term interchangeably with the phrase "radical religious groups"—denominations that are extreme in their practices or beliefs.) Members of sects like Seventh Day Adventists are much more likely than members of "most churchlike" denominations like Methodists to hold extreme beliefs such as a literal interpretation of the Bible, or to report having experienced a personal miracle or vision. Sectlike denominations like Southern Baptists would be closer in their beliefs to sects, while churchlike denominations (Presbyterians, for example) would be closer in their beliefs to the "most churchlike."[22] Those designations are consistent with standard definitions of religious radicals, who express beliefs that distance them from mainstream culture. The figure shows that those theological classifications correspond to patterns of social behavior, as Iannaccone's club model predicted: sect members also spend more time within their congregations, and are more tightly connected socially with fellow members. When compared with members of very churchlike denominations, the more sectlike the denomination, the more often members attend church, and the more of their closest five friends belong to the congregation (3.2 for sect members versus 1.3 for the members of the most churchlike denominations).

The more sectlike the denomination, the smaller it is in membership and the more socially isolated its members are from the outside community—as measured by their memberships in groups other than church groups. Figure 3.3 illustrates these patterns. Small size and social isolation would make social control easier and cooperative production more efficient, as the club model of religious communities predicts. This is

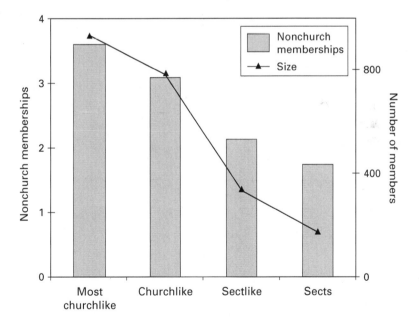

Figure 3.3
Congregation size and isolation

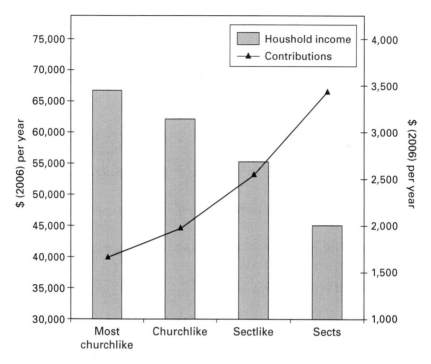

Figure 3.4
Denominations, income, and charity

evidence of the social effect of religious prohibitions on people's allocation of time and loyalty: the more sectlike the denomination, the fewer
outside activities members take part in, as reflected in less membership
in nonchurch organizations.

Economic aspects of the denominational spectrum are also consistent
with Iannaccone's predictions, as shown in figure 3.4 which reports on
household income and charitable contributions by denomination, all
expressed in inflation-adjusted dollars. Household income (on the left
scale) is lower the more sectlike the denomination, though charitable
contributions (right scale) are higher. Members of sectlike denominations
enjoy less income partly because they have completed less education; the
same data reveal that sect members had about two years less education
on average than members of most churchlike denominations. Consistent
with Iannaccone's prediction of higher cooperation within communities,

the more sectlike the denomination, the more generous members are in their charitable donations, despite lower income. Across all these measures, sectlike denominations and churchlike denominations line up in order between the sects and most churchlike, forming a denominational spectrum.

That denominational spectrum applies to Jewish congregations as well. Reform congregations have a very liberal theology and impose minimal rules on members of their large, relatively affluent congregations. Ultra-Orthodox Jews, as we've seen already, observe a very strict form of Jewish religious practice, in small, much less affluent congregations, creating extremely tight social units. Conservative congregations tend to be closer to Reform on all these measures, while Orthodox congregations are closer to ultra-Orthodox, forming a Jewish version of the denominational spectrum described above for Christians.

These findings provide direct evidence supporting Iannaccone's basic insight about religious communities as clubs. Religious radicals are characterized not only by their theology. Their communities (sects) are also extremely tight social groups, operating active internal charity networks. These findings are consistent with Iannaccone's conjecture that *religious prohibitions have an important organizational role to play. They strengthen collective activities, such as mutual aid, by distancing members from outside activities, thus reducing shirking.*

Fertility

A reader who still harbors doubts about the similarity in behavior among religious radicals of different religions should consider their fertility. Iannaccone did not have access to these data when he conducted his initial work, but we now do. Deciding whether to have a child, and how many to have, is even more consequential than how much charity we give or where we seek our friends. Even in this very private decision, religious radicals make strikingly different choices than do members of less strict denominations.

The modestly dressed Hutterites of the upper Midwest and the Canadian Prairies are the rock stars of modern demographics. Founded in 1528 in Switzerland and Bohemia, this denomination had grown to at least 17,000 members by 1622.[23] Yet fierce persecution by both Protestants and Catholics severely depleted membership in the Hutterite community, almost destroying it. In 1762 the sixty surviving members found refuge in the Crimea, benefiting from the timely protection of Catherine the Great. Between 1874 and 1877, that community emigrated en masse to South Dakota, where, now numbering 443, the Hutterites established their settlements. Like other Anabaptist sects, they lived in strict communes, allowing no private property. Over the next seventy years, the Hutterites set the world record for natural population increase, growing from 443 members to 8,542, a 4.1 percent annual rate of increase! That remarkable population growth rate implies twice as many members every seventeen years. In their honor, demographers have dubbed their population growth rate the *Hutterite standard*—the effective maximum growth rate of a population benefiting from modern standards of nutrition and healthcare. Hutterites were socially isolated enough from the rest of the American population that most of their population increase was due to high fertility, not to recruitment of outsiders to the fold.

Fertility has no direct connection to terrorism, but it has everything to do with religious radicalism and the strict prohibitions sects impose on women's behavior. The subject of fertility is worth exploring for two reasons. First, fertility provides another marker of clublike behavior, which we will use to monitor to what extent radical Islamists fit the club model. Second, fertility will provide an example of how clubs respond to changes in policy. Remarkably, we will see that the policies of modern, secular governments have real effects, even in the bedrooms of the most exotic of religious radicals.

Fertility rates are easier to understand if we express them using the more intuitive measure of lifetime births per woman. Demographers do that in two ways. One is to ask women who are past childbearing age how many children they have had. That measure is clear enough, but it has the weakness of missing current changes in fertility while we wait for women to have their final child. An alternative is to calculate a measure called the "total fertility rate" (TFR for short), which predicts how many children a young woman would have if, over her lifetime, she experienced the current birth rates of women of different ages. For instance, if as a teenager this hypothetical mother had as many births as current teenagers, in her twenties she had as many births as women currently aged twenty to twenty-nine, and so on, then her TFR would be the sum of all those age-specific fertility rates.[24] By that measure, married Hutterite women achieved a total fertility rate of 9.9 children over their lifetimes, in the years 1946–1950![25]

Hutterites are Anabaptists—members of a radical religious tradition that dates back to the Protestant Reformation. They broke with Martin Luther over their belief that baptism of infants is insufficient, so that rebaptism is required of adults, at an age when an individual is old enough to decide. Hutterites are not the only rural Anabaptists with high fertility rates. Sociologist James Hurd has reconstructed family documents of Wenger Mennonites, a group of Anabaptists who split off from the Mennonites of eastern Pennsylvania in 1929.[26] Hurd's analysis reveals that married Wenger women achieved a total fertility rate of 10.28 in 1966, which exceeded the previous record, a total fertility rate of 10.11 for Old Colony Mennonites set in 1962–1966! The point is not that Anabaptists are competitive (though the sociologists of religious demography might be). The general finding worth emphasizing is that these Christian sects—all of whom practice prohibitions—manage to raise families of record size despite the economic handicap of prohibitions.

Mothers in Anabaptist sects, despite the cultural distance they keep from mainstream America, are apparently not immune to outside forces. By the 1970s, women among the Old Order Amish had chosen to reduce their fertility, a decline that paralleled the experience of other American women, so that they averaged only about 6.8 children per family.[27] Hutterite women reduced their childbearing to a total fertility rate of 6.3 by the 1980s, and even among the Wenger Mennonites total fertility declined to an average of 8.3 children by the mid-1990s.

How does the fertility of ultra-Orthodox Jewish women compare? Given the prohibitions and mutual-aid mechanisms that these radical religious Jews share with Anabaptists, we might expect that fertility among ultra-Orthodox Jewish women would be high. It is. They experienced a total fertility rate of 6.5 children per woman in the early 1980s in Israel, well above the average for Israeli women.

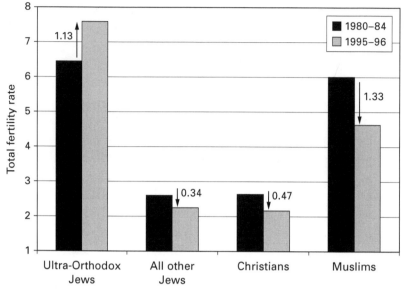

Figure 3.5
Fertility change among Israeli religious groups

Already impressive, the fertility of Israeli ultra-Orthodox women actually *rose* in the 1980s and early 1990s, reaching a total fertility rate of 7.6 children per woman by the mid-1990s, as illustrated in figure 3.5. Fertility decline has been so common in the last few centuries that demographers call it "fertility transition," and expect mothers in all cultures to eventually experience this transition to low "modern" fertility rates. Persistent high fertility, like that among the Anabaptists, is considered truly surprising. Fertility *increase* among a group of women with high fertility already is extremely rare.

It was an anomaly in Israel as well. During the same period total fertility rates declined among Israeli women as a whole (by 0.24 children), as they also did among the other major demographic groups of women within Israel: Christian Israeli women reduced fertility by 0.47 children, Muslim Israeli women experienced a fertility decline of 1.33 children, and among non-ultra-Orthodox Israeli Jewish women fertility dropped by 0.19 children. Ultra-Orthodox Israeli women in the 1980s and 1990s were somehow resisting both an international and a local trend.

The implications for the ultra-Orthodox community in Israel are staggering. Though their fertility rates do not achieve the Hutterite standard, the effect on population growth is almost the same, since relatively few ultra-Orthodox leave the fold. In the ultra-Orthodox case those fertility rates also apply to a much larger base population than the Hutterites started with. The longer life expectancies of the ultra-Orthodox today make the implied population doubling time about sixteen years. The Israeli ultra-Orthodox population in Israel did in fact double in size between 1979 and 1995, from about 140,000 to 290,000, and is on track to double again by about 2011.[28]

Is high fertility among religious radicals a purely theological phenomenon? If you ask about their fertility, Anabaptists and ultra-Orthodox Jews, regardless of denomination, give similar answers: they cite some variant of the pronatalist biblical injunction to "go forth and multiply." Anabaptists might also give thanks for the blessings of fertile soil and good weather, which have provided them with the opportunity to raise large families on prosperous farms. Ultra-Orthodox Jews might give thanks for other means of sustenance—most haven't farmed for generations. If you found a delicate way to ask, both groups would also tell you that many forms of birth control are forbidden. Yet, none of these explanations can be entirely satisfying. The rural Anabaptists of the United States are not the world's most prosperous farmers, the average Israeli ultra-Orthodox family lives very close to the poverty line, and almost every major religious denomination has some pronatalist injunction. Many religions and denominations forbid birth control altogether.[29] Yet few come anywhere close to matching Anabaptist or ultra-Orthodox fertility levels. Biblical injunctions, birth control, and income alone cannot explain why religious radicals have higher fertility than do other people of faith.

Pronatalist Prohibitions

Modern demography has an alternative way of thinking about fertility, which deemphasizes theology and birth control technology, stressing instead more practical aspects of a mother's reproductive decisions. One of the most persistent findings in economic demography is that fertility declines as a woman's education increases.[30] The economists' interpretation of that pattern is that women's education improves their market opportunities, which creates an attractive alternative to raising large families: they can spend more time earning and spending in the market and less time raising children. That might sound selfish on the mother's part until you consider what the additional earnings are spent on. The extra income allows a woman to better support her existing children, providing more food, education, clothing, healthcare, and other market goods. More spending on less children dramatically increases market resources per child. That simple logic is the gist of Gary Becker's "quality of children" theory of economic demography, which the Nobel committee cited in their rationale for awarding him their economics prize in 1992. Intuitively, education creates wage opportunities that attract women to market activities, work and consumption. Thus education distances women from work at home, including childbearing. Becker's argument links women's education and wages with fertility decisions, and is supported by plenty of evidence. Historically and in the present, women with poor labor-market opportunities have tended to have large families. As labor-market and educational opportunities have improved for women, fertility has fallen, both in developing and developed countries.

Now let's apply Becker's approach to women in a sect, complying with religious prohibitions and participating in mutual aid. Prohibitions such as forbidding motor vehicles, or not allowing women to drive, make work less attractive for mothers. Subtler but more prevalent restrictions on consuming food, alcohol, entertainment, healthcare, education, and shopping on the Sabbath, also make work less attractive because they restrict opportunities to spend the earnings. Thus religious prohibitions tend to distance women in radical religious communities from the market, pulling them back into communities and households, where bearing and raising children is a more attractive activity. In that way, religious prohibitions would be pronatalist.

Mutual aid also removes some of the risk from bearing and raising children. Since so many mutual-aid activities within radical religious communities are directed at children—education, welfare, and healthcare—a couple planning an additional child in a radical religious community can count on more support than a couple could in the general population. Should they not be able to handle the financial or emotional burden of another child, sect members know that their community will help. According to that logic, the mutual-aid network, much of which is provision of services to women by women, should also encourage fertility by removing some of the risk from childbearing.

Taken together, these two forces—religious prohibitions distancing women from work, and mutual aid reducing the cost of raising children—should predict higher fertility among religious radicals than among secular communities or mainstream religious communities. I've motivated this discussion with evidence from very radical religious groups at the extreme end of the denominational spectrums of their respective religions—Anabaptists and ultra-Orthodox Jews. Yet the conjecture is borne out in less extreme cases as well. For instance, in a survey of 860 white Protestant couples in Indianapolis in 1941, Ronald Freedman and P. K. Whelpton found that birth rates were about 50 percent above the sample average among women who were members of fundamentalist denominations (i.e., Church of Christ, Church of God, Church of the First Born, Nazarene, and Pentecostal).[31] Recalling Galileo's standard of proof, these ex post stories are an inferior form of evidence. We might have guessed that sectlike denominations would have higher fertility based on casual observation before formulating the conjecture, even if none of us had seen that particular survey about Indianapolis. A stronger test of the conjecture would come from data about behavior that ex ante we knew nothing about.

Radical Islam and Fertility

As we've seen, there is nothing particularly Christian or Jewish about religious radicals providing mutual-aid services to their communities. If their high fertility is due to a combination of prohibitions on the market activities of women and the pronatalist influence of mutual aid, then we should see the same patterns among Muslim religious radicals as well. That's important because if it is true, we can be more confident in using Iannaccone's "club" approach to study radical Islam.

Economist Ara Stepanyan and I took up that challenge a few years ago. We combed through every dataset we could find, in any country, for evidence on fertility among religious radicals.[32] We found five separate survey datasets that identified people who might be religious radicals, and that had sufficient information to estimate total fertility. Each dataset came from a different country. In all five cases the religious radicals were Muslims and the criteria for designating them as radicals were the schools their children attended. The surveys allowed us to distinguish between Muslims who sent their children to private religious schools (generally called madrassas) and Muslims who did not. The data span a wide swath of the world. From East to West, they cover Indonesia, with the world's largest Muslim population (170 million Muslims in 1992); the rural region of Matlab in Bangladesh (180,000 residents in the 1982 census, of whom 86 percent are Muslim); rural areas of the Indian states of Uttar Pradesh and Bihar (with a combined population of 285 million people, of whom 36 million are Muslims); most of Pakistan (131 million people, of whom 97 percent are Muslim); and Côte D'Ivoire in Africa (16.8 million people, of whom 35 to 40 percent are Muslim). These data also span various religious traditions within Sunni Islam.

In four of those five locations—Indonesia, Uttar Pradesh and Bihar in India, Bangladesh, and Pakistan—the analysis produced sufficiently

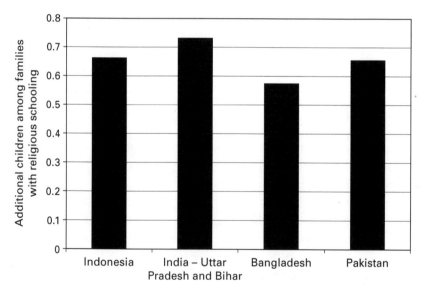

Figure 3.6
Higher fertility among Muslim religious radicals in four countries

precise estimates of differential fertility to merit reporting. Our measure of fertility in all cases was the number of surviving children for the oldest age group of women in the sample, typically age thirty-five and older. *In all four cases religious radicals had higher fertility*, as illustrated in figure 3.6. Families that we classified as religious radicals had 0.67 more children on average in Indonesia, 0.77 more children in the Indian provinces of Uttar Pradesh and Bihar, 0.58 more children in Bangladesh, and 0.66 more children in Pakistan. In the fifth location, Côte D'Ivoire, the fertility differential was 0.81, but less precisely estimated.[33]

One might suspect that higher fertility is due to living a more traditional, rural lifestyle. To make sure that our estimates were not confounded by those factors we calculated them only after accounting for the effects on fertility of education, living in rural areas, and being Muslim.[34]

All in all, parents who send their children to Islamic schools, in data from five different countries, show characteristics that are familiar from our analysis of radical religious Jewish and Christian communities. First, those families have higher fertility. Second, they distance their children from education that will provide high earnings in the market—we'll estimate the cost of that decision in lost earnings below.

To be sure, higher fertility does not indicate that Muslim families in developing countries who send children to madrassas are *as* segregationist toward the mainstream culture as are Anabaptists or ultra-Orthodox Jews. It does suggest, however, a denominational spectrum in Islam like those in Christianity and Judaism. Using differential fertility as a measure of distance from mainstream religious practice indicates that we might think of Muslim families whose children attend a madrassa as the equivalent of Nazarenes or Pentecostals, as opposed to a more mainstream "churchlike" denomination such as Presbyterians, along an analogous Christian denominational spectrum.

To sum up the chapter, the club approach provides us with a surprising insight, that is, mutual aid and prohibitions cluster together in radical religious communities for a very practical reason: prohibitions allow communities to control shirking in the provision of mutual aid and other communal activities. Our next task is to understand the role of sacrifices in controlling shirking before we can apply these insights to the central question: Why do religious radicals excel at violence and terrorism?

Older students in madrassa and yeshiva: Studying Koran in Lahore, Pakistan (undated); Studying Talmud in Bnei Brak, Israel, May 2006. (AP Photo/K.M. Chaudary; Uriel Sinai/Getty Images).

4

Sect, Subsidy, and Sacrifice

Then when he has completed one year within the community, the Congregation shall deliberate his case with regard to his understanding and observance of the Law. And if it be his destiny, according to the judgment of the Priests and the multitude of the men of their Covenant, to enter the company of the Community, *his property and earnings shall be handed over* to the Bursar of the Congregation. . . .

But when the second year has passed, he shall be examined, and if it be his destiny, according to the judgment of the Congregation, to enter the Community, then he shall be inscribed among his brethren . . . *his property shall be merged* and he shall offer his counsel and judgment to the Community.

—Community Rule of the Qumran sect, first century, describing the surrender of property required of new members following their two-year trial period[1]

Iannaccone provided a clever explanation for religious prohibitions with his club model. As we've seen, his approach is supported by evidence: religious radicals from different cultures show strong similarities in their prohibitions, mutual aid activities, and fertility, be they Christian, Muslim, or Jewish. Yet we still haven't explained *sacrifices*, yeshiva attendance, or the lethality of clubs at terrorism.

Let's return to the puzzle of sacrifices. Sacrifices grate on economists like fingernails on a blackboard, because they involve a most uneconomical destruction of resources. In biblical times, religious sacrifice included burnt offerings, vows of celibacy, and vows of abstinence—all expensive to reverse, and some even impossible to reverse.

Sacrifices are quite common among communal religious sects. The *Yahad* (literally "united") were a sect of Jewish religious radicals who chose to live in isolation at Qumran, on the northwestern shore of the Dead Sea, two thousand years ago. Members surrendered all of their property to the community in return for acceptance. We know this because they carefully compiled their community rules on scrolls from which the epigraph above is taken. Their writings lay undisturbed for almost two millennia in dry caves, among the other Dead Sea Scrolls, until Bedouins accidentally discovered them in the mid-twentieth century.

Ancient Israel in the first century was an incubator for many religious groups, including early Christians.[2] The historian Josephus writes that the Essenes, a larger Jewish sect of that period, also required that new members surrender property, and undergo a trial period and a series of theological tests. As archeologist and Qumran scholar Eyal Regev points out, all three of those requirements of new members—surrender of property, trial period, and test—were required by nineteenth-century Christian Shakers as well, and are currently required by Hutterites.[3] These parallels are remarkable. The founders of these modern radical religious groups are unlikely to have read Josephus and could not have read the Scrolls, which were not discovered until 1947. The Amish and Mennonites today have similar rules but do not practice fully communal property. Shakers and members of the Qumran sect had another sacrifice in common: they disavowed marriage, childbearing, and sexual relations. (Shakers were both male and female. The Qumran sect may have been entirely male.)

Activities early in life that preclude schooling are also a form of sacrifice, at least from the point of view of an economist (and a parent) because we think of schooling as an investment. Education increases earning potential later in life, in both developing and developed countries. For that reason education is best obtained early in life so that the benefits, those higher earnings, can be enjoyed for longer. How could a religious requirement that reduces income, such as madrassa or yeshiva attendance, survive centuries during which religious communities scraped by on incomes close to subsistence?

Consider the image of students studying in madrassa in the upper of the two chapter-opening photographs figure. Such students spend years learning the holy texts by rote, even in non-Arabic-speaking countries, where they most likely would not understand the text they are memorizing. While this is an education, it is hardly an investment in future earnings. On the contrary, it comes at the cost of secular lessons not learned—in reading, writing, arithmetic, or a trade—that could prepare students for further education and higher-wage jobs, or for a well-paid occupation. This type of sacrifice is common among ultra-Orthodox Jews as well, who are captured studying in yeshiva in the lower of those two photographs. The current generation of ultra-Orthodox Jews in Israel, as we will see, hold the record for years of religious study. Most radical Christians also have poor educational outcomes, because they limit years of education for their children. Why would a parent sacrifice a child's future income by sending her to study in a school where basic skills are not well taught? The same puzzle applies to years devoted to missionary work by young adults. Why incur the cost of lost years of schooling by spending time early in life doing missionary work, as is common among U.S. Mormons, for example?

Iannaccone's observation of collective activity among religious radicals led to a second critical insight, one that can explain religious sacrifices. A club engaged in collective activity, such as mutual aid, must be very selective about who it chooses as members. It must exclude shirkers. They will not only take up space at seminars (in my academic example), but they will also draw more than their share of favors from neighbors while not carrying their weight at barn raisings or other mutual aid activities. A mutual aid club with too many shirkers will face more demands on its' services than it has resources, bankrupting the collective.

An example may help illustrate how a sacrifice can usefully exclude shirkers. Imagine that you are a member of a radical religious group in some remote village. A young suitor arrives, seeking to marry your daughter. The young man stands there awkwardly, wearing his best suit of clothes, telling you earnestly that he worships your daughter. He describes with passion how he will contribute to the community, raise your grandchildren to keep the faith, and care for you in your old age.

"Of course he worships my daughter," you think. "Any sane man would." But as he speaks you imagine, in the manner of protective parents, how the young man might do exactly the opposite of what he promises: draw support from the community when the children are young; raise them to be skeptics; and then—when he gets himself established economically and his turn comes to give back to the community—he will run off with your daughter and your grandchildren to a good job in the big city, abandoning you to care for yourself in old age.

This is truly a dilemma for you, the parent. Anyone can promise to be a good citizen—to your family and to your community—but it might be a decade until you will be able to verify the young suitor's seemingly earnest commitment. The life cycle of mutual aid dictates that people tend to draw services (health, education, safety, and social services) when they are very young or very old, and pitch in to help others community when they are middle-aged. By the time you can test his commitment it will be too late. He will already be your son-in-law and father of your grandchildren. Based on the young suitor's promise alone, how can a parent know if he is the community-minded altruist he says he is, or a materialistic shirker plotting his escape to the attractions of the market, in the big city? You need some sign of his intentions *now*, before the wedding. Some demonstration of his commitment to mutual aid would help you decide.

Then the young man says something critical: "I've spent the last few years studying in holy pursuits and want to spend a few more." Depending on the community, that may mean study in religious seminary, community service, or perhaps missionary work.

That changes everything, because he has demonstrated commitment! If he were secretly interested in eventually leaving for a high-paying job in the big city he would be off studying in a secular school accumulating earning potential, or off working, gaining work experience. The last thing a materialist would devote his time to would be activities with little or no return in the market. The suitor's commitment to forgo future earnings demonstrates to you that the young man is not a materialistic shirker. He may not go on to be wealthy, but you can be sure he is not thinking of running off to a high-paying job in the secular world. Your grandchildren may be poor, but you will at least see them, and your son-in-law will be there to contribute to the mutual aid pool that functions as your social insurance.

Now imagine the ultra-Orthodox setting, in which the young man just committed himself to spending time in yeshiva (1.8 percent return on a year of education) rather than secular schooling (9.4 percent return). It seems counterintuitive to a parent and especially to an economist that you would prefer a son-in-law who prefers the worse investment. Yet it is important to remember how economies of mutual aid work. The community cannot retain most of the members with high wage potential, who will forgo mutual aid, preferring to buy education, health, and social services in the market. Those high-wage individuals are on their way to less strict, less demanding, and less supportive denominations that free up their valuable time. The son-in-law whom you can count on to remain loyal to the strict, radical religious community is the young man who prefers community service and the worse investment (at least in narrow pecuniary terms). sacrifice demonstrates long-term commitment

That example illustrates the idea of an efficient sacrifice. Sacrifices are wasteful in the narrow sense; they destroy value and opportunities. Yet a social norm in which individuals destroy personal opportunities is useful in the broader sense. It allows people to demonstrate their commitment. That explanation covers the ancient practice of sacrificing animals. It also explains current practices common to religious radicals: sacrificing years of secular schooling to community service, years of study in religious seminaries, and years of missionary work. *The idea of an efficient religious sacrifice is Iannaccone's second great insight into religious sects.* He must share some credit, though, with the great Jewish rationalist scholar, Moses Maimonides. As the epigraph at the beginning of the previous chapter indicates, Maimonides hinted at a similar conclusion some eight centuries earlier, in Egypt.

People of faith raise two major objections to Iannaccone's efficient-sacrifice argument. The first is that seminary attendance, missionary work, and community service are not sacrifices at all, but productive activities that people find fulfilling. Fulfillment is not inconsistent with interpreting these activities as sacrifices—forfeiting some good or option in a way that will be expensive or impossible to reverse—in order to demonstrate commitment. Yet interpreting these activities *solely* as sources of personal fulfillment does not explain the two related behaviors: why sacrifices are more common among radical religious groups providing mutual aid than among less strict denominations, or why sacrifices tend to occur early in life, when demonstrating commitment is important.

The second major objection raised by people of faith is that this reasoning is agnostic about the ethical and religious content of study, missionary work, circumcisions, or other sacrifices. That's absolutely true. In fact, sacrifices as demonstrations of commitment are common in many nonreligious organizations. Moreover, some of these groups would be ethically abhorrent to believers—such as the Mafia, gangs, and other criminal organizations, which have violent and destructive initiation rites. Fraternities expose new recruits to public ridicule by hazing and to private ridicule through drunken rituals. Military units and sports teams often impose painful or embarrassing initiation rites on new members. Tribes require rites of passage, which can involve pain, personal risk, or self-mutilation. Communes such as the early Israeli kibbutz, which was entirely secular, had the same requirement as the Shakers and Essenes: initiates surrendered all personal property, so that a member might be required to donate her mother's wedding dress to the communal supply of work clothes.

The communes with the strictest sacrifices seem to have been the most successful. That certainly was true of nineteenth-century utopian communes in the United States, such as the Shakers, Amana, Oneida, Harmony, Zoar, and Jerusalem. Shakers, for example, renounced their relatives, committed to forgoing sexual relations, and surrendered their property. Yet their communities grew and thrived, including twenty-two separate villages and thousands of members at one point.[4] All these initiation rites have a common characteristic: a high cost to the members, who distance themselves from opportunities outside the group by submitting themselves to it. A common element among all these groups is a collective activity threatened by shirking—such as mutual aid—so that the group depends critically on preventing shirking. Of course the theological content and spiritual activities of radical religious groups have almost nothing in common with the partying of fraternities or the boozing of fraternities and football teams. That's why the ethical objection misses the point: regardless of the ideology or theology of the group, collective activities that rely on loyalty make up-front sacrifices a useful cohesion-building instrument. Sacrifices allow prospective members to demonstrate commitment, distinguishing themselves from shirkers.

It's not about the ideas, that induce devotion.
It is the structure of the group *Sect, Subsidy, and Sacrifice*   101
    - mutual aid incentive
    - sacrifices   - prohibitions

To summarize, regardless of theology, religious radicals of different religions share common behavioral patterns. Costly and demanding sacrifices, strict prohibitions, and extreme theological positions tend to cluster in communities with large doses of collective activity, mutual aid, a relatively low income membership, less (secular) education, small congregations, and a self-segregating attitude toward the mainstream culture. That clustering of characteristics was recognized by sociologists Max Weber and Ernst Troeltsch, who labeled it the "church-sect" distinction.[5]

Iannaccone's contribution was explaining *why* prohibitions, sacrifices, and collective activities cluster together. Mutual aid and other collective activities make communities sensitive to shirking, so mutual aid communities employ sacrifices to weed out shirkers; they employ prohibitions in order to segregate themselves and reduce shirking opportunities. Economists and sociologists call that type of group structure an economic *club*, a term we can now expand to include not only religious sects, but also communes, fraternities, gangs, and other groups that engage in collective activity whose benefits are exclusive to members. Sacrifices and prohibitions flow from the logic of clubs. To learn why, it may help to consider a more familiar example: vows of commitment and prohibitions on infidelity flow from the logic of *couples* for the same reasons. A couple is also a social unit engaged in mutual aid and other cooperative activity—activities that are very vulnerable if there is shirking or defection.

Subsidized Sacrifice

Armed with the logic of clubs, we can predict how religious radicals will respond to outside support, government action, and economic conditions. That is important for two reasons. First, before we use the club model to study terrorism, we would like to be able to further test its validity. Like any rookie theory, it should be tested at every opportunity. Second, our ultimate aim is to formulate new, practical ideas for societies dealing with modern religious radicals. The recent history of the Israeli government's relationship with ultra-Orthodox Jews provides a wealth of data, illustrating the extreme reaction of clubs to subsidies.

A first useful step is to explain how clubs respond to changes in their economic environment. To illustrate, let's return to the example of the suitor and your daughter, but with a new twist. Imagine that just before the suitor walked in your door and began earnestly describing his willingness to sacrifice for community and family, something wonderful happened. The radical religious community your family belongs to was blessed with a huge donation, a subsidy that it would use to expand schools and clinics, build a new community center, upgrade the youth club, introduce early childhood education, make the streets of your community safer, and even provide more generous stipends for seminary students. These improved services, however, will also attract opportunists. A suitor can now expect a more comfortable standard of living if he marries your daughter. Now the suitor, who was alone in the last example, is standing among dozens of others, milling about on the doorstep like the suitors of Penelope in Homer's *Odyssey*, waiting for a chance to marry into your devout and (now) very supportive community.

How will you distinguish the sincere young man in the last example, from the crowd of potential shirkers now crowding your doorstep? They all tell the same story of earnest devotion. Now that the subsidy has sweetened the pot, they are *all* willing to do what only the truly committed young man was volunteering to do in the previous example—spend a few years sacrificing their secular education and work experience to devote themselves to holiness. Membership in the subsidized club is more attractive now, so even less committed young men are willing to sacrifice in order to join.

You have no choice. The old demonstration of commitment is no longer sufficient to allay your fear that deep down the young suitor is just like the others, a shirker. You will have to ask for *more years of sacrifice* on the part of a prospective son-in-law. How many more years? Enough to scare off the last of the shirkers and leave the sincere, committed young man alone in your living room. To be sure, you will ask for this increased sacrifice with some hesitation, since every extra year in a seminary will prevent the young man from working to support your daughter and grandchildren and reduce future earnings. Yet, just as a wealthy parent is constrained by the need to protect his or her children from suitors who seek only to marry into money, you must protect your children and community from suitors who seek only the benefits of marrying into a mutual aid club. So you demand a larger sacrifice of your future son-in-law in return for allowing entry into the family and community, which is to say, the club.

How big an extra sacrifice is required to scare off the last shirker, leaving only the committed young suitor in your living room? It's hard to say; the necessary sacrifice could be very large. For example, the smallest necessary increase in sacrifice that leaves just one committed suitor might be *greater* than the benefit to the young family from the donation the community received. Why? Because the extra services provided might be more attractive to the potential shirkers than they are to club members (including the dedicated suitor)—who have already organized their community to meet their own basic needs. In that case the donation can actually become a curse. It makes community members worse off because the sacrifice that the outside subsidy triggers more than outweighs any benefits. That's an extreme example, but it illustrates the point. A small donation or subsidy to a club can induce a very large increase in sacrifice.

The general mechanism illustrated by the suitor example is this: A sacrifice that is used to demonstrate commitment must be expensive to the demonstrator (otherwise it would indicate nothing about commitment), so he will provide the minimum necessary sacrifice. That necessary minimum will increase with the value of membership in the club, because a more valuable club attracts more opportunists (potential shirkers). So a subsidy to the club that increases the value of membership necessitates an increase in required sacrifice. If the club chooses to increase the value of membership in a way that is particularly attractive to potential shirkers, the increase in required sacrifice might be quite large.

With the logic of subsidized sacrifice under our belts, let's return to what I called "the mystery of the missing dads" in the previous chapter, the strange decline in employment among Israeli ultra-Orthodox Jews in the 1980s and 1990s that got me hooked on studying religious radicals. Perhaps an increased subsidy to the ultra-Orthodox communities of Israel made them more attractive to prospective members? According to

the club model, that should have increased the length of yeshiva attendance necessary to signal commitment, extending durations of yeshiva
attendance and reducing labor-force participation. The only piece still
missing in that puzzle would then be the increased subsidy—which is
exactly what happened. To explain how requires a short digression on
ultra-Orthodox political parties and their role in Israeli politics. (As we
will see later, the Israeli case is less a digression than a useful example
of a general problem. An important source of religious conflict in the
Middle East is the inherent tension between the aspirations of radical
religious politicians and the responsibilities of government to other
citizens.)

From the late 1970s until recently, Israel has had two large voting
blocs. This division expresses a left-right split in the electorate over
foreign policy, which allocates to each side 35 to 45 percent of the vote
in a given election. The left has been more willing to concede territory
in negotiating a peace treaty with the neighboring Arab states and Palestinians. The right has been less willing make territorial concessions,
either because they suspect the intentions of the neighbors or because
they have a stronger religious attachment to the West Bank, Gaza, and
the Golan Heights. Ultra-Orthodox political parties, though their constituency is only 5 to 10 percent of the electorate, have typically com-
manded the swing vote in the Israeli parliament. In their view, foreign
policy is in the hands of the Almighty, so they can credibly threaten to
join either left- or right-wing blocs to form a coalition government. This
status as a swing voting bloc has allowed the ultra-Orthodox disproportionate influence over every Israeli coalition government, left or right,
since Menachem Begin created his first right-center coalition in 1977,
the government that removed the cap on the number of draft deferrals
for yeshiva students.

With gut-wrenching issues of war, peace, and power on the line, the
larger parties in Israeli politics have been willing to pay a high price
for the critical support of ultra-Orthodox parties in forming coalition
governments. The most bruised veteran of these negotiations is current
Israeli President Shimon Peres, who once complained: "The ultra-
Orthodox told me, cast your bread on the water. I cast entire bakeries."[6]
The price of ultra-Orthodox support for coalition governments has

included generous stipends for married men in yeshiva, direct funding of yeshivas, and a set of subsidies that discriminate in favor of the ultra-Orthodox, including reduced tuition in preschools and elementary schools, reduced property taxes, and reduced health insurance premiums, among others. Ultra-Orthodox parties have also lobbied effectively to increase the generosity of various nondiscriminatory support systems from which they benefit disproportionately because of their low incomes. Increased child allowances, which are increasingly generous per child as the number of children in a family grows, have also benefited from consistent support from the ultra-Orthodox lobby.[7] In addition, ultra-Orthodox politicians have pursued a contentious political agenda, attempting to impose religious prohibitions through secular law in such areas as dietary restrictions (*kashrut*), sabbath observance, and abortion. They have insisted on an Orthodox definition of Judaism in Israeli civil law. This constitutes an important and emotional issue for Jews, both in Israel and abroad, since Israel's "Law of Return" grants any (recognized) Jew citizenship on arrival. In addition, through control of government ministries, the ultra-Orthodox have created jobs for their clerics and other officials, especially in the Ministry of Religion.

Here, finally, is a possible explanation for the missing dads—that is, why yeshiva attendance among the Israeli ultra-Orthodox expanded so rapidly after the late 1970s in Israel and is so much more extensive than yeshiva attendance among ultra-Orthodox Jews in other countries. The Israeli government steadily increased subsidies to Israeli ultra-Orthodox communities, unintentionally forcing young men to spend even more time in yeshiva to demonstrate commitment. In terms of the "suitor at your doorstep" example, the government, in effect, crowded the doorstep with potential shirkers, attracting them by enriching the club with subsidies. To distinguish themselves from the crowd of potential shirkers on the doorstep, who were merely attracted by the larger subsidies, committed recruits were obliged to signal commitment by further increasing their level of sacrifice—or risk being asked to leave the premises.

In concrete terms, the argument goes like this. In an ultra-Orthodox community outside of Israel, say in Brooklyn (or historically in Israel or Europe), perhaps three to five years of yeshiva after high school are sufficient to demonstrate commitment to the community and prove that you're not a shirker. In Israel, since the 1990s, if a man leaves yeshiva "early," at age thirty-five, it's unclear if he is really committed or if he has been in yeshiva up until now merely to avoid military service and collect other subsidies. So he must remain a few more years in yeshiva after his draft exemption, typically five more, to demonstrate his commitment.[8] Comparing the subsidized community in Israel to that in New York or Montreal (where we have reliable survey data), this argument implies that *the effect of subsidies has been to delay entry into the labor force by fifteen to twenty years for ultra-Orthodox men in Israel!*[9]

The subsidized-sacrifice argument can explain our existing puzzles, but how can we tell if it constitutes a valid explanation or is just a clever rationalization? To really convince an empirical scientist one must meet Galileo's standard of proof: challenge the conjecture with fresh data and see if it is refuted—data you hadn't seen when you worked out the idea in the first place. Luckily, Israeli politics provided some data of that nature as well.[10]

In 1984, the ultra-Orthodox political party fractured at the national level. A group of ultra-Orthodox politicians of Sephardi origin (Jews from North Africa and the Middle East, also known as Mizrachi) split to create a party called *Shas*.[11] The split had many causes, but one was resentment of the preferential treatment given to the Ashkenazi (European) ultra-Orthodox by their Ashkenazi-dominated institutions and political party. Shas immediately became the largest ultra-Orthodox political party, expanding its support by drawing the votes of Sephardi Jews who were not ultra-Orthodox away from secular parties. Bolstered by that additional constituency, Shas became *by itself* the swing voting bloc in the Israeli parliament. Its leaders used their newfound political leverage to engineer sharp increases in funding for their own system of Sephardi ultra-Orthodox schools and social welfare institutions. From 1984 onward, subsidies to Sephardi ultra-Orthodox communities increased even faster than the growing subsidies to Ashkenazi ultra-Orthodox communities.

The subsidies that Shas showered on its constituency allow us to test the subsidized-sacrifice conjecture. The conjecture predicts that yeshiva attendance should have increased more quickly among the Sephardi ultra-Orthodox than among the Ashkenazi ultra-Orthodox from 1984

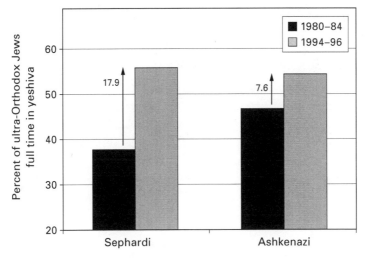

Figure 4.1
Yeshiva attendance of Sephardi increases faster than that of Ashkenazi

on, when subsidies began rising more quickly for Sephardi than Ashkenazi ultra-Orthodox institutions. The results (based as before on Israeli labor-force surveys) are illustrated in figure 4.1. While full-time yeshiva attendance rates among ultra-Orthodox Ashkenazi men increased by 7.6 percentage points, from 46.8 to 54.4, full-time yeshiva attendance rates among Sephardi ultra-Orthodox men increased by a full 17.9 percentage points, from 38 percent to 55.9 percent![12] A standard economic model of labor supply does not predict anything close to that sharp a drop in employment, in response to a subsidy to incomes and local public services. Thinking about the community as an economic club provides a much better explanation.[13]

One lesson from this episode is that subsidies for religious radicals can have extreme results. In this case an increased subsidy caused almost one in five Sephardi ultra-Orthodox men who would have otherwise been working or looking for work to remain in yeshiva instead, despite the economic burden that their nonparticipation loads on them, their wives, their families, their communities, and Israeli taxpayers. Measured over a little more than a decade, the 18-percentage-point decline in labor supply among young Sephardi ultra-Orthodox men is the most extreme example of manufactured welfare dependency I've ever seen—a policy that cripples the ability of an entire community to support itself!

A more general lesson from the Israeli experience of subsidizing an economic club is that the extreme behavior of members of radical religious communities is not necessarily due to age-old beliefs, theology, or ideology—those could not have changed as fast as labor supply declined. It *is* a direct result of public policy and economic conditions. In this case the subsidies of a secular state exacerbated an existing set of community sacrifices that distance community members from the secular, market culture.

Madrassas

Is the ultra-Orthodox experience in Israel unique? As we've seen, there is nothing particularly Jewish about religious radicals providing mutual aid services to their communities, or choosing high fertility. If education with low market returns demonstrates commitment to one's religious community among ultra-Orthodox Jews, we should see the same patterns among other religious radicals.

Using the same data described above to investigate fertility, economist Ara Stepanyan and I estimated returns to madrassa (i.e., Muslim religious) schooling as well, in Indonesia, rural Bangladesh, India (in Uttar Pradesh and Bihar), Pakistan, and Côte D'Ivoire. In two of those five countries, Indonesia and Bangladesh, the data yielded sufficiently precise estimates of economic returns to religious education to merit reporting.[14] Those results, combined with the figures from Israel, are reported in figure 4.4. For each country the height of the bar labeled "general schooling" is the estimated economic return to a year of secular schooling (i.e., the associated percentage increase in future earnings), while the bar labeled "religious schooling" reflects the return to a year of religious schooling. Economic returns to religious schooling are lower than those in the secular schooling system in Indonesia and Bangladesh, as they are in Israel. In Indonesia, for each year of religious schooling a student forfeits 2.2 percent of future earnings (every year) that they would have otherwise received, had they attended the general schooling system. In

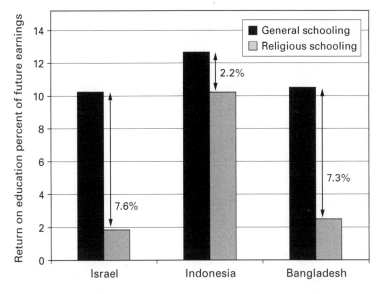

Figure 4.2
Lower returns to education for religious radicals (corresponds to note 14, chapter 4)

Bangladesh, the cost in future earnings is even higher, with 7.3 percent of future earnings lost for each year of religious schooling. Students in the Matlab region of Bangladesh sacrifice about as much per year as do students in ultra-Orthodox schools in Israel (7.6 percent).

This loss in earnings would not be a sacrifice if students had no other school to choose—just a tragedy. In all three cases, we observe in the data children in the same areas attending nonreligious schools as well, demonstrating that their parents indeed have a choice, and choose to sacrifice.

One caveat about this figure requires explanation. The estimated loss due to attending religious schools in Indonesia may be *underestimated* in the following sense. Our method does not distinguish between students attending the state religious stream and those in the private religious stream. The state religious stream follows a nationally approved curriculum, while the private religious stream chooses not to. Presumably the private religious schools have even lower economic returns than the average return in the two streams. If the average return across both streams is 2.2 percentage points lower than the general return, then the private religious return is likely even lower than that.

The larger message of figure 4.2 is this: In the two additional cases where we had enough information to estimate the economic benefits of schooling precisely, the pattern of low market returns we found among radical religious Jews held for radical religious Muslims as well. The findings for Indonesia and Bangladesh support the idea that Muslim communities that send their children to private religious schools may be understood as economic clubs as well.

Unfortunately, we don't yet have comparable estimates of returns on schooling among radical Christians. (Economist L. Choon Wang of UC San Diego has some suggestive preliminary results. He estimates that the lost earnings of the Pennsylvania Amish resulting from not attending ninth grade are even greater than the earnings lost in Israel or rural Bangladesh by missing a single year of secular schooling.[15]) Nevertheless, the little evidence we have is consistent with the club-theory prediction of a sacrifice early in life. The approach of U.S. Amish, Hutterite, and Wenger Mennonite communities, as noted in chapter 3 by James Hurd, is to deny education to their children altogether beyond the eighth grade, an increasingly expensive sacrifice in a modern education-driven economy. This modern Anabaptist approach to schooling only strengthens Iannaccone's argument that we should think of Christian religious radical communities as clubs that require sacrifice.

To recap, we've added another characteristic to the list of religious radicals' common behavior across religions, countries, and cultures. Insisting on education with poor market returns, or forbidding education altogether, seems to play the role of sacrifice. These expensive restrictions on schooling are an additional behavioral characteristic of radical religious communities, joining the various forms of prohibition, mutual aid, and high fertility that we've examined already. That commonality reinforces the idea that we can apply the insights of the club model developed to explain the behavior of radical religious Christians and Jews to radical Islamists as well. Moreover, we've seen evidence of an exotic implication of the club model: clubs are surprisingly responsive to changes in policies, and in unintuitive ways, so that small interventions can have extreme and sometimes unintended consequences.

Subsidized Prohibitions and Fertility

To further explore how clubs respond to changes in social policies, I want to return to our discussion of high fertility, another characteristic common to religious radicals across religions. While one might think that high fertility is an intimate decision, insulated from policy by personal values, tradition, and strongly held theological beliefs, we will see that the fertility choices of religious radicals can change quite quickly in response to changes in incentives.

So far we've seen two related conjectures relating fertility, religious prohibitions, and mutual aid: first, the more mutual aid in a community, the stricter the prohibitions; second, the stricter the prohibitions, the higher the fertility. We can test those conjectures if we can observe some changes in the levels of mutual aid available to families. Conveniently enough for this research, Israel's government increased subsidies to ultra-Orthodox communities in the 1980s and 1990s in a way that improved ultra-Orthodox mutual aid provision, as we've seen. How does a club model predict that the fertility choices of female members should respond to increased public subsidies and the accompanying increases in mutual aid? The answer takes a little figuring out—which we'll get to in a moment. Once we know it, we can take that prediction and test the model by comparing it to data from the episodes of increased subsidy in Israel.

In exploring the effects of subsidies on clubs I've emphasized so far the effect of improved services on people that want to join (in the suitor example). Now consider members who might choose to *leave*. Attrition is a persistent problem that all the denominations I've mentioned face. Putting aside theology, imagine the calculation of a young man or woman thinking of leaving a mutual aid club. It would go something like this: "Would I rather observe all the prohibitions and take on the sacrifices in return for all the services that the community provides, or leave, behave as I please, and buy those services in the market?" That sounds a little materialistic, but it need not be. The young person weighing options might take into account their religious feelings, as well as their empathy for family and friends. Weighing the costs and benefits of leaving, psychic or material, is a process that young men and women who grow up in radical religious communities and communes eventually must undertake. They typically do so in their late teens or early twenties, before marriage. The Amish actually have a customary trial period, *rumspringa*, in which young single men and women are cut some slack in the enforcement of prohibitions, including permission to leave the community, while deciding. (Amish teenagers on rumspringa were the stars of the reality cable TV show *Amish in the City*.) Israelis born on a kibbutz (communal villages that are generally secular) have a similar norm.

The possibility that members might leave must be on the minds of religious communities when they set norms. Prohibitions that are overly strict will chase away members, especially unmarried youth, who often look for ways to rebel against their parents in any society, and whose parents would naturally like to keep their children and grandchildren close. Communities face a constant trade-off in setting norms about prohibitions. If they enforce too strict a dress code, or crack down excessively on movies and the Internet, for example, they might risk losing members. On the other hand, if they are too lax with prohibitions, then the benefits of prohibitions will be lost: members will spend too much time in the mainstream culture, weakening the quality of collective activity, including mutual aid. For community leaders, choosing the right level of strictness requires trading off the benefit of retaining members on the one hand, against the cost of being too lax and allowing mutual aid to suffer as members pursue options outside the community.

Subsidies ease that trade-off by reducing the attraction of leaving. A subsidy spent on collective activities—making worship more attractive or improving the quality of services provided through mutual aid, for example—makes remaining in the community more desirable to members who might be considering leaving. That, in turn, allows the club to tighten prohibitions without risk of losing those members. Since prohibitions improve the quality of collective activities, that process is self-reinforcing, and collective activities might be doubly strengthened by subsidies. Despite the increase in strictness, membership will not decline. It may well grow, if the benefits of improved services made possible by subsidies outweigh the cost in stricter prohibitions.

What does that imply for the effect of subsidies on fertility? Radical religious clubs will respond to subsidies by increasing the strictness of religious prohibitions, as I've just argued. Increased prohibitions will in turn increase fertility through Gary Becker's "distance from the market" mechanism described above—they increase the cost of working for mothers and decrease the benefits of shopping, encouraging women to shift into nonmarket activities, chief of which is having and raising children.

Do radical religious clubs actually use outside subsidies to improve services for members? That's clearly what we've seen among the Hezbollah, Hamas, and ultra-Orthodox Jews. If we include law and order as a service, it is true of the Taliban as well. Do subsidies empower religious club to impose stricter prohibitions? That's the pattern we saw in Lebanon and Afghanistan; religiosity, as expressed in burkas and prayer, increased in Shiite communities in Lebanon when Iran subsidized Hezbollah. Subsidies and military aid to the mujahideen in Afghanistan were accompanied by increases in visible signs of religiosity. A similar increase in religiosity accompanied the expansion in provision of social services by the Muslim Brotherhood (which would spawn Hamas) in Gaza and the West Bank.

The logic of clubs also implies that even without an outside subsidy, an increase in social needs can cause members to increase their compliance with religious prohibitions. Even if the quality of services provided by the club is unchanged, a decline in the ability of government to provide basic services, such as security, electricity, education, or welfare services, will allow religious radicals who provide those services to demand stricter adherence to religious prohibitions. Members who would have considered leaving the club when outside options were good will instead remain demonstrably loyal if the club suddenly becomes their sole provider of necessary services, allowing the club to ratchet up prohibitions without fear of losing members. That's consistent with the increase in visible religiosity in the Shiite suburbs of Baghdad when al-Sadr's forces became the most reliable providers of basic services.

Now that we understand how outside subsidies increase a club's prohibitions, we can test whether subsidies affect fertility. If it is really true that a subsidy can cause changes in religious norms powerful enough to alter something as intimate as fertility decisions, that would constitute compelling evidence for thinking of religious radicals as mutual aid collectives—or economic clubs. High fertility among Christian Anabaptists and ultra-Orthodox Jews was explained earlier as the result of religious prohibitions imposed on women, distancing them from working in the market. If subsidies increase prohibitions that apply to women, then we should see *increases* in fertility. From a research perspective, fertility has the great benefit of being both observable and quantifiable, in contrast to the strictness of religious prohibitions, which is more subjective by nature. So fertility changes are ideal for testing the conjecture of *subsidized prohibitions*—that is, that subsidies to a club with pronatalist prohibitions will increase fertility.

Increased subsidies to Israeli ultra-Orthodox Jews, as I discussed above, began in 1977 when ultra-Orthodox politicians used their position as swing voters in the Israeli parliament to successfully lobby for large transfers of subsidies and services to their communities. Ultra-Orthodox leaders used those resources to augment a system of services provided to their communities through mutual aid. The "subsidized-prohibition" argument predicts that those subsidies should have induced stricter religious prohibitions and increased fertility. Anecdotally, that increase in religious prohibitions occurred, though it is hard to document. The timing of the fertility increase among ultra-Orthodox Jewish mothers, on the other hand, is clearly documented and consistent with the subsidized-prohibition argument. As we have seen, ultra-Orthodox women added over a child to their total fertility, which increased as subsidies did, between the early 1980s and mid-1990s, from 6.5 to 7.6 children per woman.

How can we be sure that increased fertility was caused by increased subsidies? The differential increases in subsidies between Sephardi and Ashkenazi ultra-Orthodox communities provide strong evidence. Recall that Israeli government subsidies to the Sephardi ultra-Orthodox lagged behind those to the Ashkenazi from 1977 through 1984, when Shas captured the balance of power. From then on subsidies to the Sephardi ultra-Orthodox accelerated and may have even caught up. The

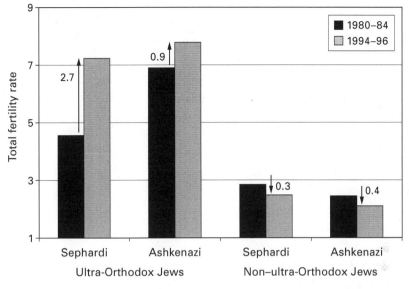

Figure 4.3
Fertility change—denomination and origin

"subsidized-prohibition" explanation for high fertility among religious radicals implies that fertility among Sephardi ultra-Orthodox women should have increased faster than that among Ashkenazi ultra-Orthodox women from 1984 onward.

Figure 4.3 describes what actually happened, allowing us to check the club model's predictions against the Israeli data. To the right are bars representing Sephardi and Ashkenazi non-ultra-Orthodox Jewish women, just over 95 percent of adult Jewish women in the mid-1990s. Their total fertility rates fell by 0.34 and 0.35 children respectively. Second from the left are Ashkenazi ultra-Orthodox Jewish women, whose fertility increased by 0.89 children on average. The far-left bars represent the total fertility rates of Sephardi ultra-Orthodox women. They increased from 4.57 to 7.24 children in just over a decade, an increase of 2.67 lifetime children per woman!

The velocity of this increase in births by Sephardi ultra-Orthodox women is quite exceptional in modern demography. The difference between it and the increase among Ashkenazi women (2.67–0.89) is 1.78

children.[16] The faster growth in fertility for the women in the more subsidized denomination provides further evidence for the subsidized-prohibition argument implied by the club model of radical religious groups.

Recalling the evidence on how yeshiva attendance (i.e., sacrifice) responded to changes in subsidies, figure 4.3 implies that religious prohibitions respond to subsidies as well. Fertility, in turn, responds quite dramatically to changes in religious prohibitions that affect women. Combining the data on fertility increases with that on yeshiva attendance discussed above, the evidence is piling up in support of the idea that public policy toward radical religious clubs really does matter; it can induce dramatic changes in members' behavior. That will be worth bearing in mind when we consider approaches governments might take to religious radicals.

How Many Radical Islamists?

If we're convinced by the evidence that the club approach is a useful way of thinking about religious radicals, then here's one way we can apply that insight. Religious schooling among Muslims predicts low educational returns and high fertility. If we accept those as markers of clublike behavior, then those markers are useful for another reason. They give us a rough measure of the incidence of religious radicalism, which one might think of as the size of the radical religious population where clubs might exist and of the core constituency that Islamist political parties can aspire to gain support from.

For the five countries in which we could measure attendance at Islamic schools, figure 4.4 reports on the proportion of Muslims (actually, adult Muslim women) living in families in which any member attended a religious school. The prevalence of Islamic schooling is quite high in the rural villages of Uttar Pradesh and Bihar (16.4 percent) as well as in Indonesia (14.1 percent)—where the estimates include the both private and public religious schooling. Yet the prevalence is below 5 percent in Bangladesh, Pakistan, and Côte D'Ivoire. Subsequent analysis by other scholars using more complete data sources yields an even lower estimate

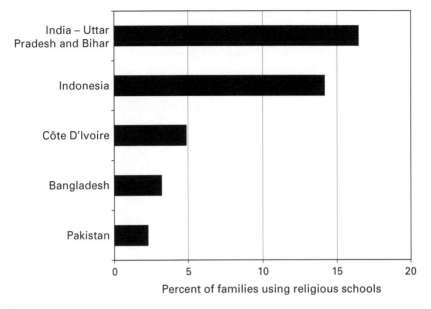

Figure 4.4
How many radical Islamists?

for Pakistan, and reveals that even among families in which one child attends Islamic schools, often other children do not. Thus figure 4.6 may actually overstate the proportion of Pakistani children in Islamic schooling.[16] The data indicate that across all these countries, the underlying core constituency that supports radical religious views, and might support political Islamists in elections or provide a recruiting pool for radical Islamist rebels, is much smaller than one might suspect based on media accounts.

Figure 4.4 also underlines how much can be learned from just a little bit of inexpensive data collection, once we have a theory to guide what we're looking for. All of the results and insights in this chapter were made possible by the addition of a question about the "type of school attended," to existing survey forms, at a collection cost of pennies per observation. (In fact, had the question not been on the Israeli version I would have never launched this research agenda in the first place.)[18]

Recap

We have covered a lot of ground in this discussion of clubs, so before returning to an analysis of violence by religious radicals, this is a good time to review the peaceful interlude that these last two chapters provided. Iannaccone set out to explore the puzzling behavior of religious radicals with the tools of economics and returned with a surprisingly useful explanation: radical religious groups, or sects, operate as economic clubs. They collectively provide both spiritual services and an entire array of concrete social services through mutual aid systems. Sometimes that communal structure is explicit—for example, among early Hutterites who operated formal communes, or in the Indonesian Pengajian, which has a formal redistribution rule. More often the mutual aid contract is implicit, as it is among ultra-Orthodox Jews. To protect that mutual aid club against shirkers, members require sacrifices of each other as demonstrations of commitment. Religious prohibitions also help reduce shirking among members by distancing them from market opportunities and strengthening collective activity. Radical religious clubs are just an extreme example of collective activity that is quite common within religious congregations. Religious radicals are at the high-commitment, high-collective-activity end of a spectrum of religious denominations found in Judaism, Christianity, and Islam alike. The more collective activity in a denomination, the stronger the religious prohibitions and sacrifices. That club logic also applies to communes, fraternities, gangs, and other nonreligious organizations, as Iannaccone anticipated in his study.[19]

Changes in economic opportunities and in government policy toward radical religious clubs can trigger extreme responses, because their levels of sacrifices and prohibitions are very sensitive to the possibility that shirkers will join, on the one hand, or that nonshirking members will choose to leave the fold, on the other. The prosperity of American Anabaptist farming communities apparently worked like a subsidy, inducing extremely pronatalist norms and lifestyles among Anabaptist women, who achieved record-high fertility in the nineteenth and twentieth centuries. Subsidies to the social service provision network of Israeli ultra-Orthodox Jews induced a dramatic increase in sacrifices in the

1980s and 1990s as well as a precipitous decline in work; young men stretched yeshiva study into their forties on average to prove their commitment to the community. The same subsidies induced an increase in prohibitions and a sharp increase in the fertility, especially among Sephardi ultra-Orthodox women.

We know much less about the internal organization of radical religious groups among Muslims, despite intense media attention. There is widespread anecdotal evidence of social service provision by Muslim religious charities. Our evidence on families who send children to madrassas in various Asian countries reveals markers of clublike communities: low economic returns to schooling and high fertility. In the denominational spectrum these families look, on average, less extreme than Anabaptists and more like, perhaps, a U.S. denomination like the Pentecostals or the Church of God. Even using that broad definition of religious radicals, those families are far from a majority in the five countries for which we could find evidence. The majority of the population is likely to be more moderate in their religiosity. Consistent with the implications of the club model, we've also seen that when Islamic radicals are subsidized, religiosity can increase quickly, allowing religious radicalization, as we saw in Afghanistan, Lebanon, Palestine, and possibly among Shiites in Iraq. The same increase in religiosity can occur when Islamic radicals become the principal providers of some basic public services, such as security or welfare services.

The broad parallels between religious radicalism in Christianity, Judaism, and Islam suggest an underlying model that we can draw on for insights. Now that we have a way of thinking about religious radicals and the communities they live in, we're prepared to return to two central questions: Why are religious radicals such effective terrorists and insurgents? And how should the answer inform a response?

Religious authorities and forensics team search wreckage of bus after Hamas suicide attack, Jerusalem, Israel, March 1996. (AP Photo/Eyal Warshavsky).

5

The Hamas Model: Why Religious Radicals Are Such Effective Terrorists

We must examine the costs and benefits of continued armed operations.
—Mahmoud al-Zahar, founding member of Hamas, quoted in *Al Quds*, East Jerusalem, October 1995[1]

The "Hamas Model"

In October 2005 a major earthquake shook the mountains and valleys of Kashmir, the disputed region that sits uncomfortably between northwest India and Pakistan. While the epicenter was in Pakistani-administered western Kashmir, the destruction traced a broad arc along the intersections of the Eurasian and Indian plates, from Karachi in southwest Pakistan, north into Afghanistan, east across northern Pakistan, through Kashmir, and into India. Over seventy thousand people died, mostly in Kashmir. Millions were left homeless. In the earthquake's aftermath humanitarian needs were acute—especially in the poorly governed hinterlands of Kashmir. Remote villages with road access blocked by landslides desperately required medical care, food, and sometimes even help extracting survivors from the rubble. National and international aid efforts were immediate but disorganized. Some of the most nimble providers of aid were reported to be bearded young radical Islamists.

Der Spiegel reporter Susanne Koelbl describes twenty-five-year-old Mohammed Maqsood, a "militant" in Kashmir who would not shake her hand or even make eye contact with her—a female journalist.

Men like Maqsood were the first aid workers to arrive in the disaster zone. . . . They conducted systematic searches for survivors in the rubble of ruined buildings, often digging with their bare hands. In the first two days following the earthquake the bearded young men seemed to be the only ones with a well-functioning network—both in Muzaffarabad, the capital of the Pakistani state of Azad Kashmir, and in the completely devastated settlements of Bagh and Balakot. Many local residents owe their lives to these aid workers.

Today Maqsood is the acting director of the Al-Rahmat Trust Camp, a refugee camp for earthquake victims in central Muzaffarabad. It's an open secret that the organization is the civilian wing of a banned guerilla organization, Jaish-e-Mohammed . . . and its fighters are battling Indian security forces in the Indian section of Kashmir.[2]

Under the subheading "The Hamas Model," journalist Koelbl goes on to describe these "militants": "Their politics and policies resemble those of the militant groups Hamas and Hezbollah in the Middle East, where radicals have filled the vacuum left by the state. They develop social institutions and help address the local population's day-to-day survival needs. In the long term, this social role also helps the local population identify with the respective groups' political goals."[3] Describing a different Islamic aid group, *Jamaat-ud-Dawa*, she writes:

The organization, with its many camps and hospitals, ordinary schools and Koran schools, is the region's strongest and most powerful Islamist aid organization. It is closely associated with the banned Lashkar-e-Tayyaba, or "Army of the Pure," which, like Jaish-e-Mohammed, sends its fighters into the Indian section of Kashmir to kill soldiers and blow up military barracks. Both groups are also suspected of having committed the 2001 attack on the Indian parliament in New Delhi.[4]

Lashkar-e-Taiba subsequently dispatched the Mumbai terrorists in November 2008, according to the admission of the surviving attacker, Mohammed Ajmal Kasab. They are responsible for over 170 deaths in suicidal attacks on a packed train station, luxury hotels, and a Hassidic religious center. Indian authorities also hold Lashkar-e-Taiba responsible for a number of other murderous terrorist attacks, including the July 2006 train bombings in Mumbai, which killed 211 people. The dissonance is jarring: empathy for earthquake victims and proactive dedication to their well-being on the one hand, and murderous disregard for the lives of other civilians on the other.[5]

That same disturbing dissonance characterizes all of the violent groups I've described already. While it is reassuring to realize that these terrorists are neither theologically brainwashed drones, nor the psychopathic killers of B movies, it's hardly a consolation to know that people who are effective at providing humanitarian assistance, education, and healthcare to their own constituency, are at the same time so deadly when it comes to outsiders.

Compared to older terrorist organizations the current cohort of radical religious terrorists all started out relatively short on training and experience, yet the Taliban, Hamas, and Hezbollah nonetheless quickly developed into the most destructive rebel organizations in their respective conflicts. I think the central question about modern terrorism is this: If religious radicals are neither blinded by theology nor psychopathic killers, then why, when they turn to violence, are they so effective at it? This chapter suggests an answer, using the logic of defection constraints and economic clubs developed above, and turning to data from the Middle East for evidence. The first step in the argument is to see violent religious radicals as their constituencies do, as economic clubs.

Origins of the Model

Social service provision dates back to the very beginnings of modern political Islam. Hasan al-Banna, the first political Islamist of the twentieth century, was a gifted schoolteacher in the Egyptian city of Ismailia, on the west bank of the Suez canal. A charismatic preacher, al-Banna would lecture in the mosques and even in the coffee houses in the evenings. Together with six laborers, he founded the Society of Muslim Brotherhood at age twenty-two in 1928. Like other religious thinkers at the time, al-Banna opposed European and secular influences. He advocated a return to traditional Muslim values, the strengthening of families, and an Islamic approach to social and political issues.[6] Unlike other organizations, the Brotherhood took practical action under his leadership. Al-Banna and his followers raised money and built a mosque, and then two schools (one for boys and one for girls) as well as a social club.

Using freshly declassified State Department and CIA documents, sociologist Ziad Munson took a new look at the history of the Muslim Brotherhood in 2001. He describes al-Banna's organizational model:

Each new branch of the Society followed a similar pattern of growth. The organization would establish a branch headquarters and then immediately begin a public service project—the construction of a new mosque, school, or clinic, the support of a local handicraft industry, or the organization of a sports program. This private social service infrastructure grew quickly and became an important part of the Egyptian social, political and economic landscape.[7]

The Brotherhood grew exponentially. They organized youth groups, charities, trade unions, and night schools for workers. Eventually they even owned factories. Al-Banna's organization expanded to fifteen branches by 1932, when he relocated himself and their headquarters to Cairo; and to three hundred branches by 1938, with a membership estimated at between 50,000 and 150,000. By 1949 the Brotherhood's two thousand branches throughout Egypt included between 300,000 and 600,000 members.[8]

The Brotherhood filled a demand for educational, cultural, social, and medical services left unmet by government. Yet a club is not a government—in order to motivate members (who are generally volunteers) not to shirk on their work for the club it expels them for shirking and excludes nonmembers from access to services. Munson writes: "Muslim Brotherhood public works brought millions of Egyptians into contact with the organization and its ideology. They helped overcome potential free-rider problems within the organization, as resources such as schools and clinics served as *selective incentives* for Muslim Brotherhood members and potential recruits."[9] To be clear, the "free riders" that Munson describes are the shirkers in the mutual aid examples of the last chapter.

The Brotherhood established a tiered membership structure early on, by 1935. Lower-tier members paid dues, held a membership card, and had access to the social service network and mosques. At higher tiers, the Brotherhood required more commitment, including an oath of allegiance, Koranic studies, and physical training. This structure allowed the organization to select suitable candidates among the large pool of lower-tier members who sought services, then train and indoctrinate them. Once suitably selected and prepared, higher-tier members could be entrusted with more sensitive jobs.

The social service network also created an organizational base that protected the Muslim Brotherhood against repression, which the government quickly resorted to when the Brothers became involved in politics. For the first decade the Brotherhood remained apolitical, concentrating on building social service institutions and preaching personal piety. That changed when two political currents merged into a perfect wave of opportunity. The first was the 1936 general strike in Palestine, a rebellion of Palestinian Arabs against both the British—who governed Palestine under a mandate from the League of Nations—and Jewish settlement. The rebellion in Palestine gave the Brotherhood a chance to show solidarity with an anti-imperialist movement without actually endangering themselves by rebelling in Egypt against British control of the government. The second current was the terribly unpopular collaboration of the Wafd party with the British. The Wafd party had previously gained widespread support by waving the banner of Egyptian nationalism, so their implicit acceptance of British rule was considered a betrayal. In 1941 the Brotherhood seized the political opportunity, running candidates in elections and calling for both social reform and British withdrawal. The British responded by banning the party and arresting leaders. Yet by this time the Brotherhood was difficult to suppress. Its broad membership base made it resilient to the loss of leaders. They easily weathered the storm. The British soon went back to concentrating on the war effort and released the Brotherhood leaders.

That organizational base, built on the social service provision network, would prove critical in surviving the next, more severe, round of repression. Previously, sometime around 1939 al-Banna and the Brotherhood leadership had reluctantly established a militia, the "Secret Apparatus," in response to internal pressure from more militant leaders. After the end of World War II, the Apparatus began attacking British and government targets. The government responded by legally dissolving the Brotherhood in December 1948. The Apparatus took revenge later in the same month, assassinating Prime Minister Mahmud Fahmi al-Nuqrashi. Al-Banna condemned the assassination, protesting to the authorities that he could not control the militia with a crackdown in place and his organization officially dissolved. His pleas of innocence did him no good. Al-Banna was shot in the street by government agents in February 1949. Yet, despite losing its charismatic founding leader, suffering fierce repression—which included the arrest of four thousand members—the

Brotherhood again proved resilient, managing to retain the loyalty of members and of its constituency.

The Free Officers coup of 1952 led to an even more serious challenge. The new president, Gamal Abdel Nasser, and the coup leadership had allied themselves with the Brotherhood to gain power. Yet the organization and the new government were quickly in conflict. The Brotherhood demanded power sharing and was incensed, among other things, over the British-trained officers' refusal to ban alcohol. In October 1954 a Muslim Brother attempted to assassinate President Nasser. Or perhaps he was framed. Either way, Nasser emerged a hero and exploited the opportunity. He legally dissolved the Brotherhood, had six members hanged, imprisoned thousands, and launched a protracted campaign of arrest and torture that would last for a decade.

Nasser also took an additional, critical step that the British and the previous Egyptian government had not. He nationalized the Brotherhood's social service provision network and operated it as part of the Egyptian government. That counterinsurgency strategy was singularly effective: without its schools and clinics the vast organization withered, and to this day it has not recovered its political strength or organizational ability. The threat to Nasser's government dried up with it.

A virulent new strain of Islamist revolutionary theology grew in the hostile environment left by the Brotherhood's political failure and Nasser's successful suppression of their operations. One of the jailed and tortured leaders was Sayyid Qutb, who had edited the Brotherhood newspaper. In prison, Qutb developed the extreme principles that became the basis of current jihadist theology. Just a few years earlier the Muslim Brotherhood had been willing to cooperate with secular officers to overthrow the government and expel the British. Now those former allies, Nasser's officers, had their jailers torturing Qutb and the other Brotherhood leaders. A new approach was needed. Qutb argued that the Western values of individualism, colonialism, capitalism, and Marxism had not only failed; they were a symptom of *jahiliyya*, the chaos that engulfed the world before the time of the prophet Mohammed. This reversion to pre-Islamic chaos had been brought on not by foreign rule, but by secularism—a denial of the will of the Almighty. His solution was clear: prepare for a jihad to overthrow the usurpers, both foreign and secular governments, in Egypt and abroad, and to establish Islamic states in their place. Qutb preached that under the circumstances violent revolt was a religious duty, even against Muslim nationalists. Until that revolt was feasible, he called on his followers to self-segregate Islamist communities from the secular culture, so that they could survive.

The Egyptian Brotherhood and the Egyptian clerical establishment largely rejected Qutb's theories, as do most Muslims.[10] His view of violent jihad as a religious requirement is controversial and generally not accepted on theological grounds. Jihad for most Muslims is a personal mission of pious self-improvement and service to others.[11] Muslims generally interpret Islam as tolerant of other cultures, permitting violence only in self-defense and never in religious matters. Qutb claimed that violence is permitted because Islam is under siege, but that argument is generally rejected. Nasser's government had Sayyid Qutb hanged for treason in 1966. But his brother, Mohammed Qutb, survived to publicize his works, and would eventually personally influence Al Qaeda leaders Ayman al-Zawahiri and Osama bin Laden. Through that link Sayyid Qutb's writings would provide the foundation for Al Qaeda's political theology of global jihad.   Muslim Bros ~ the Hamas-org

While it is easy to lump al-Banna and Qutb together, understanding the broad influence of the Muslim Brotherhood requires carefully distinguishing al-Banna's organizational model from Qutb's theology. Al-Banna's major innovation was not theological but organizational. He invented what is now called the "Hamas model"—an Islamic social service provision organization that can quickly evolve to exploit political opportunities as they arise, all with the goal of enabling personal piety and eventually establishing an Islamic state. This organizational model generated the exponential growth and popularity of the Muslim Brotherhood from the late 1920s through the late 1940s, long before massive oil revenues were available to subsidize present-day Islamist charities. Al Qaeda, today's bearer of Qutb's ideological torch, is harshly critical of the Muslim Brotherhood, rejecting their willingness to participate in elections as an abandonment of the duty of violent struggle against corrupt usurpers of power, Muslim or otherwise.[12]

Al-Banna's approach to Islam was strict but would hardly qualify him as a theological radical. He was on the conservative edge of the mainstream, arguing for a more literal reading of the holy texts. His stance included strict prohibitions concerning individual conduct, such as dancing and gambling, which mainstream Muslims might allow, and a rejection of all things Western, such as theater, films, and foreign styles of dress. The club approach predicts that those stricter prohibitions should have contributed to the success of the Brotherhood's social service provision network, though the social service component of the Brotherhood's history is terribly understudied and we currently have no direct evidence with which to test that conjecture.

Whether the internal workings of Muslim Brotherhood charities and communities are economic clubs, like those of radical Christian and Jewish sects—which are much better documented—is an open question. On the one hand we have no direct evidence. On the other, the Muslim Brotherhood under al-Banna did practice exclusionary provision of services, and service provision seems to be accompanied by a stricter set of religious prohibitions than those practiced by the surrounding society. Furthermore, there is the puzzle of who pays for the social services. Like the Christian and Jewish radical religious clubs, the Muslim Brotherhood manages to provide extensive services without formal tax authority or an outside revenue stream. Economist Timur Kuran of Duke University estimates that charitable contributions (*zakat*) in other Muslim countries make up less than 1 percent of income among the general public, indicating that volunteer labor would be necessary to keep such a large network running.[13] We do know that, whatever their internal workings, al-Banna's model of Islamist charities combined with politically active Islam has spread successfully and widely, with Muslim Brotherhood chapters now established in countries and communities throughout the Muslim world.

Under the subsequent Egyptian presidents, Anwar el-Sadat and Hosni Mubarak, the Muslim Brotherhood was technically forbidden to engage in political activity but was generally tolerated, with occasional waves of arrests and government repression. President Sadat, who succeeded Nasser in 1970, freed members from jail and co-opted the Brotherhood in an effort to present himself as a more Muslim leader as he consolidated power. The organization's influence has grown since, as its rebuilt social service networks—financed since the 1980s with revenues from zakat—

have outperformed those of the government. Sadat would not survive his experiment with co-opting the Brotherhood. In October 1981, as he reviewed a military parade, a truck full of troops halted in front of the review stand and opened fire on the presidential party, killing Sadat and eleven others. The troops were loyal to the Egyptian Islamic Jihad, an outgrowth of the Muslim Brotherhood that espoused a jihadist theology influenced by Qutb.

President Hosni Mubarak, Sadat's successor, has taken a middle course, allowing the Muslim Brotherhood to compete unofficially in tightly controlled elections while brutally suppressing the Egyptian Islamic Jihad. (He has good reason. The Egyptian Islamic Jihad ambushed Mubarak's presidential motorcade during a visit to Ethiopia in June 1995, narrowly failing in their attempt to assassinate him). In the Egyptian parliamentary elections of 2005, Muslim Brotherhood candidates ran as independents. Despite strict government control of both the media and the election process, Brotherhood-affiliated candidates won one-fifth of the total seats and formed the largest opposition bloc.

Hamas

With the history of the Muslim Brotherhood as background, the birth of Hamas appears familiar. Palestinian-born Sheikh Ahmed Yassin returned to Gaza in the early 1970s from Egypt, where he had joined the Muslim Brotherhood as a university student.[14] He vitalized local branches of the Brotherhood by following al-Banna's standard procedure: build an organizational base of social service provision and wait patiently for political opportunities. The Israeli occupational government and foreign aid providers left him lots of service provision opportunities: Gaza had a tremendous unfilled demand for new mosques, schools, clinics, youth groups, and the like.

The Brotherhood managed to supplement local charitable giving by soliciting funding from Muslims abroad, especially after the oil crises of the 1970s initiated a flood of oil revenue from the world's economies into the Persian Gulf. They also found a way to gain revenue and political power with the help of an unlikely ally: with the tacit approval of the Israeli administrators, to whom the Brotherhood looked like a placid

counterbalance to Yasir Arafat's Fatah, they gained control over important mosques and the substantial *waqf* property attached to them.[15] (A
waqf is a religious trust established according to Ottoman law. The most
famous waqf is that which controls the Haram al-Sharif, the Temple
Mount, in Jerusalem. Since waqf property is not taxed, much private
wealth was historically channeled into these trusts, so that a waqf associated with a mosque or charitable institution can retain significant assets.)
Mishal and Sela (2000) report that about 10 percent of the agricultural
land and other real estate in Gaza belongs to various *awaqf* (plural of
waqf).[16] Between these three sources of revenue—local charity, transfers
from Muslims abroad, and proceeds from waqf properties—Yassin's
branch of the Brotherhood gathered the resources to grow its service
provision network.

Yassin's initial reluctance to get involved in the nationalist, territorial
struggle with Israel would have been sensible, considering the odds
against expelling the Israelis and the Brotherhood's dismal history with
its Secret Apparatus in Egypt. As we've seen, though, internal pressure
from younger members, combined with the threat of being left out of a
popular uprising—the first Intifada—eventually prompted Yassin to
reluctantly authorize a militia, Hamas, in late 1987. The new name
would have been an attempt to distance the militia from the social service
institutions, which might be vulnerable to repression, as the Muslim
Brotherhood's network of institutions in Egypt had been.

Why did Hamas turn to terrorism? The Oslo Accords of 1993 launched
a peace process between Israel and the Palestine Liberation Organization
(PLO) designed to create an eventual Palestinian state. That process
had delivered the leadership of the Palestinian Authority (PA) to Yasir
Arafat's secular Fatah movement, the dominant organization in the PLO.
Familiar as Yassin had to be with the Brotherhood's history in Egypt,
the threat must have been clear. Nasser's secular nationalist state had
shattered the Brotherhood's dream of an Islamist state in Egypt. Now
Arafat was threatening to do the same by creating a secular *Palestinian*
state. Yassin ridiculed Fatah for collaborating with the occupiers, painting them into the role of the Egyptian Wafd—this time with the Israelis
cast as the British colonialists. Terrorism against Israeli targets allowed
Hamas to present themselves as the true nationalists. Hamas did not

need Qutb's global jihadist ideology to turn to terrorism. The possibility of Fatah gaining a Palestinian state simply created opposing political agendas and a political opportunity that could be captured through violence. At first violent resistance against Israel was designed to position Hamas as a nationalist organization like Fatah. Later it was designed to undermine Fatah by crippling the peace process.

When political opportunities emerged Hamas seized them. First, the Oslo process stalled in the mid-1990s. Then economic conditions on the West Bank and in Gaza worsened. These developments allowed Hamas to brand Fatah as corrupt collaborators. Hamas, their reputation enhanced by both a thriving social service provision organization and lethal acts of terrorism, could present themselves as an alternative, both honest and brave. In January 2006 they chose to participate in Palestinian parliamentary elections and won—surprising even themselves. That victory set off a crisis, because Israel, the United States, and Europe cut off the international aid that supported the Palestinian authority, leaving the Palestinian Authority unable to pay civil servants' salaries. Though Hamas nominally held power, they lacked the resources to govern. As discussed above, that electoral victory set off a chain of events that led to Hamas seizing Gaza, rocket attacks on Israeli civilians, and the Israeli incursion into Gaza in December 2008. Though they lost that battle, Hamas can now aspire to win the reconstruction and to make further political gains at the expense of Fatah.

In summary, the so-called Hamas model was introduced and developed in Egypt, by al-Banna's Muslim Brotherhood. The Hamas theology is not jihadist, in Qutb's sense. Indeed, Hamas has generally distanced itself from Al Qaeda and global jihadists. Like the original Muslim Brotherhood in Egypt, their political aspirations are domestic. Hamas aspires to solve the problems of Muslim Palestinians by establishing an Islamic state. Their first step was to set up a social service provision network, just as al-Banna had done in Ismailia, which was accomplished by the early 1980s. After that, they were poised to seek political power, by violence if necessary, and with the help of Iranian allies if it suits their purposes.

In this sense, Hamas is *not* a terrorist organization using social service provision as a front to disguise its other activities, as is sometimes claimed.[17] The social services came first. As recently as 2001, Israeli terrorism expert Reuven Paz wrote of Hamas, "Approximately 90 percent of its work is in social, welfare, cultural and educational activities. These are important elements of Hamas's popularity that keep it closely tied to the public. Hamas is more effective than most PA institutions, which is not surprising considering the difficulties and corruption of the PA. Its only real competitors are several nongovernmental organizations that cannot or do not want to translate their work into political influence."[18] Hamas is better understood as a radical religious, social service-providing organization, in the mold of al-Banna's Muslim Brotherhood, which adopted terrorism in order to achieve its political goals.

Social Service Provision by the Taliban, Hezbollah, and al-Sadr

The roots of the Taliban also contain aspects of the "Hamas model": a radical religious social service provider with political aspirations. The Taliban trace their origins back to refugee camps run for Afghans in Pakistan by the Jamiat-e Ulama-I Islam (JUI), a small Pakistani Islamist political party. The JUI are fundamentalists, following the Deobandi educational tradition. The Deobandi began in India in the nineteenth century as a reaction to British rule, when they rejected instruction in English—the language of the colonial power. Deobandi schools have a strong antisecular bias, teaching mostly religious subjects. They are supported by charity and awaqf, with additional donations coming from Saudi Arabia since the 1970s.[19] Deobandi schools expanded rapidly in the 1980s in Pakistan, partially because of supportive government influence over waqf assets. Pakistani journalist Ahmed Rashid describes the JUI-Taliban connection:

Throughout the [Afghan civil] war in the 1980s the Jamiat-e Ulama-I Islam had quietly built up a support base among the Durrani Pushtuns living in Baluchistan and the North West frontier Province, opening up madrassas and carrying out relief work in the refugee camps.

   The Pushtuns that belong to the JUI have a great deal in common with the Taliban. Both come from the Durrani tribes that straddle the porous border between Afghanistan and Baluchistan. The activists of the JUI are Deobandis, followers of a fundamentalist reformist sect that interprets Islam, particularly its injunctions against women, extremely strictly.[20]

During the Afghan campaign against Soviet occupation JUI madrassas adopted a militant jihadist stance, with the approval and support of the Pakistani Inter-Services Intelligence organization (ISI), the CIA, and Saudi Arabia, all of whom supported the rebels as a means of expelling the Soviets from Afghanistan.

After the Soviet retreat in 1989 the CIA lost interest, but the JUI madrassas and relief network on the Pakistani side of the border remained, eventually giving birth to the Taliban in 1994. I've already described the consensus view of Taliban origins according to foreign scholars. The Taliban's own version emphasizes provision of a critical service, public safety. Here it is, as told by Australian journalist Anthony Davis:

> The official Taliban version of history traces the genesis of the movement to a humble madrasah in the Singesar village of Kandahar province's Maiwand district where Mohammad Omar, a former mujahid, was studying. Long incensed by the excesses of predatory Mujahideen bands on the provincial highways where arbitrary "taxation," robbery and rape had become a depressing norm, he and thirty comrades finally decided to take up arms in the summer of 1994. On a wave of popular anger, the movement grew from there.[21]

Anthropologist David Kilcullen reports that the resurgent Taliban have returned to providing judicial services in Afghanistan. "By mid-2008, the Taliban were operating 13 guerrilla law courts throughout the southern parts of Afghanistan—a shadow judiciary that expanded Taliban influence by settling disagreements, hearing civil and criminal matters, and using the provisions of Islamic shari'a law and their own Pashtun code to handle everything from law disputes to capital crimes."[22]

We explored above the critical role of social service provision in the development of Hezbollah. In a nutshell, Hezbollah's early leaders were active in Lebanese Shiite charities. With the benefit of Iranian funding, they quickly expanded their social service provision network, triggering an accompanying expansion in visible religiosity.

As we have seen, social service provision also played an important role in the history of the Mahdi Army, Muqtada al-Sadr's militia in Iraq. Al-Sadr's father, Mohammad Sadeq al-Sadr, built an extensive charity network in the 1990s to serve Shiite Muslims in Baghdad and southern Iraq when the sanctions-depleted government of Saddam Hussein cut back services to Shiites.

Those two organizations, Hezbollah and the Mahdi Army, have a close theological affinity. Both are political-religious organizations built by students who studied in the Shiite holy cities of Iran and Iraq. Those two Shiite militias are quite distinct theologically from the three Sunni organizations: the Taliban, Hamas, and al-Banna's Muslim Brotherhood. What all these groups share, though, is the "Hamas model"—political radical Islam combined with social service provision.

Why Religious Radicals Are Such Lethal Terrorists

The charitable activities of Hamas, the Taliban, Hezbollah, and al-Sadr's militia are confusing to most observers, considering that we first heard these names in the context of violence and terrorism. However, there *is* an organizational logic that links the benign and the violent activity. Here's where economics can help.

Let's reconsider the two young men in the Taliban trade route example of chapter 2. We had them manning a dusty checkpoint in southwestern Afghanistan, somewhere on the Kandahar-Herat route. A convoy is coming into view as it rounds a corner and the men are considering their options: defect, steal the convoy, and start a new life in Turkey; or remain loyal and accept their (much smaller) share of the toll. Recall that they waved the low-value ($10,000) convoy safely through, since defection wasn't worth it for their $430 net profit. On the other hand, if they were offered a high-value ($100,000) convoy, they would defect and steal it. For that reason a high-value convoy would never have left Kandahar in the first place, since its theft was predictable by the organization, if not the client. The two young men illustrated the defection constraint—the largest-value convoy that can be sent down the road without operatives stealing it. That illustration made two general points about loyalty. First, loyalty is critical in lawless places, since there is no legal system to enforce contracts. Second, only an organization that can convince clients of the loyalty of its subordinates will be able to credibly commit to securing its clients' goods along a trade route.

What we now know about the background of those two Taliban members as religious radicals allows us to understand why they are unlikely to defect. All those years reciting the holy texts in a Deobandi-style JUI madrassa in their refugee camp did very little to prepare them for a new life elsewhere, say running a grocery store as refugees in Turkey. They lack the practical and social skills to get by in a foreign culture, not to mention the ability to run a small business. Without a secular education the poorly educated pair of Taliban guards at the checkpoint have very limited outside options, both in a cultural and in an economic sense. For the sake of argument, assume that any given pair of Afghan Mujaheddin, with only a rudimentary education and very little skills, will defect if they can capture a convoy worth at least $30,000. Then the defection constraint (the smallest-value project that will trigger defection) for these two Taliban members would be much higher, perhaps a $50,000 convoy. They are so poorly suited to making do in an unfamiliar environment that it will take a larger net profit from defection to induce them to try.

The poor outside options of Taliban foot soldiers have wonderful implications for the Taliban organization. The driver of the lead truck in a $40,000 convoy need not worry about being held up, since he knows that the Taliban guards at the checkpoint are not tempted by treasure and economic emancipation in a foreign land. The owner of the goods in that truck may have other worries, but Taliban defectors stealing his shipment is not one of them. The two Taliban foot soldiers at the checkpoint are under the control of their masters, for lack of outside opportunities.

In turn, the mafia of smugglers in Quetta (across the Pakistani border from Kandahar) and the ISI in Pakistan could be sure that the Taliban were a disciplined organization that could control their troops and thus keep their promises. If the route were first conquered, the Taliban could protect it and open it to trade. That trade route revenue, as we saw earlier, allowed the Taliban to grow, financing the conquest of more and more provinces.

It might seem counterintuitive at first, but here at last is an explanation for why the Taliban could protect trade routes for their clients while the former mujahideen of Afghanistan could not. It was not that they recruited talented personnel with outstanding outside options. Quite the opposite. The Taliban could succeed because they had a reservoir of personnel whose outside options were so poor that their loyalty could be depended on, even when the temptation to defect, steal the convoy, and start a new life on the outside was high.

That logic of creating loyalty by recruiting troops with low outside options applies to many types of coordinated violence. In this instance the trade route had to first be conquered before it could be controlled. That involved capturing the commanding territory, the second militia activity we considered in chapter 2. Think of the commanding territory as hills and consider again that second defection-constraint example—capturing a hill.

In that example the key decision was made by the Taliban soldier considering whether to loyally provide cover fire for his comrades running uphill toward the enemy at the top, or not. He could accept a bribe from the enemy, stop shooting, and doom the attack to failure. Where would he spend the bribe money, though? Certainly not in the Pashtun areas of Afghanistan or Pakistan, which a defector would be wise to flee as fast as a stolen taxi could carry him. Eventually he wouldn't be safe in any part of Afghanistan, if he correctly predicted the Taliban conquest. And what language would he speak? How would he ensure that he was not being cheated in business? What job could he work at? A moment of quick reflection might indicate to the typical Taliban soldier that his lack of outside options makes the offered bribe fall below his personal defection constraint—in this case the smallest bribe that will tempt him into defection. He shoots cover fire loyally for the Taliban. The battle is won, the hill is captured, and the trade route will be secure. Revenue will flow in from the tolls. A few years later the conquest of Afghanistan will be complete.

The young Taliban soldier on the hill shooting cover fire, in an introspective moment, might have asked himself a critical question that brings us back to clubs: Who *did* decide to destroy his outside options by sending him to an inferior school? It wasn't the Taliban, though they benefited, since he was already well through madrassa when they got organized in 1994. It may have been the JUI, who organized traditional Deobandi schools in the refugee camps, rather than schools that taught more universally marketable skills. Or it may have been his parents, if they chose the madrassa over some alternative school to send him to, or over a different place to live.

The short, simple answer is that we don't know. To this day, there's precious little information available to researchers about the educational alternatives of Afghan refugees in the poorly governed western provinces of Pakistan. A longer, more troubling answer is this: even if there were better, secular schooling options for Afghan refugee children in Pakistan, their parents may still have chosen to send them to Deobandi-style madrassas that limit their economic options as adults.

To understand why, recall the earnest young suitors on the doorstep, vying to join radical religious clubs; or the radical Christians in the United States, choosing to limit their children to a middle-school education. People often choose to sacrifice an educational opportunity if it allows them to signal commitment and thereby gain admission to a club, perhaps a mutual aid club, which provides an attractive set of services. If a madrassa education was the cost of admission to the JUI mutual aid network in the refugee camps, then parents may have chosen that education for their children even if they had an alternative. Moreover, considering their options for obtaining basic services such as security and healthcare for their families, those parents would have been making the best choice for their families. Thus, no one necessarily forced the future Taliban fighter to receive an inferior education that limited his outside options. It could have been a wise choice, made with the understanding that even if religious education would not open the door to a good job, it would open doors to membership in a local radical religious service-providing club.

The puzzle of the Taliban limiting their outside options is really just a variant of the puzzle we saw among radical religious Christians and Jews. Why would *anyone* choose to submit to a life with poor outside options? That's the logic of sacrifice. By limiting outside options one incurs a cost, which signals to a community that you can be trusted. That signal, in turn, makes you an attractive member of some sort of collective production cooperative. Usually that cooperative production activity is benign—mutual aid—but if a need or opportunity arises, religious radicals sometimes press the advantage that their loyal networks provide to be effective at coordinated violence.

In this sense, the surprising attractiveness of members with poor outside options applies to militias just as it applies to mutual aid clubs. The Taliban could count on the loyalty of their members because they knew that members' outside options were awful. So they could guarantee safe trade routes, conquer Afghanistan, and hold it. In that singular achievement, capturing and holding Afghanistan, the Taliban outperformed not only their rivals, the ex-mujahideen warlords who had expelled the Soviets, but also the Soviets. At this writing even the combination of U.S. forces, NATO allies, and the Afghan government control far less of Afghanistan than the Taliban did at their peak, for one thing because they have a resurgent Taliban to deal with.

Terrorist Clubs

A similar argument invoking loyalty can explain the effectiveness of radical religious groups at terrorism. The disturbing diagram from chapter 2 illustrating the target and operatives is reproduced here as figure 5.1.

Operative 1 of Hamas, say, has his orders; the target has been chosen and the attacker has been recruited. He needs a few more operatives to carry out the planned attack. He considers recruiting operative 2, carefully thinking over operative 2's level of commitment. What about operative 2's outside options? How does he know that operative 2, once recruited to the plot, will not immediately call the Israeli General Security Services? The Israelis can afford to pay much more for information than Hamas can pay their operatives.

Operative 1 thinks through how much the Israelis will pay for the information that would save this particular target—the value of the

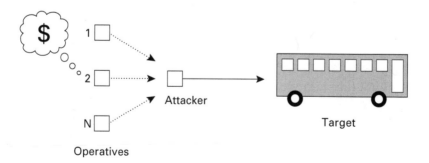

Figure 5.1
Terrorist attack

target to the victim. Then he considers operative 2's *defection constraint*, taking into account the services Hamas provides to operative 2's family (healthcare, security, religious services, and so on), and factoring in the outside options operative 2 might have in an Israeli witness protection program. Those outside options, in turn, have been influenced by how much time operative 2 has spent in prison, signaling commitment—but not accumulating human capital. Operative 1 checks that the value of the target (the possible payment for information) does not exceed operative 2's defection constraint, satisfying himself that operative 2 will remain loyal. He takes a deep breath and makes the call. Or perhaps not. He might instead advise headquarters that if they are going to stick with operative 2, they should choose a lower-value target.

Operative 1 probably knows operative 2 fairly well. Publicly available documents do not reveal a lot about the common background of Hezbollah, Hamas, or Taliban operatives, but we can speculate based on what we know about the organizations in general. They might have attended a madrassa together and probably spent time together engaged in some kind of social service provision. In the case of Hamas, they could well have bonded in prison, after being arrested for some type of rebellious offense, such as throwing stones at an Israeli patrol. Those stones didn't shorten the occupation or even hurt the Israeli soldiers. However, they did take months and often years away from studying, gaining work experience, or raising a family—an expensive sacrifice of time by any account. From an operational point of view the important point is this: all other factors being equal, more loyal operatives allow the organization to attack higher-value targets.

The social service provision network is therefore important to loyalty for a number of reasons. First, demonstrations of commitment to a mutual aid club or some other form of collective activity—the sacrifices—show that an individual cares less about the material gains (which would come from defecting) and more about loyalty to the club. Second, the sacrifice directly reduces outside options, in the form of years of investment in schooling forfeited while in a madrassa or in jail, for example. Third, an operative and his friends and family may depend on the network for security, education, healthcare, and other services. If he defects they could be excluded, or they could be shunned in subtler ways—like the main character in *Paradise Now*, a Palestinian film released in 2005 about a pair of suicide attackers, one of whom is tormented by reminders from community members that his father collaborated. If operative 2 spent time in a Hamas-run community service organization, served prison time, and has family members dependent on Hamas-provided services, he is more likely to have a high defection constraint, making him very likely to remain loyal.

Social service provision also makes terrorism more effective through *harvesting*: the more individuals the social service provision network comes into contact with, the more opportunities it has to find an individual predisposed to having high commitment as an operative or attacker. Finally, there's the willingness of nonmembers to share incriminating information with the authorities. For example, an Iraqi living along a main road may hear some unusual activity in the middle of the night, as a Sadr operative sets an improvised explosive device (IED)—a roadside bomb. He could report the incident and perhaps collect a reward anonymously. Yet this noncombatant is less likely to inform if Sadr's social service network is a better provider of essential services than whoever might take over if Sadr's local organization were replaced. To summarize, social service provision can increase the loyalty of members in many ways: by weeding out shirkers through sacrifice, by lowering outside options, by leverage, by harvesting, and by affecting how much information nonmembers share with authorities.

the more you harvest, the more likely you'll find the right person

Evidence

The club approach's strong implication—that social service provision makes for more effective terrorists—can be tested against data. If terrorist organizations with a social service provision base can really take on higher-value targets without risking defection, then we should observe in data that they are more effective than other terrorists. An awful but appropriate measure of effectiveness is lethality: the number of fatalities per attack. *A measure of effectiveness is the measure of lethality.*

Eight major terrorist organizations were active in Lebanon and Israel/Palestine between 1968 and 2006. Figure 5.2 reports on their lethality—fatalities per attack—and on the number of attacks.[23] The vertical bar counts fatalities per attack, which are measured on the left axis. The

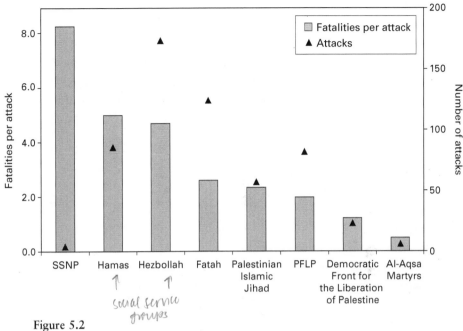

Figure 5.2
The lethality of terrorist organizations

triangle indicates the number of attacks over the survey period, measured on the right axis. Starting on the left, the most lethal organization is the Syrian Socialist Nationalist Party (SSNP), which averaged 8.3 fatalities per attack, but only carried out three attacks. The next two organizations were the most horrible sources of terrorism in the region during that period. Hamas killed 432 victims in 86 attacks, for an average of 5.0 fatalities per attack. Hezbollah amassed a death toll of 829 in 174 attacks, for an average of 4.8 people killed per attack. The other major terrorist organizations in the region have been less lethal, both in victims per attack and in total number of people killed. They include Fatah (the dominant wing of the PLO, led by Yasir Arafat until his death in 2004), 124 attacks, 2.7 fatalities per attack; the Palestinian Islamic Jihad (PIJ), 57 attacks, 2.4 fatalities per attack; the Popular Front for the Liberation of Palestine (led by Ahmed Jibril), 82 attacks, 2.0 fatalities; its splinter organization, the Democratic Front for the Liberation of Palestine (led by Naif Hawatmeh), 23 attacks, 1.2 fatalities per attack; and finally the

Al-Aqsa Martyrs Brigade, a wing of Fatah, with 6 attacks and 3 fatalities, or 0.5 fatalities per attack.

The two social service providers, Hamas and Hezbollah, are clearly more lethal than the other terrorist groups (if we put aside the three attacks by the SSNP). None of the other organizations have a social service provision function.

An important insight comes from focusing on the Palestinian Islamic Jihad, a religious terrorist organization much smaller than Hamas and Hezbollah. Its members are Sunni religious radicals with roots in the Egyptian Muslim Brotherhood, like Hamas. If anything the Islamic Jihad's theology is more violent than that of Hamas. The PIJ broke with the Palestinian Muslim Brotherhood in the late 1970s, feeling that the Brotherhood was too moderate. Theologically it is closer to Qutb's maximalist view of a pan-Islamic state achieved through jihad. The PIJ has been active longer than Hamas as a violent organization and has had more consistent foreign support (their head office in Damascus is generally considered to be sponsored by Iran). They have also been trained in Lebanon by Iranian Revolutionary Guards and Hezbollah, unlike Hamas. Yet the PIJ lack a social service provision network, and, consistent with the defection-constraint argument, they are much less lethal than the other radical religious organizations, Hamas and Hezbollah. Their level of lethality is similar to that of the secular nationalist organizations, all of which lack a social service provision network.

The club approach maintains that Hamas and Hezbollah should be more lethal than the other terrorists, not because of their theology but because of their club structure; their defection constraints are less binding, allowing more lethal operations without fear of defection. The data support this conjecture. Hamas and Hezbollah average 4.9 fatalities per attack, as reported in figure 5.3—more than twice the lethality of the other organizations, which average 2.3.[24]

These data are consistent with the anecdotal evidence we've seen already on the Taliban in Afghanistan and al-Sadr's militia in Iraq. *Social service provision is a key indicator of the ability of terrorists to be lethal*, as the logic of clubs and defection constraints implies.

Returning now to Kashmir, the club model can provide some insight into the lethality of Lashkar-e-Taiba (LeT), perpetrators of the Mumbai

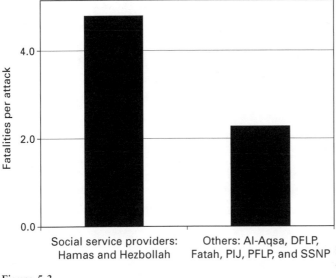

Figure 5.3
Social service providers are more lethal

killings. LeT is one of four rebel groups attacking civilians in Indian Kashmir, in a bid to force India to cede the territory. This group "is one of the largest and best trained groups fighting in Kashmir, and almost all its cadres are foreigners—mostly Pakistanis from madrassas and Afghan veterans of the Afghan war. . . . It collects donations from the Pakistan community in the Persian Gulf and UK, Islamic non-government organizations, and Pakistani and Kashmiri businessmen."[25]

LeT is the violent wing of Jamaat-ud-Dawa, an Islamist political/educational movement with a large following among poorer Pakistanis. Writing in 2002, before LeT was banned, political scientist Saeed Shafqat of Columbia University explained that LeT hosted an annual religious congregation with a million attendees, adding that "LeT congregations are dominated by the lower-middle classes, traders, merchants, petty government employees and mostly young men from various parts of Punjab and some from NWFP [North-West Frontier Province]."[26]

LeT was founded in 1987 by two faculty at the Engineering University in Lahore, principally by Professor Hafiz Saeed, son of a family of refugees from India, a devout Muslim with a master's degree in Arabic and

Islamic Studies. The late 1980s were a growth period for radical Islam in Pakistan. The government of General Zia encouraged political activity by Islamists as part of a broad program of Islamization, partially designed to counterbalance the liberals who had supported the previous government of Ali Bhutto. Moreover, with the Afghan war against the Soviets in full swing, the ISI was funneling foreign funding to radical madrassas that were willing to train jihadists.

Saeed built an educational compound that provided instruction of three types. First, they taught a puritanical version of Islam, which included banning television and pictures. Second, practical technical skills were provided, including practical courses in science and technology. The third component was military training, for jihad in Afghanistan and Kashmir.[27]

Rather than selecting on the sacrifice of outside options, as we've seen among other religious radicals, the LeT had a different selection mechanism:

Training of Mujahiden is done in two stages. The trainers are also divided into two categories: ordinary trainers and specialist trainers. The first stage of training of ordinary trainers comprises 21 days. But before this training, the trainees are asked to go in the society for 15 days on a Dawa tour, where they are expected to preach [to] others. Then there is a three-month waiting period, after which a character evaluation and assessment of the trainees is made from the people of the area. After about four months of evaluation and assessment, the second phase of training starts. This training imparts skills in warfare and guerilla tactics: how to throw a bomb, how to operate a rocket launcher, carry loads and march through mountainous areas, the tactics of guerilla warfare. This training combines three months of religious and commando training.[28]

Yateendra Singh Jafa, who administered counterterrorism operations in Kashmir as an officer of the Indian Police Service, remarks on the "high degree of tactical skill and grit" of LeT terrorists, operating in a hostile environment in (Indian) Kashmir. He cites examples in which they attacked Indian Army camps and outfought Indian troops. Jafa attributes their tactical ability to training and experience fighting with the Taliban in Afghanistan.[29] Quantitative measures from international terrorism data support that inference; the LeT conducted twenty-six attacks through the end of 2007 in Kashmir and elsewhere in India, averaging 6.8 fatalities per attack, even higher than the average of Hamas and

Hezbollah.[30] Those figures do not include the November 2008 attacks in Mumbai, which provide further evidence of LeT's lethality.

Citing Indian Army sources, Jafa describes the LeT's misogynist implementation of purportedly Islamist dress codes, in a manner that evokes the brutality of the Taliban they trained with:

> The Indian army has collected evidence of the attempts of the terrorists to turn Kashmir into a fundamentalist Islamic society. In 2001, the LET directed that women should wear full-bodied veils (Burqas) and has tried to enforce the dress code with singular cruelty. On 23 July 2001, they abducted and gang raped a 16-year-old girl of Batpora Sallar, Anantnag district. On 2 August 2001, they killed a young woman in the same village. On 3 August 2001, they shot and critically injured a Muslim girl in village Bulbul, Nowgam, Kupwara district. On 7 August 2001, they threw acid on the faces of two young women teachers at a school in Srinagar. . . . All these victims had violated the LET's dress code.[31]

LeT activities are apparently broadly approved by their constituency, as Saeed Shafqat reports (though it is unclear whether all the awful details are recounted). "Upon return from various jihads, the Mujahideen narrate their stories in front of congregations, where they are received with respect and admiration."[32]

While it would take further study to confirm the resemblance, LeT does seem to fit the Hamas model of a club, at least superficially. LeT practices strict prohibitions and requires a selection period, though not necessarily sacrifice, of full members. It also operates religious seminaries and schools (under the name of Jammat-ud-Dawa[33]), trains preachers, provides medical care for the poor in Pakistan, and offers earthquake relief in Kashmir.[34] At the very least, the club model seems to provide some insight into Lashkar-e-Taiba's tactical abilities; its cadres are particularly lethal terrorists.

When Terrorists Fail

The logic of defection constraints can also help us understand why some terrorist organizations fail. The Jewish Underground, discussed above, had military training, weapons, and a theology that sanctioned killing, if not a full-scale Armageddon. Yet they provided no concrete social services within communities. Its members failed when they tried to recruit an operative who was not committed enough and who was manipulated into informing by the Israeli GSS. The Jewish Underground is like a Jewish equivalent of the PIJ, theologically motivated, ready, willing, and able to do horrendous damage, but a weak club—lacking the social service provision capacity that would allow it to prevent defection and leaks when planning high-value attacks. By the time members attempted to wreak the havoc that they aspired to, the Jewish Underground had overreached its defection constraint and suffered an intelligence leak. The entire conspiracy was then successfully prosecuted.

Two decades later another group of Jewish terrorists organized, this time among ultra-Orthodox (rather than Orthodox) members of the West Bank settlement of Beyt Ayin. The Beyt Ayin conspirators must have been subject to much more intense surveillance by the Israeli GSS, coming after the initial Jewish Underground and after the assassination of Israeli Prime Minister Yitzhak Rabin by an Orthodox Jew linked to West Bank settlers. Yet the Beyt Ayin conspirators, despite GSS efforts, almost succeeded in detonating a bomb outside a girls' school in East Jerusalem in April 2002, which could have killed dozens of innocent children. While the perpetrators were caught and convicted, many of the other suspected co-conspirators were eventually released for lack of evidence. In contrast to their success in prosecuting the Orthodox Jewish Underground, the GSS could not find an informant who would defect and incriminate these other ultra-Orthodox conspirators. This is the only example I know of in which ultra-Orthodox Jews have been involved in terrorism, yet it fits the pattern: clubs are more dangerous, should they choose terrorism, because internal levels of trust are higher, so that defection constraints allow for more ambitious projects.

The soccer players in Toronto fall into the same category as the Jewish Underground of the 1980s. They managed to recruit members willing to plan a serious attack and even raise funds for it, but not without recruiting at least one member who was sharing their plan with the Royal Canadian Mounted Police—in exchange for a generous reward. The only nontheological service provided was apparently soccer, which must have made defection a fairly easy decision. There are other mosques and other pickup soccer games, even for informants.

A more serious threat comes from groups that are not organizationally resilient enough to execute more than a single attack, but that still manage to cause horrendous loss of life in that first attack. The London Underground and bus attacks of July 7, 2005, which killed fifty-two commuters, fall into this category. The Underground and bus attacks two weeks later, and the subsequent July 2007 car bomb attempts in London and Glasgow, might have fit into this category as well, but luckily the terrorists had not mastered detonation techniques. These are the unguided human missiles of terrorism, fighting a hopeless battle. Once the authorities have enough information to come looking for them, their low defection constraint would preclude further attacks. For that reason these one-shot terrorists do not threaten the stability of governments or even influence policies of target governments. In fact, it's hard to imagine what it is they intend to achieve. Yet the damage is real.

Clubs and Violence without Religion

[handwritten: Club theory then has nothing to do w/ religion.]

What about religion? What's surprising about this explanation for the lethality of radical religious terrorists is that it has nothing to do with the spiritual or theological content of religion. It emphasizes mundane aspects of radical religious communities, like trust between members as well as social service provision. If that's so, then why don't other violent organizations enhance their effectiveness by using sacrifices, prohibitions, and the provision of social services to increase the commitment of members? Here's another surprise: they do.

Nonreligious violent groups often practice forms of personal sacrifices as signals of commitment. *Yakuza*, members of Japanese organized crime syndicates, have elaborate tattoos, effectively barring them from outside options—imagine the look on a prospective employer's face if a former Yakuza member were to appear for a job interview with a tattoo visible on his arm, not to mention the look on prospective in-laws' faces if a former Yakuza wanted to marry their child. The Russian Mafia and American street gangs use tattoos in similar ways to signal commitment. The Hell's Angels, a well-known motorcycle gang active in the United States and Canada, provide a different example of up-front sacrifice. Their rite of entry, as documented by the late novelist Hunter Thompson, is particularly graphic: veteran members pour a bucket of their own urine and excrement on a new member, who then rides for weeks wearing the soiled clothes.[35] The stench must effectively exclude social and economic opportunities outside the gang. They are also a fairly effective criminal gang; members have participated in drug distribution, prostitution, and extortion. Street gangs in the United States often have violent, humiliating, and demeaning initiation rites. In 2000 a teenage girl in North Carolina described how a gang "beat in" and "sexed in" new members as initiation rites, as part of her testimony in a murder trial.[36] Police report that these initiation rites are common among gangs in other U.S. cities.

Criminal organizations often find it to be in their interest to provide social services to communities. The Mafia has provided scholarships and made loans to the needy. Notorious gangster Al Capone sponsored a soup kitchen in Chicago.[37] U.S. street gangs often control petty crime, sponsor street festivals, and occasionally rough up landlords at the request of tenants. The Yakuza of Kobe provided disaster relief after the earthquake of 1995. This type of service provision is probably a long-term investment in keeping residents from sharing information with the authorities, as in a "Hearts and Minds" approach to insurgency or community policing,[38] though it may also serve a club function of allowing potential members to signal commitment.

Successful nonreligious violent groups have also sprung from social service provision organizations. Good examples are the *Haganah* and its elite strike force, the *Palmach*, Jewish militias of prestate Palestine, which would eventually serve as the core of the Israeli military. Both organizations were drawn disproportionately from the population of Israeli kibbutzim. On these rural agricultural cooperatives, young men and women demonstrated commitment by surrendering personal property on entry, and practiced collective production and mutual aid. The close-knit Palmach units that these communities produced formed a dedicated and extremely accomplished militia, the most effective of Israel's War of Independence.

A terrifying violent organization that *is* religious is the Japanese Aum Shinrikyo cult of the 1990s, the only terrorists to ever stage a biological weapons attack. Aum Shinrikyo had all the characteristics of a club: sacrifices, prohibitions, and mutual aid—in this case a full-fledged commune. Historian Daniel A. Metraux writes, "It is a small voluntary group of strict believers who choose to live apart from the world. It defies Japanese society and withdrew from it."[39] Aum used sacrifices to select devoted members, through voluntary acts of physical "mortification," and required that they make "huge" donations.[40] Once admitted, members adhered to strict prohibitions, including "limitation on the forms of participation with outsiders, refusal to take part in common societal activities, peculiar habits of eating and abstinence, and . . . even peculiarities of dress."[41] Further, "Aum followers . . . donate all of their assets to the cult and move into Aum communes as adherents who completely cut off their association with the outside world for a communal life of little sleep and meager meals."[42]

With draconian sacrifices and prohibitions in place, the leaders of Aum Shinrikyo managed to carry out an audacious weapons development program in the early 1990s without being compromised by leaks or defection. They developed techniques to manufacture automatic rifles, acquired and tested laser weapons, bought a large Soviet military helicopter, developed the deadly biological weapon sarin in their laboratories, made plans to develop a much deadlier biological weapon (the botulism bacillus), and even reportedly investigated a nuclear weapons option in discussions with Soviet scientists—all apparently without the knowledge of the Japanese authorities.[43] When Aum Shinrikyo did unleash their sarin, in a coordinated attack on five subway trains, Tokyo was paralyzed. Twelve commuters died and some five thousand were injured. Only afterward did police realize that seven unexplained deaths the previous year in Matsumoto City were also due to an attack by Aum. Most troubling, perhaps, is that Aum Shinrikyo reportedly had a stockpile of raw materials sufficient to produce orders of magnitude more sarin. (Metraux speculates that Aum leader Shoko Asahara had a political motive—he was planning to destabilize the Japanese government with terror attacks, then launch a violent coup.)[44] All told, Aum provides a chilling illustration of how tightly a club can guard information, even about very high value attacks, and how much lethal potential a violent club can harbor.

Gratuitous Cruelty

The logic of controlling defection may explain another disturbing characteristic of radical religious militias, their propensity to be needlessly cruel to residents, including coreligionists. One might think that a religious group that aspires to set up a government would try its best to make itself popular with local residents. Yet radical religious organizations often go out of their way to make life worse for the populations they aim to govern. Hamas imposes general strikes on Palestinians, shutting down businesses that are barely surviving as is and restricting access to shopping for hungry households. One of their first leaflets in 1988 called on Palestinian day laborers to stop working in Israel, at a time when those wages accounted for four-tenths of all income in Gaza. The Muslim Brotherhood's "Apparatus" in the 1940s targeted judges and public officials, reducing the ability of government to provide services. Muqtada al-Sadr's Mahdi Army in Basra is infamous for harassing women who don't wear veils. In a horrific incident reported by the International Crisis Group, "Sadrists hit a woman attending a student picnic, tore off her clothes, and then shot to death two students who tried to intervene—all in front of the police. The woman, humiliated, killed herself shortly thereafter."[45] Targeting Muslims and harassing women is absolutely contrary to mainstream Muslim tradition. One of Mohammad's first goals was to emancipate women. While this abuse might be explained as an attempt to increase control by terrorizing the local population, it is hard to see how control of women provides any tactical gain. That suffering inflicted on noncombatants seems to be entirely gratuitous.

The gratuitous violence inflicted by the Taliban on the Afghan population is the most shocking. Civilians were massacred. Religious sites were desecrated, including the Buddhas of Bamyan, glorious statues carved in a mountainside, 180 feet high, which had been standing since the sixth century. The statues were destroyed though they posed no conceivable cultural threat—Afghanistan has no Buddhist minority. Homosexuals were cruelly executed by dropping a wall on them. Women were beaten publicly for the slightest offense, including purportedly drawing attention to themselves by wearing shoes that squeaked when they walked. Eventually the women of Kabul, the capital, were secluded in their homes, with windows covered to keep them out of sight. Humanitarian aid workers objected to a ban on women in hospitals, threatening to leave—a withdrawal that would cripple hospital care in Kabul, including care for children. The Taliban's response was to tell them to go.

Perhaps the Taliban were just vicious and evil by nature? That's conceivable, but inconsistent with their dedication to Islam and their loyalty to each other. It is also not consistent with how they acted in their home territory. In the Pashtun southern regions of the country, despite their conservative traditional code, women would not be humiliated in public and could expect to be defended if a stranger attacked them. Seclusion was imposed on women in the conquered capital city of Kabul, but not in the home city of Kandahar.

The need to control defection provides a possible explanation for seemingly gratuitous insult, violence, and destruction. When asked why the Taliban were willing to go to such lengths to seclude women in Kabul, one commander implied that the strictest possible prohibitions on women allowed him to control his troops.[46] The commander did not explain how this worked, but our defection-constraint argument can. How would a soldier defect or shirk in Kabul? He could do what young men do everywhere—fraternize. But then he might show up late and tired for work in the morning, and worse—he might share information with his new friends. Both these actions would undermine the Taliban commander's ability to govern by force. Yet if the troops establish a reputation for cruelty to women and the local population, that outside option of fraternizing is severely undermined. The more the local population hates the soldiers, the less of a discipline problem commanders would have in the cities, especially in the relatively cosmopolitan city of Kabul. An awful aspect of this method of controlling the cadres is that most of the cost is borne by innocents. To implement this sacrifice of an outside option (in this case the option of defecting to the local population) for even a small number of troops who might defect, the damage to a full city, including women and children, could be immense.

This explanation for gratuitous damage, especially as it applies to women, is an interesting rationalization. Unlike the model's other implications offered above, I can't think of a way to formally test it with data. Yet it has a parallel in the approach the Taliban apparently implemented in controlling their local governors. It was not uncommon among Afghan mujahideen for factions and subfactions to defect in return for some payment, often by foreigners. The Taliban apparently rotated local governors to the battle front or back to headquarters in Kandahar if they showed signs of creating a local power base, which would have allowed them the strength to switch their allegiance. Governors who were particularly despised by the local population could remain longer.[47] Here again, harsh treatment of the local population would have its reward. From a defection-control perspective, rotating governors or abusing and repressing the population would be useful to the organization, not because it improved governance or control over the population, but because it improved the Taliban's control over governors and troops, preventing their defection by reducing their outside options.

Objections

[handwritten marginalia: Terrorist leaders are rich. This goes against club theory services. that members rely on social need since rich ppl don't need social svcs.]

In the public discussion after the September 11 attacks, many commentators suggested that terrorism was caused by economic deprivation. A number of studies seemed to refute that argument, showing that terrorist attackers are generally at least as well educated and well off as their neighbors.[48] Mohammed Atta, the lead hijacker, was a well-off college student. Osama bin Laden is a multimillionaire. Isn't this evidence against the club approach, which implies that poor operatives are more likely to be loyal recruits than rich operatives, since the poor operatives have worse outside options?

A related objection is implicit in the findings of terrorism expert Peter Bergen, who studied the backgrounds of seventy-five high-profile terrorists and found that most of them did not attend a madrassa, one of the core institutions of a radical Islamist club.[49]

There are two problems with using individual data on terrorists to understand an organization's structure. First, organizations often draw in members with very different backgrounds and motivations. Some join because they want to serve a cause, while others seek a group of friends, and still others find that it's a good job. Radical religious terrorist organizations seem to include many suicide attackers who, for whatever reason, are hell (or heaven)–bent on self-destruction. Yet suicide attackers and idealists are not the weakest link in a terrorist organization, because the defection constraint seldom applies to them; the organization may be able to determine their loyalty by testing their commitment in some other way. Second, we know that terrorist organizations select members carefully for missions, assigning more able operatives to higher-value targets. For example, Al Qaeda, faced with a choice of who to send to flight school in Florida, would naturally choose from among its small membership of disaffected college students in Europe rather than from the thousands of terribly schooled Yemeni and Afghan members it was training in Afghanistan. Research on Palestinian terrorists also shows evidence of selection, as more educated and older attackers are chosen to attack higher-value targets.[50] Thus individuals observed carrying out high-value attacks are not representative of the rank and file of the organization. Moreover, given that those attackers are the more talented members, their loyalty is likely to come from some source other than a lack of outside options.

For both those reasons we should doubt conclusions about poverty and terrorism based on the characteristics of terrorists chosen to attack the highest-value targets. It only takes a few individual to wreak tremendous damage, yet a larger organization, which can exploit a few high-profile terrorist attacks to achieve military or political goals, must be staffed with less exceptional operatives. Finding *individual* terrorists with good market alternatives does not refute what we know about the rank and file of the *organizations* they belong to. Those individuals tend to be in need of the material services that clubs provide: protection, education, healthcare, and welfare services.

Another possible objection to the analysis in this chapter is that organizations such as Hamas and Hezbollah are not clubs at all, since they provide services to nonmembers as well as members. Hamas and Hezbollah indisputably provide some services to nonmembers. The same is true of Lashkar-e-Taiba, which provided earthquake relief in Kashmir to nonmembers, as we've seen. Though these organizations claim otherwise, as far as we know those services are provided in a highly discriminatory way, with core members receiving more support than ordinary members, who in turn receive more than nonmembers, a tiered structure resembling that established earlier by the Muslim Brotherhood in Egypt.

Because of the difficulty of gathering survey data on this sensitive subject, the evidence for discrimination in service provision in favor of insiders is mostly anecdotal. One exception comes in the form of interviews that Shawn Teresa Flanigan carried out in her field research in

Lebanon. She found that "Hizballah's Foundation for the Wounded assists fighters, their families, and civilians injured during the fighting with Israel, whereas the Martyr's Foundation provided services and stipends to the families of those who die in combat."[51] Matthew Levitt reports another exception, which comes from the writings of Ibrahim al-Yazuri, a founding member of Hamas:

> The Hamas movement is concerned about its individuals and its elements, especially those who engage in the blessed jihad against the hateful Israeli occupation, since they are subjected to detention or martyrdom. The movement takes care of their families and their children and provides them with as much material and moral support as it can. This is one of the fundamental truths of Islamic work and thus represents the duties of the Islamic state. . . . The movement provides this aid through the support and assistance it gives to the zakat committees and the Islamic associations and institutions in the Gaza Strip.[52]

Levitt goes on to report (from Israeli government sources) that Hamas's institutions provide payments to the families of the imprisoned, deported, or "martyred" of all organizations, but those payments are significantly larger for the families of Hamas members.

Can the Hamas model also help us understand Al Qaeda? This book is not about Al Qaeda, though because of the sheer audacity, visibility, and lethality of its attacks, Al Qaeda has shaped many of our assumptions about terrorism. Al Qaeda does not fit the club mold: it does not provide social services to members the way Hamas does. Yet Al Qaeda clearly faces defection constraints, as illustrated by an example we saw earlier, of Jamal Ahmed al-Fadl, who had embezzled from the organization. How has Al Qaeda protected itself sufficiently from defection to carry out attacks on high-value targets? One possibility is that it recruits operatives among clubs, drawing on a network of club members who can vouch for potential operatives. This is natural for an organization that traces its roots to the Egyptian Muslim Brotherhood, as noted above. Another possibility is that Al Qaeda extends that club network by recruiting within affiliated kinship networks, as appears to have been the case for bin Laden's driver. Yet another method, apparently in use in Iraq, is to quickly send foreign recruits who have not signaled commitment, on suicide attacks; that way they have little time in the organization to be exposed to information that would make them a defection risk.

Aside from Al Qaeda, the most lethal terrorist organizations and militias today are religious radicals who actively provide social services. Consistent with the predictions of the club model, they thrive in countries where governments and markets deliver poor alternatives to those services, such as Palestine, Yemen, Afghanistan, Iraq, Chechnya, Lebanon, Pakistan, Somalia, and Sudan. Radical religious clubs actively threaten to overthrow some of those governments.

In chapter 7, in looking at new thinking about countering terrorism, I consider the issue of environments that generate strong, violent clubs. Before turning to those new approaches we next examine the most salient phenomenon of modern terrorism: the suicide attack. Suicide attacks are the most lethal tactic in use, and are committed disproportionately by religious radicals. Understanding why is essential to seeing how new approaches may be particularly useful when confronting suicide attacks.

Religious groups that offer social services are the most lethal.

Aftermath of suicide attack near government compound in Baquoba, Iraq, June 2008: a wounded civilian lies on ground, another runs for cover, and an Iraqi soldier carries an injured child. (AP Photo).

6
Why Suicide Attacks?

Levy: Why? Why don't you restrain yourselves? What will you get out of it if you attack again?
Zubeidi: It's because we have no choice. Soldiers enter armed, and you can't harm them. You can't harm a tank, 70 tons of iron, while you, what do you have? An M-16. An M-16 won't hurt a soldier's uniform.

—Zakariya Zubeidi, al-Aqsa Martyrs' Brigade commander; interviewed by Israeli journalist Gideon Levy, in the West Bank town of Jenin in March 2004[1]

"If they're so rational and well adjusted, Professor," asks a young student toward the back of the lecture hall, "then why do they blow themselves up?" He's got longish black hair, parted to the side, which matches a dark T-shirt. The skateboard propped against the last seat in his row might be his. He's leaning forward stiffly in his seat, a little nervous to be asking a question in a large class. He is asking anyway, so he must care. My students at UC San Diego sometimes have friends and relatives in the military, some serving in dangerous parts of Iraq and Afghanistan.

"Good question."

The class already knows that suicide terrorists are not psychopaths or wild-eyed religious drones. Some might be content with an emotionally satisfying answer about good and evil. But my job is to teach them to think analytically, to transport themselves out of the comfort of Southern California and think like a rebel would, like Zubeidi would, drinking coffee and smoking cigarettes in a stifling basement hideout in the West Bank town of Jenin.

Why do they blow themselves up?[2] It really is a good question. Even if an organization can find a volunteer who wants to suicide for the cause, why would the organization choose a tactic in which such a devoted member is surely lost? Suicide attacks strike us as a repugnant denial of the value of life, somehow worse than regular terrorist attacks.

Suicide attacks are a very rare tactic to choose; most modern rebellions do not employ them at all. Although there are plenty of ancient examples, suicide attacks have seldom been used in wars between countries, the most recent exception being the kamikaze pilots sent to crash their fighter planes into U.S. ships by a desperate Japanese Navy toward the end of the Second World War.

Large-scale suicide attacks were not used in modern internal wars either, until Lebanon in the 1980s, when Hezbollah began a wave of attacks, first against Israeli troops, then against American and French peacekeeping forces. The increase has been dramatic since then, from 42 attacks in the 1980s, which caused 805 fatalities, to 115 attacks in the 1990s, killing 1,331, to 210 attacks in the first four years of this century, leaving 4,839 dead, including the attacks of 9/11. Suicide attacks have gone from a rare tactic of internal warfare to a threat that makes civilians worldwide feel vulnerable.

Rebels, Insurgents, and Terrorists

To think of suicide attacks as a tactic implies considering the terrorists who direct those attacks as rebels choosing tactics. That requires an emotional leap, so it's worth thinking through carefully. Should we think of Zubeidi as a rebel? Doesn't that needlessly glorify him by comparing a terrorist who targets civilians on a bus to a romantic freedom fighter in the mountains, like Che Guevara?

First we need to be clear about terms. The definition of terrorism is controversial, but most people agree that if you target civilians—or more generally noncombatants—in pursuit of a political goal (as opposed to a purely criminal goal), you're a terrorist. Insurgents use violence but target military, police, or government officials, rather than civilians, generally with the intermediate political goal of controlling territory, and with a final goal of controlling a country. Conventional insurgency is the set of tactics used by insurgents, involving violence but not suicide attacks. Let's call them all *rebels*—insurgents and terrorists both, regardless of tactics.

One reason to compare terrorists and insurgents is that that's how Zubeidi sees himself, not as a bloodthirsty psychopath, but as a fighter for national liberation. His organization, Fatah, aspires to govern an independent Palestine as a result of this fight. He and his fellow Fatah leaders choose the tactics, so it is useful to see the situation through their eyes.

Another reason to think of terrorists as rebels is that terrorist organizations often use the tactics of conventional insurgency. Zubeidi's al-Aqsa Martyrs' are a branch of Fatah—the major component of the Palestine Liberation Organization. Fatah operatives were insurgents before they were terrorists. In the late 1960s in Jordan, Fatah, led by a young Yasir Arafat, carved out an area of control in Palestinian refugee camps and other regions with Palestinian majorities. They used classic rural insurgency tactics: ambushing patrols, executing guerrilla attacks on representatives of government, intimidating civilians, and extorting tax payments from local residents. By 1969 Fatah had marked their territory with roadblocks and governed the local population using a network of self-sustaining militia units, like Castro and Che Guevara had done in Cuba or the Viet Cong did in South Vietnam. In "Black September" of 1970 Fatah and other PLO groups forced the battle into the Jordanian capital of Amman, threatening to topple King Hussein, the Hashemite ruler of Jordan. Some reports claim that the PLO even attempted to assassinate the king. Hussein responded with martial law and a military offensive, which benefited from American and Egyptian support. The fighting included house-to-house combat in Amman and claimed thousands of casualties before the Jordanian Army prevailed. The PLO was forced to withdraw to Lebanon. They used urban insurgency tactics more successfully in the Palestinian refugee camps of Lebanon, forcing the Lebanese government into an agreement that relinquished effective sovereignty within the camps to the PLO.

Fatah is not the only rebel organization that has used both insurgent and terrorist tactics. Hezbollah successfully used the same tactics to displace Amal in Lebanese Shiite neighborhoods in the 1980s. Al-Sadr's militia has done the same in the Shiite neighborhoods of Iraq since 2003, displacing either the government or rival Shiite militias. The Taliban used insurgent tactics to conquer Afghanistan, while it uses suicide attacks today against civilians and government forces. Even the Muslim Brotherhood's militia, the Apparatus, had used similar tactics against the Egyptian government, although without success. The failed insurgents of today often become the terrorists of tomorrow.

Social scientists know a lot about rebels, and for good reason. In the fifty-four years following the Second World War, 1946–1999, 127 internal wars in 73 different countries claimed at least sixteen million casualties.[3] Compared to that staggering toll in human lives, the thousands of lives lost to suicide attacks in the twentieth century are a small tragedy, one one-hundredth of 1 percent. In rebellions, as in international wars, suicide attacks have been rare.

When do rebels choose suicide attacks? The best way to answer that question is to first examine what we know about what leads rebels to do what they usually do: choose conventional insurgency tactics. Surprisingly, the answer is *not* simply that people rebel when there's a grievance worth fighting the government over: the correlation across countries between the level of grievance in the population and whether a rebellion starts is zero.[4] Being angry is not enough. Ethnic and religious differences don't predict rebellion either. A motivating cause, be it ethnic, religious, or economic, may be necessary for rebellion, but it apparently is not sufficient to sustain armed resistance.

What does predict rebellion appears to be the balance of forces between rebels and governments, and here two patterns are clear: first, wealthier countries suffer less rebellion; second, countries with mountains suffer more rebellion. There are several possible interpretations for those findings but the most common among scholars concerns the viability of counterinsurgency: poor governments have badly equipped militaries that have trouble chasing down rebels, especially in the mountains. They suffer many rebellions that tend to last for a long time. Wealthier countries can afford to chase rebels with expensive helicopters and Humvees, tap rebel phone conversations, patrol often, train and equip special forces, and bribe rebels generously into defection. In short, rebels choose conventional insurgency tactics when they work—against weak governments and in mountainous terrain, like Cuba. And when those tactics don't work? Apparently, rebels generally give up.

Returning to suicide attacks, do conditions that favor insurgency predict suicide attacks? The answer is negative. Political scientist David Laitin and I examined data on suicide attacks throughout the world, through 2003. We found that suicide attacks are uncorrelated with the income of the attacker's country or the topography; suicide attacks are just as likely in high-income, flat countries like Israel as they are in poorer, hilly countries like Sri Lanka and Lebanon. One possible explanation is that suicide attacks might be the tactic of choice when the government is too wealthy and the land too flat for conventional insurgency to work. I return to that conjecture below.

What does predict suicide attacks? One strong predictor is violence involving targets of a different religion. Putting grievances, ethnicity, topography, and wealth aside, 84 percent of insurgencies attack coreligionists, while only 13 percent of suicide attacks do (figure 6.1). Though rebels typically attack their own governments or neighbors—who tend to be of their own religion—suicide attackers disproportionately attack members of other religions. Palestinian and Lebanese terrorism is generally Muslims killing Jews or Christians. In Sri Lanka it is mostly the Hindu Tamil minority versus the Buddhist majority, in Russia it is Muslims versus Eastern Orthodox Christians, in China Muslims versus Buddhists. In Iraq suicide attacks tend to be carried out by Muslims against coalition forces, which would be mostly Christian, and when Muslim suicide attackers target other Muslims it is generally Sunnis versus Shiites. Al Qaeda often attacks foreigners, mostly Christians, though its objective seems to be to replace governments in individual Muslim countries with an Islamic Empire. The major exceptions to this pattern are the fourteen suicide attacks carried out in the 1990s by the Partiya Karkeren Kurdistan or PKK (the Kurdistan Workers' Party), in which Muslim Kurds attacked fellow Muslims, and recent attacks in Pakistan and Afghanistan—which we will discuss below.[5]

Taken together, 87 percent of suicide attacks are carried out against members of other religions. That's a very strong pattern and particularly surprising given the evidence we've seen so far, which implied that the motivation of suicide attackers is not primarily religious. Moreover,

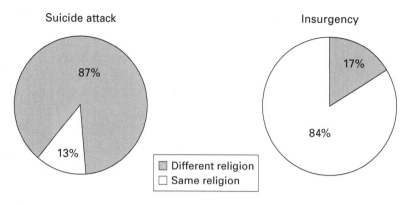

Figure 6.1
Insurgents, suicide attackers, and coreligionists

organizations that use suicide attacks *do* kill coreligionists; they just do so using conventional tactics. So why the increase in suicide attacks over the last two decades? And what does it have to do with religion?

The answer, I believe, lies in examining the process that made insurgency increasingly difficult in the period before the Iraq War. As countries became wealthier, their ability to counter conventional insurgency improved. By the end of the twentieth century the Middle East and North Africa had only two large, ongoing insurgencies, in Algeria and Turkey. In the 1980s and 1990s, long-standing insurgencies that had begun in the 1970s had been either shut down or substantially reduced in intensity by the governments of Lebanon, Morocco, and Iran. A new insurgency was suppressed within a year in Yemen in 1994 and another within two years in South Yemen in 1986.[6]

One way to understand that decline in insurgency is to recall the discussion of defection constraints and to reconsider the example of a band of insurgents capturing a hill. This time let's think of the government as the defender, with a police station at the top of the hill as the target. The insurgents follow standard procedure; they divide into groups and start taking turns running and shooting cover fire. As before, a group responsible for firing could decide to defect, stop firing, and sell out their comrades to the enemy at the top of the hill. In the "Black September" rebellion of 1970, for instance, the Jordanian police included some Palestinians, so, as in Afghanistan, the enemies could have been cousins.

Now freeze that battle for a moment and imagine what would happen if the government had a few helicopters in reserve, which may show up any moment. The business end of an attack helicopter is a sobering sight (Saddam Hussein demonstrated what a fierce weapon an attack helicopter is in Southern Iraq after the end of the first Gulf War). Should that helicopter appear, the insurgents would doubtlessly stop running up the hill and start running for cover, with the helicopter in pursuit. If the police manage to capture a few surrendering insurgents, then even those who escape will have to hide out for a while, shutting down the local insurgency. *helicopter → insurgents hide bc they cant collect payoff*

The possibility of a helicopter arriving to save the police station should play into the defection/loyalty calculation of the insurgents responsible for cover fire, since it reduces their chances of conquering the target and collecting the payoff. They are less likely to remain loyal, since the payoff they can expect from the insurgency is lowered by the probability of no payoff (or worse) if that helicopter arrives. The helicopter probability makes high-value targets look a lot less attractive to commanders now, for two reasons: first, high-value targets are more likely to have a helicopter show up to defend them; second and more important, high-value targets are now more likely to exceed the defection constraint, since the chances of collecting a share of the prize fall when the helicopter is more likely to come beating down. The chance that a helicopter might show up changed the police station from a *soft* target to a well-defended or *hard* target—that is, one with a low probability of successfully attacking and then getting away safely.

Hardening of targets can explain the general decline in insurgency in the Middle East over the 1980s and 1990s. As governments get richer and military technology improves, they gain access to helicopters, night-vision goggles, armored personnel carriers, drones, eavesdropping equipment, and a host of other ways to better control territory, defend themselves, and bribe insurgents into defection. So the range of targets available for insurgents to attack narrows and insurgency declines.

Hardening of military targets can also explain the increase in terrorism. Civilians are much softer targets than police stations, patrols, and military aircraft. Civilians are much more numerous and it's much harder to defend every last one of us. So as military targets become better defended, conventional insurgency should decline and rational rebels should change tactics, from insurgency to terrorism. Killing civilians may not be particularly effective in capturing territory—the goal of conventional insurgency—or in influencing government policy to release rebel prisoners or negotiate control over refugee camps, say. Yet, as Zakariya Zubeidi of the al-Aqsa Martyrs' Brigade pointed out in the epigraph that opened this chapter, when the military are well defended, civilians may be the only feasible targets left.

As a tactic of rebellion, attacking civilians and other low-value targets only works sometimes, and it often fails. It works if the government is scared out of the area, depriving the population of services, so the rebels can take over. Alternatively, if the rebels can goad the government (or other enemies) into responding, then a government with poor information and crude weapons may react with a campaign of indiscriminate bombing or attacks on the local population. Should those indiscriminate attacks have the unintended effect of increasing the pool of recruits for the insurgents, providing intelligence, or increasing other support— perhaps from foreign donors—then the insurgency can benefit from government "collateral damage" to the population. If the government neither flees nor overreacts, the outgunned insurgents may simply fail.

"I still don't get it." The student who asked about suicide attackers looks skeptical.

"Well, do you understand Zubeidi when he says he has no choice? He really does have limited options, right?"

"He could just give up." offers the student.

"I think that's usually what happens. But let's take a look at his other option, the suicide attack."

Suicide Attacks

Now picture the terraced hills and scattered towns of southern Lebanon in the fall of 1982. The Israeli Defense Forces had rolled into the south that summer in pursuit of Fatah and other PLO rebels. Fatah insurgents had for years exploited the absence of any Lebanese Army control of southern Lebanon to launch rocket attacks and terrorist raids into northern Israel. In a few weeks of fighting the IDF had pushed the PLO up to

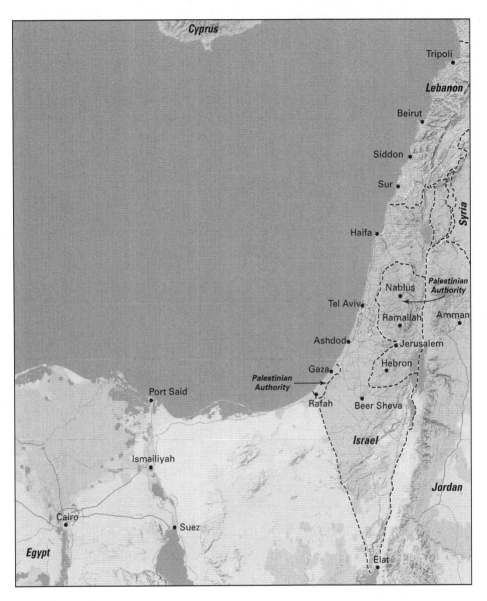

Figure 6.2
Israel, Lebanon, and the Palestinian Authority

Beirut, and was now trying to expel them from Lebanon altogether. Israeli bulldozers were digging bunkers in the hilltops, for what looked like a protracted stay. The IDF patrolled the roads in personnel carriers and tanks and dominated the skies in their fighter planes. American, French, and Italian peacekeeping forces arrived by the boatload, well trained and extremely well armed, to supervise a ceasefire, oversee the withdrawal of the PLO from Beirut, and help stabilize the Lebanese government. It was a prime example of modern asymmetric warfare; conventional insurgents were both outgunned and outnumbered. Beirut and southern Lebanon were suddenly full of hard targets.

In the meantime the Shiite student-rebels of Hezbollah had returned home from Iran and Iraq to the Bekaa valley, eager to bring Ayatollah Khomeini's fresh revolutionary ideology with them. They were advocating personal piety, establishing Islamist institutions, and aspiring to political power for Lebanese Shiites. Between them and their goal stood those well-equipped forces, the Israeli occupying army and the American and French peacekeepers.

It helps to have a picture of what asymmetric warfare looks like from the strong side. An individual soldier is often vulnerable, either riding along on top of a personnel carrier, manning a roadblock, patrolling neighborhoods on foot, or checking that a road is clear of roadside bombs (IEDs). A sniper, a grenade attack, or even a well-aimed rock could easily be fatal. Yet the ability to call in massive firepower quickly and efficiently is a powerful deterrent, making individual soldiers hard targets. Perhaps for that reason the occupying force and the peacekeepers were seldom attacked directly and when they were, casualties were relatively few for the strong side and many for the insurgents.

On November 11, 1982, in Tyre, Hezbollah changed all that. They demonstrated a viable tactic of asymmetric warfare for the weak side. Tyre is a crowded but lovely ancient Phoenician port on the Mediterranean, mentioned frequently in the Bible. In Greek mythology it is the birthplace of Europa, who was seduced by Zeus. Only fifteen miles from the Israeli border, Israeli soldiers serving there were a short drive from the safety, familiarity, and gentle beaches of the northern Israeli coastal town of Nahariya.

In Tyre, Ahmed Qusayr succeeded in driving a vehicle full of explosives into the Israeli military headquarters, and then suicided by detonating the weapon. The building collapsed, killing almost everyone inside, a total of seventy-four Israelis, Lebanese, and Palestinian prisoners.

The attack clearly illustrated how lethal suicide attacks can be. The explosives were accurately delivered to a location at which they could do tremendous damage. Little special training was necessary. The weapon was simple and not very expensive. There was no attacker left to capture or interrogate and thus no information would be leaked. Follow-up attacks would be difficult to deter. Hezbollah made a video but did not claim responsibility, which they later explained as an attempt to keep the attacker's identity a secret. After the Israeli withdrawal of 1985, once his town was no longer under Israeli control, Hezbollah would proudly show the video to Qusayr's neighbors.

My student is nodding slowly. I take a chance and ask him: "So why do they blow themselves up?"

"Because it works?" he answers.

"Exactly. It works."

I look around the room. The day Qusayr demolished the building in Tyre, in November 1982, I was training with Druze soldiers from a town in northern Israel. Some lost cousins and friends in that building. My strongest memory of that day is of young men, about the age of my students, shocked and grieving.

The suicide attack came at a high cost for Hezbollah. A loyal member had to give up his life with certainty, and that would have to be explained to his family and community. Yet the building in Tyre was a hard target. It was well guarded against assault and full of armed, trained soldiers. A conventional attack would have surely failed, leaving Hezbollah members dead or captured and available for interrogation. The suicide attack was lethal and efficient and well within the capability of a technologically inferior group of rebels.

The key insight demonstrated by Hezbollah in Tyre is this: suicide attacks allow harder, higher-value targets to be destroyed without fear of defection by operatives. Tactical failure is unlikely, because the method delivers the ordnance so precisely. The probability of information leakage is also low, since the perpetrator cannot be interrogated. Suicide attacks won't be chosen against soft targets or low-value targets, because conventional attacks are effective against those targets without the organization necessarily losing the attacker.

Evidence

The conjecture that rebels choose suicide attacks against hard targets and conventional attacks against soft targets is testable, once you know what a hard target looks like.

David Laitin and I examined data from Israel and Palestine for the first three years of the "second Intifada" (the Palestinian rebellion that began in September 2000). Palestinian rebels had both soft and hard targets to choose from during this period. Soft Israeli targets are abundant in the West Bank and were abundant in Gaza as well until Israel's withdrawal in the summer of 2005. Israeli settlers and soldiers often use roads that pass through heavily populated areas, or that are vulnerable because of their topography. Civilian settlements and military bases, though fortified, have entrances that are also fairly exposed. Some of these are also quite close to Palestinian population centers. A Palestinian attacker in the West Bank or Gaza could shoot at Israeli soldiers or settlers, or detonate an explosive, and still stand a good chance of successfully fleeing and melting unobserved into the local population.

Targets on the Israeli side of the "green" line—that is, in Israel proper—are much harder, in the sense that they are riskier for the attacker. To reach a target on the Israeli side during the second *Intifada* an attacker would have had to pass through checkpoints where his or her weapon could be discovered, and perhaps cross a security fence in order to enter Israel. Once on the Israeli side, the attacker would have to somehow avoid being identified as a Palestinian until reaching the target. If he or she succeeds in destroying the target, the attacker would still need to somehow escape without being noticed by Israeli security services or a hypervigilant public. For all these reasons targets within Palestine are much softer than targets within Israel proper.

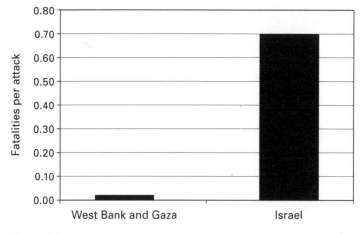

Figure 6.3
Lethality of Palestinian attacks, by location

Figure 6.3 describes the lethality of attacks by location. These data were provided by the IDF spokesperson's office and cover the period from the beginning of the second Intifada in September 2000 through August 2003.[7] Attacks include all forms of violence toward Israelis and residents of Israel, including everything from stone throwing to shooting to roadside bombs to suicide attacks. Some 17,405 incidents (96 percent) were perpetrated in the West Bank and Gaza, on the soft side of the green line. Yet 60 percent of the fatalities (511 out of 852) are on the Israeli side of the green line. While these data don't provide direct evidence on methods, the tactics chosen by Palestinian attackers on the Israeli side are clearly more lethal.

A separate data source on suicide attacks, made available by the Institute for Combating Terrorism (ICT) in Herzliya, Israel, allows us to track where suicide attacks are more likely to be used. Of 409 deaths due to suicide attacks recorded during the same period, 401 were on the Israeli side of the green line (figure 6.4).

Taken together, the evidence from Israel/Palestine supports the conjecture. Suicide attacks are disproportionately against hard targets, on the Israeli side of the green line.

The Lashkar-e-Taiba suicide attacks on Mumbai follow the same logic. The assailants could hardly have expected to be able to destroy

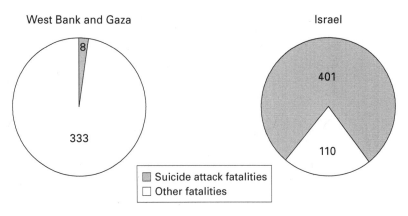

West Bank and Gaza

Israel

Figure 6.4
Suicide attacks chosen vs. hard targets

high-value targets deep in India and escape safely. In that sense Mumbai was "hard." A better bet was to carry out suicide attacks, leaving no assailant to be interrogated about their origins. The attackers might have succeeded in igniting conflict between India and Pakistan—if that was really the goal—had the last assailant managed not to be captured alive. In interrogation he revealed that they were sent by a banned terrorist organization, not by Pakistani agents.

Evidence from Iraq and Afghanistan also indicates that terrorists reserve suicide attacks for well-defended, or hard, targets. Sociologist Diego Gambetta of Oxford University compiled data on suicide attacks in Iraq for the period May 2003 through January 2006.[8] These attacks are perpetrated by three groups, former Baathists, Iraqi Al Qaeda, and Ansar al-Sunna from Kurdistan. All three of these organizations were involved in sectarian attacks and attacks on the Iraqi government during this period, yet fully 81 percent of their suicide attacks were aimed at Coalition forces. The Taliban did not use suicide attacks in conquering Afghanistan from other Afghans in the 1990s, as far as we can tell. Yet they have turned to suicide attacks increasingly since 2001 to attack military and government targets—much harder targets, now that American and other Western military forces are in place.

Coreligionists Are Soft Targets

The logic of hard targets can also explain why suicide attacks are generally a tactic chosen against members of a different religion, even though most rebellions are against governments made up of coreligionists. Recall that this is the one reliable predictor of when suicide attacks are chosen. First of all, it's worth pointing out that tactic choice apparently has little to do with empathy for coreligionists. The same rebels who use suicide attacks against members of other religions often kill coreligionists as well, when they are suspected of collaboration or are merely political rivals. Hezbollah, LTTE (the "Tamil Tiger" rebels in Sri Lanka), Hamas, and Fatah have all spilled the blood of coreligionists quite often and in very brutal ways. During the conquest of Gaza in June 2007, for instance, Hamas members assassinated Fatah prisoners by throwing them off a building. Yet these four organizations, as far as we know, have never used a suicide attacker to kill a coreligionist.

Here's an explanation. *Coreligionists are soft targets*, in the following sense. Consider what it would take to defend a crowded target like a market, bus station, or airport against attack. People come and go constantly. How can security forces somehow identify every possible assailant and all the weapons they could possibly be concealing? One fairly effective solution is profiling, predicting which individuals are the most likely to be dangerous and screening them successfully. Yet coreligionists are almost impossible to profile because they look so much like the targets. When profiling is difficult, targets are extremely vulnerable to conventional attacks. Coreligionist assailants can often simply walk up to the target, shoot, and escape by blending into the surrounding population, as John Wilkes Booth did to President Abraham Lincoln. A coreligionist has a much easier time leaving a bomb in a bus or shopping center and just walking away, since profiling is ineffective against him. He doesn't use a suicide attack because he doesn't have to.

Tactic choice by rebels in Chechnya shows the same pattern. The rebels are Chechen Muslims while the police and army are disproportionately ethnic Russians, so profiling by religion is probably straightforward. Chechen suicide attacks are reserved for Russian civilian and military targets, which would be hard targets if profiling is in use. When Chechen rebels kill collaborators, they don't waste the life of a suicide attacker on the effort.

In the exceptional cases in which suicide attacks have been used against members of the same religion, the targets were almost always extremely well protected by some method beyond profiling, so that a bomb, shooting, or other approach was unlikely to succeed. Two Al Qaeda suicide bombers, disguised as journalists, assassinated Ahmad Shah Massoud of the Afghan Northern Alliance in September 2001. He was well enough protected that they could not possibly have shot him and escaped his camp alive. The LTTE suicide bomber who assassinated Rajiv Gandhi in May 1991 was Hindu, like him. Yet as the favorite to win the next election he would have been well protected by means beyond profiling. The Egyptian Islamic Jihad members who assassinated Anwar Sadat in 1981 also carried out what they must have considered a suicide attack. The embattled Egyptian president would have also been an unusually well protected target.

That idea of hard targets also provides a possible explanation for the increase in suicide attacks over the past twenty-five years. As countries have become wealthier and better armed, conventional insurgency has become much less effective, limiting the options of rebels as conventional insurgents and pushing them to switch to suicide attacks. As the United States, Israel, Canada, and Europe have sent well-armed, well-equipped forces into battle against low-technology insurgents, rebels have responded with the tactically appropriate weapon. The West sends in hard targets; the rebels counter with suicide attacks.

In a cruel example of unintended consequences, hardening military targets induced an innovation by rebels that put targets of much greater value at risk. How large a target could a suicide attacker aspire to destroy? We could not have known the answer after Tyre, in November 1982. Yet since September 2001 the answer has been clear. Deterrence is ineffective, so if the little training, munitions, and funding required are available, the only remaining constraint on suicide attacks is the defection constraint. That makes some very high value targets vulnerable to suicide attacks, if terrorist organizations can recruit and maintain operatives who will not defect.

The sheer destructiveness of suicide attacks also makes civilians in countries far from the battle attractive high-value targets for terrorists. For example, a high-damage suicide attack in Manhattan might be easier to execute and more effectively weaken the government in Riyadh than the same attack in Saudi Arabia—at least in 2001, when Manhattan was unprepared. As Arab governments in the Middle East have hardened their targets, they have become more resilient to domestic insurgency. That process has doubtless saved human lives and suffering (though it has not necessarily improved human rights). An unintended consequence, though, may have been that rebels have forgone domestic insurgency in favor of terrorism, including suicide terrorism, and set their sights on a global set of targets, drawing foreign civilian populations into their domestic conflicts.

"So they use suicide attacks because they work, and we're all at risk? Professor, you're freaking us out here." He's grinning, but deserves an answer.

"Sorry. That wasn't my intention. Very few terrorist organizations can actually succeed at suicide attacks."

Clubs

Even in cases where standard insurgency is clearly not succeeding, most rebel groups still choose not to resort to suicide attacks. Consider the African National Congress (ANC) in South Africa, Euskadi Ta Askata-suna (ETA) in the Basque region of Spain, Aum Shinrikyo in Japan, the Red Brigades in Italy, and the Baader-Meinhof gang in Germany. None of these rebels could have hoped to succeed as insurgents. They faced wealthy governments with well-equipped militaries and police, yet they did not choose suicide attacks. Why not?

The previous chapters have prepared us to answer that question. In chapter 2 we saw that it is hard to hold together an organization that attacks high-value targets because the risk of leaks and defection is too great. Chapters 3 through 5 pointed out that religious radicals have an advantage; having already figured out how to create defection-resistant mutual aid organizations, they have a leg up at recruiting and managing low-risk operatives should they choose to engage in coordinated violence—including terrorism.

Suicide attacks are best aimed at high-value targets, as we saw above. Only defection-proof organizations can assume the risk of attacking those targets, though. For the ANC, ETA, and the Baader-Meinhof gang, suicide attacks against high-value targets were probably not worth the risk, despite the hard-target environment they functioned in, where other types of attacks were unlikely to succeed. Who is likely to succeed at suicide attacks, even in a hard-target environment? Clubs are. Hard-target environments predict not only suicide attacks, but also *who* the perpetrators will likely be: religious radicals who provide social services.

An example will help illustrate why clubs have an advantage at suicide attacks. Consider again the conspirators in figure 5.1 plotting a suicide attack on a civilian target. The target is of high value and the government has ample resources to defend it, including surveillance and large bribes to exchange for information. The weak link in the conspiracy is not the suicide attacker; as we have seen, he or she is already highly motivated, unlikely to be captured before the attack, and impossible to interrogate afterward. The method is so simple and inexpensive that the conspiracy will probably not fail because of problems with training, locating the target, financing, or arming the attacker. The combination of a high-value target and a high probability of success, should operatives remain loyal, dictates that the government will offer very generous rewards for information that will help thwart the attack. So *the weak link in this conspiracy is the defection of operatives who might be tempted by generous rewards, especially for suicide attacks*. It is here that the extraordinary advantage of clubs is so valuable; they have access to operatives already selected for their resistance to defection.

This argument for the special potency of clubs at suicide attacks, combined with what we now know about the characteristics of clubs, has two clear testable implications. First, religious radicals who provide social services will account for a disproportionate number of suicide attacks. Second, they will take on higher-value targets (i.e., more lethal attacks) when they do so.

Figure 6.5 reports on the first implication, that clubs choose suicide attacks more often. Here I use data collected by the Interdisciplinary Policy Institute for Counterterrorism (ICT) on all major terrorist attacks carried out in Israel and Palestine between 1980 and 2002.[9] Hamas, the social service provider, chose suicide attacks 35 percent of the time (40 out of 115 attacks). Among all the other organizations the average was 16 percent (37 of 235 attacks). That 19-percentage-point difference is statistically significant using the usual methods of scientific research.

Of these seven organizations the only one that does not satisfy the predictions of the model is the Palestinian Islamic Jihad, the radical Islamic terrorists who do not provide social services but do choose suicide attacks 35 percent of the time, just like Hamas. That is a particularly high rate of suicide attacks, considering that the PIJ is not nearly as lethal at suicide attacks as Hamas is, as we will see below.

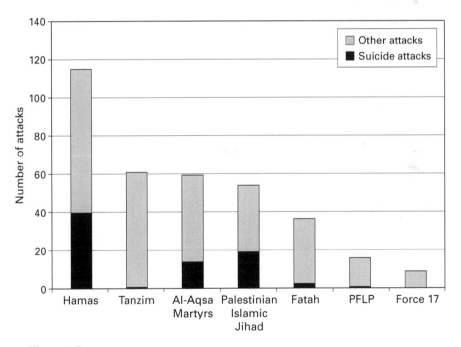

Figure 6.5
Who selects suicide attacks?

This choice of suicide attacks by radical Islamists is consistent with the evidence from Chechnya, where Russian troops actively profile and invest heavily in hardening targets. Russian ethnologist Valery Tishkov tells the story of how suicide attacks on Russians began after the arrival of Wahhabi fundamentalists from Saudi Arabia, with funding from associates of Bin Laden. The Wahhabi in Chechnya behaved like a club. They provided social services to converts, including stipends for their families. In return they required religious prohibitions: Arab dress codes, compulsory prayers, a ban on shaving beards. Women were forced to stop working. The rival religious authorities, the traditional Sufi sheikhs, *usatazes*, were banished.[10] Consistent with the predictions of our model, once religious radicals providing social services had established themselves, they could overcome pressures to defect and choose suicide attacks against hard targets.

Combining the logic of clubs with that of hard targets also provided us with a second testable implication, that clubs will choose higher-value targets, killing more individuals per attack than other organizations. To test that conjecture we again use the ICT data on suicide attacks in both Israel/Palestine and Lebanon, including all organizations that carried out suicide attacks between 1981 and 2003. These data include two radical Islamic organizations that provide social services, Hamas and Hezbollah, as well as the Palestinian Islamic Jihad, radical Islamic terrorists that do not. The data also report on four secular nationalist organizations, the Popular Front for the Liberation of Palestine (PFLP), Fatah, the Al-Aqsa Martyrs' (a Fatah affiliate), and the SSNP. Fatalities per attack and the number of attacks are reported for each of these organizations in figure 6.6

The message of this figure is consistent with what we saw for all terrorist attacks, in figure 5.3 of the previous chapter: radical Islamists who provide social services are much more lethal at suicide attacks than are the other groups, including the Palestinian Islamic Jihad, which at four fatalities per attack is much less effective at terrorism than Hamas and Hezbollah. To be sure, weak organizations that do not provide social services, such as the secular nationalists and the PIJ, are a real threat to civilians. Yet the greater threat by far comes from the strong clubs—religious radicals who provide social services to members and have

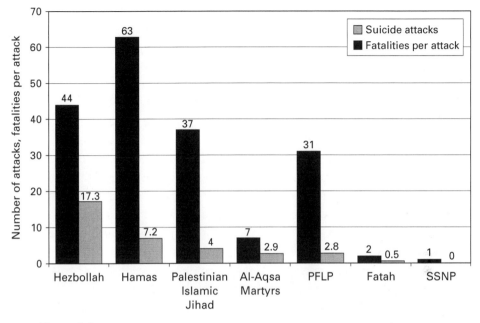

Figure 6.6
Lethality of suicide attacks, by organization

chosen violence. These organizations are particularly dangerous in "hard-target" environments, where they use suicide attacks.

Data from Iraq are consistent with what we've learned from Israel and Palestine. Diego Gambetta reports casualty statistics for 152 suicide attacks committed in Iraq between May 2003 and January 2006 for which he can identify the organization of the perpetrator by broad affiliation.[11] The three groups are Sunni former Baathists, Al Qaeda in Iraq, and Ansar al-Sunna—an organization of Kurdish Islamists. Among these three, the radical Islamists were clearly more lethal: Al Qaeda averaged 39 fatalities per attack over 41 attacks. Ansar al-Sunna averaged 28 deaths per attack (8 attacks), while the Sunni Baathist groups averaged 10 fatalities (103 attacks). Unfortunately, we know almost nothing about social service provision among these organizations or about other means they might have to recruit carefully and reduce defection. Al-Zarqawi, who led Al Qaeda in Iraq for most of that period, apparently built his organization around a group of Islamists who bonded while they served in a Jordanian prison, as mentioned above. Yet little else is known about them, or members of the other groups, at least from open sources.

Alternative Explanations

So why *do* religious radicals blow themselves up? I've offered one explanation, but it is worth considering others. Suicide attacks are more terrorizing, I think, since they communicate so vividly how vulnerable we all are, in airplanes, buses, and offices. Suicide attacks also cut viciously through the casual social ties that bind societies across religious, ethnic, or national groupings, making us suspect strangers of other religions, ethnicities, and backgrounds. In sowing terror and seeding suspicion, suicide attacks are insidiously effective. Suicide attacks also have tactical advantages, which are worth reiterating: they are relatively inexpensive, deliver explosives precisely to a vulnerable point, and leave no informant to be captured and interrogated. These are all compelling reasons for rebels to choose suicide attacks as a weapon, but they can't explain why so *few* organizations worldwide do so.

Other explanations offered are tied to religion. Religious radicals have developed what look like cults of martyrdom that glorify suicide attackers. All the major terrorist organizations that use this hideous method, religious or secular, extol the dedication of their suicide attackers in their media campaigns. That may be important, but as we've seen, there is really no shortage of individuals, religious radicals or otherwise, who are willing to give up their lives for a cause. The Tamil "Tigers" (LTTE), who carried out the most suicide attacks for years in the 1980s, are likely atheists—being nominally Marxists. Whether a cult of martyrdom is essential or not, none of this explains why religious radicals who provide social services are more successful at suicide attacks than religious radicals who do not.

Robert Pape, who wrote an important book[12]—the first to methodically analyze data on suicide attacks—has pointed out that they tend to be concentrated in places with a foreign occupier, such as Iraq, Palestine, or Afghanistan, or at least places with a foreign presence, such as Saudi Arabia or Lebanon. With the data he had available, that explanation is hard to distinguish from the "hard-target" argument, since foreign occupiers tend to be well defended. More recent suicide attacks in Turkey and Pakistan are less supportive of the foreign-occupier hypothesis. Foreign occupation also cannot explain why suicide attacks are used more on the Israeli side of the green line than on the Palestinian side, why religious radicals who provide social services are more lethal at them, or why suicide attacks are used so often against well-defended nonoccupiers such as Shiite Iraqis, Rajiv Gandhi, Ahmad Shah Massoud, or the sailors of the *USS Cole* in the Yemeni port of Aden. A "hard-target" explanation provides insight into all these cases.

The Future of Suicide Attacks?

The future bodes ill for conventional insurgents. The mountains won't get lower and targets will likely get harder. Governments are getting richer, at least outside of Africa, and both the counterinsurgency technology and the training available from allies is improving. Moreover, we may be entering an era in which the militaries of Western countries are increasingly placing hard targets in the paths of rebels, as they engage in state building in unstable countries such as Bosnia, Afghanistan, and Iraq. While those trends are good news for vulnerable governments, they do predict more suicide attacks, both locally and globally.

As a strategy chosen when conventional insurgency fails, today's suicide attacks are reminiscent of the hijackings and hostage taking that Yasir Arafat's PLO perpetrated in the late 1960s and early 1970s. That experience is worth reviewing because of the insight it provides into the ongoing evolution of both terrorist and counterterrorist methods.

By the late 1960s, Fatah and the other PLO groups controlled enough territory in Jordan and Lebanon to train in, but were not strong enough to overthrow the governments of Jordan, Lebanon, or Israel using conventional insurgency tactics. Arafat turned to spectacular international airline hijackings, a method that successfully captivated the international media and focused the attention of governments on the Palestinian cause. In July 1968 an El Al Boeing 707 from Rome to Tel Aviv was hijacked to Algiers, where the PLO held the twenty-one Israeli passengers and crew hostage for thirty-nine days. In September 1970, during the "Black September" rebellion, the PLO hijacked four flights by Western carriers, from Frankfurt, Zurich, Amsterdam, and Bahrain. Three were forced to land on an airstrip in the Jordanian desert in territory controlled by the PLO (the fourth was too large and was diverted to Cairo). After evacuating the 310 passengers and crew, the terrorists invited international media to film as they staged the explosion of the aircraft. With the passengers held at gunpoint, the PLO began bargaining for release of its operatives jailed in Europe and Israel. Over the next two weeks some of the hostages were rescued by the Jordanian military, as part of its victory over the PLO, while some were indeed exchanged for PLO prisoners held in Europe.

Counterterrorism evolved to meet the threat. Israel, Europe, the United States, and the other countries whose airplanes were being targeted introduced passenger inspections and other security improvements, which remain in place today.

Thwarted by improved commercial airport security, the PLO evolved as well, turning to an even more spectacular method. Before the dawn of September 5, 1972, eight "Black September" terrorists found a soft target: Israeli athletes asleep in their dormitory in Munich's Olympic village. Two were killed immediately. The terrorists held the other nine as hostages, demanding in exchange hundreds of Palestinians jailed in Israel, as well as Baader, Meinhof, and other terrorists held in Germany. The German authorities dragged out negotiations with the PLO terrorists through a long day, all broadcast in real time around the world. That night they attempted a rescue that went horribly wrong, ending in a gunfight that lasted until 1:30 in the morning. By the time the last terrorist was killed by the German forces, the nine athletes and one German police officer were also dead.

European and American civilians were being taken hostage, and hundreds of millions of television viewers around the world were suddenly engaged, all in the name of a cause that most previously had never heard of. Though PLO operatives were failing as insurgents, the hijackings and the Munich massacre gave the organization media exposure, support among its constituency, new recruits, and new opportunities to extort concessions and money from governments, just as the suicide attacks of 9/11 did for Al Qaeda.

Unlike suicide attacks, though, the threat from hostage taking, airborne or otherwise, was quickly contained. Israel secured its airplanes, never allowing another hijacking. The German police had been taken by surprise in Munich and botched the rescue. Yet the Germans, British, and French governments responded quickly to the Munich massacre, setting up special counterterrorism units that could deal effectively with hijackings and hostage situations. In 1978 the German GSG-9 successfully rescued all eighty-six hostages on a Lufthansa flight hijacked to Mogadishu. In 1980 a British SAS unit saved nineteen of twenty-one hostages held at the Iranian Embassy in London.

Two years later, in November 1982, Hezbollah demonstrated the next evolutionary step: the high-casualty suicide attack has proved to be much more difficult to contain using military and police methods of counterterrorism. Hardening civilian targets shifts risks from one airport to another and even from the United States to other countries, but it may not have reduced the global risk overall, since suicide attacks are so difficult to prevent altogether. Defensive actions against terrorists using suicide tactics are unlikely to shut down the threat, and the cost of those defensive actions has been astronomical, both in money and in travelers' time. Special counterterrorism units are effective, but only with very precise intelligence about the perpetrators. And it only takes a few suicide attackers slipping through the cracks to do tremendous damage.

"That's not entirely reassuring, Professor. So what can we do about it?"

The next chapter examines a possible evolutionary response: moving away from reactive counterterrorism to proactive, constructive solutions that use what we now know about radical religious groups and hard targets to design new approaches to dealing with suicide attacks in particular and terrorism in general.

Iraqi troops distribute food rations in the impoverished Sadr City district of eastern Baghdad after U.S. forces suppress militias, May 2008. (Ali Yussef/AFP/ Getty Images)

7

Constructive Counterterrorism

Counterinsurgency is armed social work; an attempt to redress basic social and political problems while being shot at.

This makes civil affairs a central counterinsurgency activity, not an afterthought.

—Dr. David Kilcullen, Lieutenant Colonel. Australian Army[1]

In 1973 PLO Chairman Yasir Arafat had a terrorism problem. The campaign of hijacking and hostage taking and the spectacular attack on athletes at the Munich Olympics had exposed his cause brilliantly to the world. These bloody acts had also made recruitment and political extortion much easier. Now, having achieved international standing, further violence threatened to undermine the new image Arafat sought to project. The PLO was being vilified as a bloodthirsty terrorist organization just when he wanted to become the foremost statesman for the Palestinian cause. Terrorism had become a liability on his path to international legitimacy. It was now critical to somehow keep his cadres of accomplished terrorists—young men whose violent acts had been lionized and celebrated—under control.

A senior PLO official recalled the PLO's dilemma, in an interview conducted decades later by Bruce Hoffman, a scholar of terrorism at Georgetown University: "We had a group called the Black September Organization. It was the most elite unit we had. . . . We could send them anywhere to do anything and they would lay down their lives to do it. No question. No hesitation. They were absolutely dedicated and absolutely ruthless."[2] Aside from the Munich attack, the Black September Organization had assassinated Jordan's prime minister, hijacked a Belgian aircraft, and attacked targets in Germany, the Netherlands, Great

Britain, Sudan and Greece. They were itching for more action. How could the PLO leadership shut them down before they undermined Arafat's diplomatic ambitions?

Hoffman describes the solution that Arafat and his staff devised: "Finally they hit upon an idea. Why not simply marry them off? In other words why not find a way to give these men—the most dedicated, competent and implacable fighters in the PLO—a reason to live rather than to die?"

And that's what they did. Arafat and his deputy, Abu Iyad, offered the hundred or so Black September operatives a generous outside option: an apartment in Beirut, $3,000, a gas stove, a refrigerator, and a television. Best of all, they recruited a hundred lovely young Palestinian women to the cause. If the operatives married, the PLO would shower them with all of those rewards. In addition, the terrorists qualified for a $5,000 baby bonus if they had a child within a year.

Their incentives worked marvelously. Not only did former Black September operatives give up violence; the formerly ruthless killers refused to even travel abroad on nonviolent PLO business, for fear of being arrested outside of Lebanon and separated from their new wives and children. The Black September Organization was retired and has not been heard from since. Arafat, his dogs of war safely domesticated, would go on to address the United Nations in November 1974, famously imploring "Do not let the olive branch fall from my hand!" In 1975 the PLO was granted observer status at the United Nations.

In the same article Hoffman describes how the Northern Ireland prison service weaned hardened IRA and Loyalist operatives from violence, using a similar incentive-based program. The service studied the domestic situations of prisoners and granted selected prisoners a home visit. At home, the jailed terrorists would see aging parents, lonely young wives, and children who needed parenting. After the visit, these chosen prisoners were offered shortened sentences with more frequent family visits, if they agreed to certain conditions: integrated cell blocks (Catholic and Protestant), nonviolent behavior, vocational training, and counseling. None of the inmates who took up that option ever returned to violence. Both the IRA and the Loyalists suffered attrition in prisons that had previously been their strongholds.

In a nutshell, the message of the previous chapters is consistent with the approach that Arafat and the Irish prison service adopted. Strong terrorist clubs insulate themselves against defection by dampening the options of operatives outside the club. Clubs can be weakened by taking the opposite tactic, *improving* outside options. Even men with a history of horrible violence respond to domestic incentives, however mundane these may seem.

How Terrorist Clubs Succeed

One way to think about how to cripple the most lethal religious terrorists, the clubs, is to pay attention to what we've learned about how those organizations reduce defection. We've discussed six methods in the previous six chapters. First, clubs destroy the outside options of members through up-front sacrifices of educational opportunities or work experience. Second, they recruit carefully from within a nonviolent organizational base—charitable groups that provide social services. Third, social services are not only a source of recruits; they also provide leverage over veteran members. That works because clubs generally provide services in a discriminatory, exclusionary way: only members receive services and more valued members receive more services. That leverage is enhanced if members and their families are desperate for services, a situation that a terrorist club can engineer if competing sources of social services—the government or NGOs—can be suppressed. So it shouldn't surprise us to see rebel clubs attacking police stations and government agencies or destroying reconstruction projects, including bridges, schools, and hospitals—as we have seen in Iraq and Afghanistan. The greater the rebels' monopoly over the usual functions of government, the more leverage they have over their own members. Fourth, clubs can augment the leverage social services provide by improving the quality of services provided, which is in turn possible with outside subsidies or with a revenue stream from smuggling, drug trafficking, or other illegal activity. Fifth, rebel clubs attempt to monopolize political representation, taking it out of the hands of government and political rivals—often by using violence to intimidate or eliminate organizations vying for the same constituency—as al-Sadr's militia does among Shiite Iraqis, Hamas does among

Palestinians, Hezbollah does among Lebanese Shiites, and the Taliban does among Pashtun Afghans. Political power may be their ultimate goal, but even if it is not, a monopoly over political representation provides leverage over followers, just as a monopoly over any other public service does. Sixth, rebel clubs create distance between members and the culture they could possibly defect to—a possible explanation for the hideous brutality against women, and the widespread repression of women practiced by the Taliban and al-Sadr's Mahdi Army, for example.

Radical Islamists thrive when governments allow them to pursue these methods with impunity, ceding provision of basic social services, such as security, education, and healthcare. Beyond Iraq, Lebanon, Palestine, and Afghanistan, weak or dysfunctional governments have also allowed radical Islamists to establish government-like levels of social service provision—including provision of basic security—in many countries at various times, including Somalia, Nigeria, Algeria, Chechnya, Kashmir, Tajikistan, Yemen, Bosnia, and the southern Philippines. When the Soviet Union collapsed, the weak governments that replaced Soviet rule in central Asia could not prevent the proliferation of radical Islamic activity, including social service provision and sometimes militia activity. As author Ahmed Rashid points out, that process was reminiscent of a similar upsurge in Islamic communities when the czarist Russian Empire collapsed seven decades earlier.[3] Clubs filling a vacuum left by dysfunctional governments are not a strictly Islamist phenomenon. It was out of the weak governance of southern Italy after the Second World War that another economic club—the Sicilian Mafia—resurrected itself.

Expanded social service provision by religious communities is in itself a wonderful thing. Clinics, schools, community centers, and even foot patrols restoring order, must be a welcome relief from ineffectual or absent government provision of the same services. The majority of what radical Islamists do is inherently constructive and often fills a pressing humanitarian need, such as the postearthquake relief they provided in Kashmir. Yet there are two problems with ceding social service provision to religious radicals. First, when the method of provision is a mutual-aid club, it will necessarily be exclusionary. Exclusion of nonmembers from services, ostracism ("shunning") of defectors, and the maintenance of social distance from outsiders—sometimes to the point of abuse—must eventually be part of the package in order to control free riding. Second, in the minority of cases in which religious radicals choose violence, they have the potential to be, as we have seen, extremely lethal at it, so much so that the very survival of governments may be threatened. What if religious radicals simply become the government? We'll return to that question in the next chapter, putting it in a broad historical context. For now our focus is on the nuts and bolts of constructive approaches to counterinsurgency and counterterrorism that the club approach suggests.

Constructive Counterterrorism

The benign activities of religious clubs strengthen their violent capabilities, but that also has a wonderful implication: a government that seeks to undermine the potential for lethal rebellion among religious radicals has a menu of nonviolent options. It can limit the lethality of terrorist clubs by countering the tactics that clubs use to insulate themselves from defection.

First, enhance outside options for rebels and potential rebels. That is to say, provide the basic prerequisites for good jobs in the legitimate economy: thriving markets and quality educational opportunities. Anything that enhances the labor-market opportunities of potential defectors tightens the defection constraint rebels face on terrorist activities, making it easier for the government to bribe conspirators into defection. The more receptive operatives are to bribes and a subsequent transition to legitimate employment, the safer high-value targets are; that's because when outside options improve, attacks on high-value targets become so liable to result in defection that the action becomes prohibitively dangerous for the club.

Enhancing outside options is most effective when clubs choose suicide attacks. If clubs are using suicide attacks, then high-value targets are threatened. Those are the targets whose security is most enhanced by a strategy of enhancing outside options. The reason is this: the highest-value targets are those for which the largest bribes for defection will be paid, so if an operative is going to defect at all, it will be to expose the high-value attack—the one that carries with it a large bribe (i.e., reward) for information, rather than a small one. The higher the stakes, the more a security policy should depend on improving outside options and offering generous rewards for defection.

Creating jobs, enhancing educational opportunities, and building prosperity seem like straightforward recommendations from Development Economics 101. Yet in an ungoverned space, economic development is more complicated because *projects can be captured.*

A. Heather Coyne of the U.S. Institute of Peace tells a story from her fifteen months as a Civil Affairs Officer in Baghdad that illustrates the problem of captured projects. Early in the occupation of Iraq, an army colonel was charged with controlling Sadr City, the overcrowded, run-down, violence-prone section of Baghdad with a large and poor Shiite population. In an attempt to build authority and support for a moderate local council, the colonel initiated a street-cleanup program. The U.S. Army offered to pay $10 to anyone who showed up one morning to help clean up the streets. It would be a quick, simple way to create jobs and provide a basic service.

Coyne describes what happened next:

The project had actually been running pretty smoothly for a while and he had the idea of going out and talking to the people who had been participating, to get their feedback. It turned out that they were just so enthusiastic about the program. They said: "We love this program. We are so happy about it. We have money in our pockets. We can care for our families. It shows concern for the communities. We are so grateful for this program.

And we're so grateful to Muqtada al-Sadr for doing this program."

The Colonel did a double take, and said: "No, no. This is the army program, and the district local council. We're doing the program."

They said: "No. Muqtada al-Sadr is doing the program."

Colonel: "Why do you think that? Why do you think it's Muqtada al-Sadr?"

And they said: "Because Muqtada al-Sadr told us that it was his program."

Sadr agents had been infiltrating the program, going around telling everyone that this was Muqtada al-Sadr showing his concern for the community, and nobody else had told them anything different, so they believed them.

So the Colonel was crushed. All credit for his great idea was going to the Army's arch nemesis.[4]

As far as conventional development economics goes, the colonel achieved his goal, providing jobs. Yet he failed in his true objective—

weakening the rebel al-Sadr who was competing with the government for control of Sadr City. The program actually accomplished the *opposite*, strengthening al-Sadr and undermining the local council, since—as far as local residents were concerned—the temporary jobs and cleaned-up streets had been delivered by al-Sadr. In the minds of local residents, al-Sadr could presumably withdraw those services if they misbehaved, so that the program increased his control over their neighborhoods. Al-Sadr could exploit a program in his territory to strengthen his organization because he could infiltrate and capture the program. This cautionary tale illustrates a general principle: economic development and governance can be at odds when the territory is not fully controlled by government.

There's another, even less subtle, way in which the intuition we have about economic development in well-governed spaces leads us astray. Western businesspeople often look at a place with high unemployment and low wages, like Iraq, Afghanistan, South Lebanon, or Palestine and immediately think of ways to attract foreign investment and create jobs. That approach misses a basic rule of economics: investment chases profit opportunities like air rushes into a vacuum. If investment is absent, we should first figure out why investors are not rushing in. The problem is often not a lack of local funds. In Palestine during the second Intifada, for example, the local population had about $3 billion in savings; these financial assets were sitting idle in banks, not locally invested or invested abroad. If *local* entrepreneurs—who understand local conditions best—are not investing, foreigners should be asking why. The problem might be the physical risk to assets, it may be the lack of reliable infrastructure, it may be a failed legal system, or it may be the suspicion that profits will be seized by some corrupt official or warlord like al-Sadr, who can snatch the profits from local private investment as quickly as he can capture the credit for a public works program. Without security, infrastructure, minimal rule of law, and some protection from extortion by corrupt officials, private investment will be negligible and public investment, including job-creating reconstruction projects, will often be wasted.

Second, compete directly with the rebels in social service provision. The southern suburbs of Beirut are bomb-scarred and riddled with bullet holes marking three decades of civil war and invasion. Majority Shiite, these suburbs are also bursting with population, having absorbed refugees and migrants from the underdeveloped and war-torn Shiite villages of South Lebanon (in much the same way that Sadr City has absorbed economic refugees from rural Iraq). There is no public hospital.

Hezbollah operates two of the three private hospitals—where women may not visit male patients.[5] Hezbollah also collects garbage. It provides water and manages an electricity grid. It runs schools—both madrassas and mixed schools, which teach a combination of the government-approved curriculum and religious studies. It provides vocational training. Many Hezbollah schools and hospitals began by providing services only to the families of Hezbollah fighters but later expanded to provide for others, though their militants pay lower fees and presumably still get priority treatment.[6] Why would Lebanese Shiite Muslims support a Lebanese government that does a poor job providing basic services, when Hezbollah has demonstrated an ability to do a far better job, using a combination of donations and Iranian funding?

What's wrong with this picture? What's wrong with charities providing municipal and social services in general? There would be no problem, if those charities were not building loyalty for a political organization that seeks to undermine government, and if that organization did not embody tremendous potential for violence, both domestic and international.

Yet shutting down those charities would be a cruel and shortsighted response. It would deprive residents of essential services, leaving some families without education, healthcare, or welfare services. A shutdown would arouse even more anger, delegitimizing the government. Worse, into the chaos of a social service provision vacuum would inevitably step some *other* opportunistic actor, perhaps with greater potential for violence. Disproportionate response is what outgunned rebels pray for.

A wiser approach is for government to compete: providing security, water, garbage collection, power, education, healthcare, welfare services, and all the other services that residents in developed countries have come to expect from their government. Truly competing means providing services in a nondiscriminatory way. Nondiscrimination sends a strong message: it communicates to members of all ethnic or religious groups, minority or majority, that they have an outside option to sectarian or ethnic rebel organizations.

As we saw in the case of the Taliban, security matters—it was the basic service they provided first, apparently winning them a constituency. Historian Richard English points out that the Irish Republican Army did the same; it initially established a foothold among Irish Catholics, and then entrenched itself, by providing security from sectarian violence that local government did not.[7]

As we saw in the case of Egypt, President Nasser provided a crude but positive example of this constructive approach to preemptive counterinsurgency in the 1950s. He nationalized the schools, clinics, and other social service institutions of the Muslim Brotherhood, effectively shutting down their organizational base for two decades. Since its appointment in June 2007, the government of Palestinian Prime Minister Salaam Fayyad, which controls the Palestinian West Bank, has attempted to implement a similar strategy. It has tried to use a combination of social services delivered by government and foreign-funded nongovernmental organizations (NGOs) to compete directly with the social service network provided by Hamas. Fayyad's aim was clear: to prevent Hamas from successfully seizing the West Bank, either through elections or by violence, as it did Gaza in June 2007. Whether in a future unity government this basic service provision will be credited to the government, or captured by Hamas, is an open question.

Competing to provide basic services is a matter of enhancing outside options, which tightens the defection constraint. It deprives terrorists of high-value targets that are otherwise vulnerable to attack without fear of defection.

Third, protect service providers. Rebel clubs will attack providers of basic services. They recognize how dependent they are on their nonviolent social service–providing organizational base, and therefore see competing providers of those same services as a threat, be they government employees or well-meaning volunteers from NGOs. Lieutenant Colonel Kilcullen, a veteran Australian counterinsurgent with a doctorate in anthropology, puts it bluntly: "There is no such thing as impartial humanitarian assistance or civil affairs in counterinsurgency. Every time you help someone, you hurt someone else, not least the insurgents. So civil and humanitarian assistance personnel will be targeted."[8] For that reason it's not enough to provide services. Service providers need protection, which requires plenty of trained security personnel. I'll return to the organizational problems this raises below, but suffice to say that just as few marines signed up to nation-build, even fewer employees of NGOs enlisted with the intention of getting shot at.

Competitive service provision cannot be naive. Services provided by NGOs can be captured by rebels and turned to their benefit, just as the colonel's job-creation program in Sadr City was captured. While a captured service meets the humanitarian objective, it strengthens rather than weakens rebels.

NGOs and international aid providers often face dilemmas. For example, should a United Nations agency have allowed the Muslim Brotherhood to deliver aid for them in Gaza, as they did for years? Or should they have subcontracted that job to a less efficient operator who posed less of a threat to the occupational government? While the UN aspires to remain neutral, that aspiration is unrealistic in the context of a political conflict; no aid can be truly neutral in a place where governance is in dispute.

The greater the control a rebel club has over the territory, the worse the dilemma. In Afghanistan under the Taliban, international aid organizations were completely vulnerable, as they struggled to provide food, education, health, and welfare services to a suffering local population. The Taliban did their best to capture those services, forcing organizations to discriminate according to stringent Taliban prohibitions, not allowing women to enter hospitals, for instance. When the aid organizations stuck to their principles, threatening to leave rather than discriminate against women, the Taliban response was flippant: let them leave. Since the Taliban controlled the territory there was no choice. The NGOs left, depriving communities—including women and children—of healthcare.[9] An aid organization has no good way to resolve this dilemma.

Yet what is a dilemma for an aid organization, which must be noncoercive by nature, should be a simple choice for a government capable of controlling territory and interested in countering terrorism:

- Do not provide services that will be captured.
- Provide competing services.
- Protect the providers.

Fourth, reduce rebel revenues. This is subtler than it first appears. Clearly, if rebels finance their activities through smuggling and drug running, as the Taliban do in Afghanistan, reducing that flow of income has multiple benefits. Yet other cases are not as clear. What if rebels collect charitable donations and use them to pay exclusively for benign activity, like education and healthcare? As we have seen, those charitable activities increase the potency of the rebel threat, should the charitable organization turn to violence. For example, the Israeli occupational administration allowed the Muslim Brotherhood to capture waqf assets in Gaza, as we saw in chapter 5. Though the Brotherhood was nonviolent at the time, it was a historic mistake. It allowed the Brotherhood to strengthen the organizational base that would eventually support Hamas. In a parallel example, the Palestinian Authority for many years allowed donations from Gulf states to flow directly to Hamas in support of that organization's charitable work, including social service provision, rather than supporting government provision of the same services. Similarly, Lebanon allows Gulf states to donate reconstruction funds directly to Hezbollah, strengthening its organizational base in competition with the government, rather than insisting that foreign donations support Lebanese-government reconstruction efforts.

Here's a subtler case of misguided policies that subsidize terrorist clubs. Pakistan and Afghanistan inadvertently generated revenue for rebels in the 1990s, through poorly designed tariff and duty agreements on goods landing in the Pakistani port of Karachi but bound for Afghanistan, creating what amounted to a "full-employment act" for Pashtun smugglers. The agreement was presumably designed to help the landlocked Afghan economy, allowing goods to be imported in bond (i.e., without duties or tariffs charged) at Karachi, and then transported through to Afghanistan, which could then levy its own duties and tariffs on arrival. That would have been fine, except that the Afghan-Pakistani border was insecure: smugglers easily diverted the goods, avoided paying tariffs and duties in either country, and established a duty-free pipeline of consumer goods into Pakistan via Afghanistan. Rather than simply agreeing to let the Pakistani government charge tariffs and duties in Karachi, and then transfer that revenue to the Afghan government, the money both governments lost subsidized Pashtun smugglers on both sides of the border. The smugglers, in turn, eventually subsidized the Taliban through the fees they paid to move goods along Taliban-controlled trade routes.[10]

Indirect methods of reducing rebel revenue can also help weaken rebel clubs. Rebels often thrive on smuggling illicit goods bound for Western markets. A reduction in heroin prices in Europe, for example, would have directly reduced the smugglers' revenue earned by the Taliban as they rose to power in the mid-1990s. The same is true of rebels in Afghanistan today and possibly also in the Federally Administered Tribal Areas (FATA) of Pakistan, where opium profits often make rebel forces better armed and better paid than government troops. The Revolutionary Armed Forces of Colombia (FARC) is another terrorist organization that finances itself with revenues from the drug trade, in this case from cocaine. (The Bekaa valley east of Beirut, where Hezbollah was initially established, was a major opium production and distribution center during the Lebanese civil war, under the protection of Syria, though it's unclear if Hezbollah gained revenue from production.) Legalizing drug use—that is, treating illicit drugs as controlled substances that are legal to grow and regulated by government—has other social costs. Yet it might be worth considering as a way to stabilize Afghanistan, Colombia, and perhaps western Pakistan, where the government is outgunned and outbribed by wealthy narcotics traders. Petroleum is legal, of course, but by the same token, curbing global demand for petroleum would not only have environmental benefits. It would also reduce funds available for donation to Islamist terrorism and to Islamist social services provided by rebel organizations that compete with governments, not only in the Middle East, but in many other parts of the Muslim world as well.

Returning to the dilemma of social service provision, is there a way to weaken religious rebels without cutting social services to communities in need? Yes. Consider the Shiite minority in Lebanon, which is poorly served by its own revenue-strapped government but receives generous support from the Iranian government through Hezbollah. If foreign governments were to provide humanitarian aid through local governments, such as the Lebanese, Palestinian, or Afghan governments, rather than through Hezbollah, Hamas and Taliban-linked charities, the humanitarian objective would be achieved without strengthening the organizational base of rebels.

This brings us to the delicate topic of whether governments effectively provide services to their own residents in the first place. One argument foreign donors often make for contributing to the Islamists is that certain governments are corrupt and unworthy of their charity, while the Islamic charities are effective providers of services. In this sense improving the capacity of allied governments to provide services in an honest, transparent, and effective way is a critical component of counterinsurgency and counterterrorism efforts. For example, a seemingly mundane issue such as improving the logistics of tax collection is a form of foreign aid that improves social service provision by local governments, by providing a tax base to pay for those services. Dealing with corruption and the representativeness of government is harder, because it generally requires a system of outside monitoring, through the legal system, political pressure, and an active civil society. Returning again to the Fayyad government, in June 2007 it proposed a creative solution to its own lack of capacity: partnering with (secular) NGOs in providing services in areas where it recognized that its own departments required assistance.

Fifth, remember that civil society matters. Many developing countries effectively grant religious politicians a monopoly on political representation by default, when they thoroughly suppress political activity outside of mosques and other places of worship. Representation is a public service that citizens of democracies take for granted, yet it is rare and precious in much of the developing world. Breaking the religious monopoly on opposition politics, by allowing a secular opposition to function, weakens radical religious clubs by providing an alternative form of political expression (an outside option) to members. Providing that alternative requires protecting competing elements of civil society from being intimidated by either government or religious radicals, who—as previous chapters have argued—have an advantage at organized violence and therefore at intimidation. If government does not allow safe ways to exercise freedom of assembly and freedom of speech, rival political groups can be expected to either be intimidated into suppression or to organize their own rebel cells.

What's Wrong with the Old-Fashioned Methods?

This is not an argument for planting roses in rifle barrels or naively dispatching the Peace Corps in shorts and sandals to quell terrorism. No act is neutral, no matter how benign. Competing in social service provision, economic development, and political development, and cutting off revenue streams all require a muscular commitment to security and enforcement.

The old-fashioned methods of counterterrorism and counterinsurgency are not sufficient to confront the modern threat of radical religious rebels. Once expensive security and enforcement are in place, the soft targets have become hardened but they are still not secure. In that environment weak rebels may abandon insurgency altogether, as Fatah did in Jordan after their defeat in 1970, but strong rebels will turn to terrorism and suicide attacks. The rebel groups with the organizational strength to do so today are generally radical religious clubs. Once clubs turn to suicide attacks, further hardening of all the targets is very expensive because there are so many targets to defend. For example, Coalition forces invest in securing a police station in Afghanistan, making it safe from conventional attack. Rebels adapt and change their tactics to a suicide attack. But if they must give up a suicide attacker, why waste him on the local police station? They might start eyeing government offices in Kabul or Islamabad, or perhaps airports or train stations in Europe. The cost of defending all potential targets is enormous.

What about taking offensive rather than defensive approaches, namely, "capture and kill"? These approaches have their place, but the U.S. Special Forces have a saying: "A defection is better than a capture; a capture is better than a kill." Why? The answer recalls what Sam Popkin learned in Vietnam. Dead rebels are easily replaced. Captured rebels reveal information. Defectors reveal even more. Competing with radical religious sects in their benign activities—social services, politics, and markets—weakens them by improving outside options, inducing defection. Offensive approaches have their place, but they apparently work best when complemented by a flow of information from informants and defectors.

Moreover, "capture and kill" by itself is not sustainable. Ambassador Henry (Hank) Crumpton has the right look for a spy; the nondescript appearance of a man who could be from anywhere. Wearing a jacket and dress pants, he could blend into the background of a hotel lobby or bus station anywhere from Sydney to Beirut, looking like a midlevel manager on a business trip. Crumpton was responsible for the initial intelligence effort that allowed Coalition forces to break the Taliban in 2001. Despite the loss of Northern Alliance commander Ahmad Shah Massoud to a Taliban suicide attack, Crumpton and his men quietly toured Afghanistan shortly after 9/11, organized an alliance of local fighters, identified targets for air strikes, and most likely negotiated a provisional power-sharing arrangement as well. The effort was a remarkable example of small, smart, high-tech warfare in support of local allies. American forces numbered only a few hundred Special Forces troops on the ground, who suffered only one casualty in the first month of fighting. The Taliban had collapsed within two months, when Kandahar fell on December 7, 2001.

Hank Crumpton called his job "the first 10 percent." The other 90 percent—securing the territory, stabilizing the government, and developing the economy—is not the job of the CIA or the Air Force. Yet he freely admits that the first 10 percent is not sustainable. In his words, "Disrupting enemy networks in the war on terrorism is an essential activity, but it can only take us part way to success. We must also work with our partners to find alternative ways to meet people's social and economic needs and prevent them from gravitating toward extremist networks."[11] A capture-and-kill approach is not sustainable because it only removes the current threat. If the result is a weak government without the resources to meet basic needs, then *some* social service provider will step in. During the Cold War that alternative provider was likely to be communist. Today in the Muslim world it is likely to be radical Islamist, using the "Hamas model."

During the two years following the collapse of the Taliban, the "lost years" of Afghan reconstruction, the United States and its allies tragically underspent on improving social services and governance in Afghanistan. The Taliban, retrenched and rehydrated with smuggling revenue, at this writing again constitute an existential threat to the Afghan government.

Where to Start?

The junior officer's eyes darted nervously from me to the general, an imposing man with a gnarled face and an amused smile. The Pacific Special Operations Command has a tradition of annually gathering senior special forces officers from allied countries bordering the Pacific to discuss their common concerns. I briefly addressed their plenary session one morning. In the afternoon, not having anything better to do with the outside speaker, they invited me to participate in a small informal brainstorming session with senior officers. Around a circular table sat a group of formidable looking men in well-decorated uniforms, representing several Asian countries with a history of active insurgency. Most had junior officers sitting beside them to translate.

Our table lacked a moderator so, spotting a research opportunity, I took the initiative. "Tell me," I asked, "what's your standard procedure when you move into a poorly governed space?"

Translators whispered in the ears of colonels and generals, while the Americans and other English speakers waited politely. One officer nudged his translator, spoke with authority, and then nodded to the translator, who explained in English. It went something like this: "First we gather intelligence. Then we secure the territory. Next, we ask local leaders and the population what services they need. We meet their requests if we can. If we do a good job and provide security, they feed us information about the insurgents, who we set out to ambush." I thanked him and looked around the table for a reaction. A commander from a different country took his turn, spoke with a most serious expression, then motioned to his own translator, who proceeded a little nervously: "First we gather intelligence from the local villagers. We then secure the territory. Next we poll the local population about their needs. Then we provide them as best we can . . ." I stopped taking notes and looked at the translator to see if he was joking. His eyes darted nervously from me to his commander, then to my immobile hand holding the pen and back to my eyes.

Realizing my mistake, I resumed taking notes: ". . . give us information that leads to the capture of the insurgents." The English speakers at the table kept poker faces and looked around for a diplomat. "Interesting that there's so much agreement," I managed to summarize, as we moved on to the next speaker, and the drama repeated itself.

The point is that special forces the world over have developed a doctrine that dates back at least as far as the British "emergency" in Malaya. After securing the territory, they ask the locals what they need and provide it as fast as possible. If Hank Crumpton promised an airdrop of humanitarian assistance, he made sure it was there within three days: food, tents, and even toys. His working assumption was that the local population knows what it wants and that local leaders know what makes them vulnerable to competition from insurgents, just like good politicians anywhere.

It seems incongruous, massive special forces officers with necks and shoulders like linebackers, expounding on the importance of building schools, paving roads and digging wells. Yet an increasing number of special forces, marines, and army officers think this way, because they have successes to show for it, most recently from the shift in tactics that accompanied the "surge" of early 2007 in Iraq. The surge included not only an increase in troop strength but also change in tactics: forces were redeployed from large bases to smaller outposts, soldiers dismounted from vehicles to patrol on foot, and a greater emphasis was placed on speaking to local leaders. Improved communications apparently led to improved provision of municipal services that Iraqi communities actually valued, which was certainly the case for the most basic service of public safety.

True, many of those defeated insurgents who informed this doctrine were communists, not Islamists, yet they were clublike in their behavior: providing services, perhaps by stealing rice from landowners in Malaya and sharing it with the peasants. Yes, today the rebels use suicide attacks, but as we have seen, that has mostly to do with the asymmetry of forces, not with theology.

The Malayan Precedent

The modern doctrine of counterinsurgency has deep roots in Malaya, where the British faced a formidable, experienced insurgent organization from 1948 through 1957. The communist Malayan Races Liberation Army (MRLA), led by Chin Peng, had a jungle to hide in. They had also benefited from extensive training in guerrilla warfare—by the British themselves—during the Japanese occupation. Early in their campaign, the MRLA managed to ambush the British High Commissioner in his car, assassinating Sir Henry Gurney in October 1951. The new counter-insurgency campaign was designed in 1952 by his replacement, General Gerald Templar, with the assistance of Lieutenant General Harold Briggs, his "Director of Anti-Bandit Operations." Eight years later the British left Malaya in the hands of a stable, allied government, with the insurgency suppressed. Templar's strategy was based on intelligence and service provision: gather intelligence, secure the area, and provide services. Then gather better intelligence; which informs ambushes and raids by small groups of British troops. This is now standard practice for counterinsurgents throughout the region, as my brainstorming session with the generals made clear.

The MRLA were capable of deterring collaboration with credible threats of violence and they moved freely within the population. They were not a modern club, because they lacked a social service provision base. Nevertheless British military historian Sir Robert Thompson writes that competent services provided by the government—schools, clinics, running water, electricity, and security for the ethnic Chinese—were necessary for the flow of intelligence that allowed insurgents to be located and eventually defeated.[12] Thompson went as far as to state that conquering an area was pointless without providing services afterward in order to hold it.

One aspect of service provision was conversion of the police force from an instrument of the government in enforcing a police state to a public service provider in what the British call the "constabulary tradition" (and Americans might call "community policing"). That conversion was implemented by London Police Commissioner Arthur Young. Young had gained experience commanding the Italian police force after the Allied conquest of Italy during the Second World War. The police, rather than the military, became the principal collectors of intelligence, which in turn guided ambushes and other counterinsurgency operations.

Providing services, while distancing a half million ethnic Chinese Malayans from jungles populated with MRLA, was expensive. It also involved transfers of population that would be unacceptable today:

This resettlement program, which moved the poorest tenth of Malaya's population into more viable areas with good roads, sewage, water, and electricity, helped to solve one of the country's most serious social problems. It gave large numbers of Chinese peasants security in land title for the first time and brought them into a friendlier relationship with the government. Politically, the transfer program contributed toward a reorientation of thinking among the people who had hitherto comprised the most unstable and least reliable element of the civilian population.[13]

How expensive was it? Though it is hard to distinguish civilian development from military expenditure, it is still useful to get at least a rough sense of the cost of the Malayan campaign to the British. Estimates as the time put it at £720 million over the period 1948–1957,[14] which is $21.4 billion in today's dollars.[15] That amounts to $286 per Malayan per year over ten years, or $765 per ethnic Chinese Malayan (who were about 37 percent of the population and the constituency of the rebels), or $153,000 per year for each of the 14,000 combatants and support troops that the communists could field.[16] That's an overestimate, because there would have been some cost to administering Malaya even in the absence of an insurgency, but even if we deflate by an estimated 20 percent to cover those expenses,[17] repressing the Malayan insurgency was hardly cheap. Yet despite the expense, the results were outstanding. The insurgency was quelled, and when the British finally returned home, they left a friendly government in charge.

A similar approach worked for the British in the Middle East. Some of the SAS veterans from Malaya were eventually deployed in the monarchy of Oman, at the southeastern tip of the Arabian Peninsula. They were dispatched to help repress a rebellion that had begun in 1957 in the western province of Dhofar, bordering Yemen. The rebels were Marxists, yet they had managed to gain the support of the conservative Muslim rural tribes with the promise of first expelling the tyrannical Sultan Taimur and then providing municipal services. A turning point came in 1970, when the Sultan's son, Qaboos, deposed his father with British support. Qaboos offered amnesty and cash rewards to defectors, and invested heavily in health and education. To punctuate the young sultan's commitments, British SAS teams included doctors and veterinarians. British-trained Omani troops followed a "conquer-and-hold" strategy, accompanied by civil affairs teams who dug wells, built schools, and opened clinics. The rebellion was quelled by 1975.[18]

A more recent example of constructive counterterrorism is the work of the U.S. Special Operations forces against the Abu Sayyaf Group on the southern Philippine island of Basilan. Though only 5 percent of Philippine residents are Muslims, the southern islands have a Muslim majority. Abu Sayyaf is an Islamic terrorist organization responsible for attacks, kidnappings, and extortion in the Philippines and Malaysia, including the bombing of a ferry in Manila that killed 114 people in February 2004. The southern Philippines have hosted training camps for Indonesian Jamaiya Islamia terrorists under the protection of the Philippine Moro Islamic Liberation Front (MILF). The Abu Sayyaf group is small and as far as I know provides no social services. They used Basilan as a safe haven and base of operations.

American involvement began in January 2002. While the Philippine armed forces provided security, U.S. Special Forces conducted surveys, which indicated that local priorities were water, security, medical care, education, and roads. The U.S. Special Forces helped the Philippine government respond to these needs, building roads and improving schools, hospitals, and mosques. When the local population increased its support for the Philippine military presence, they provided information that led to the capture of Abu Sayyaf operatives.[19] The Abu Sayyaf group reportedly left Basilan in 2004, allowing the Philippine military to draw down forces and triggering a return of teachers and other professionals.[20]

Is this the same strategy that General David Petraeus implemented in Iraq? It is very similar. During his tour commanding the Mosul region,

Petraeus was converted to thinking constructively about counterterrorism. Those views were reflected in his subsequent revision of the U.S. Army field manual on counterinsurgency which he coauthored with Lieutenant General James Amos of the Marine Corps in December 2006, a few months before returning to command forces in Iraq:

The integration of civilian and military efforts is crucial to successful COIN [counterinsurgency] operations. All efforts focus on supporting the local populace and HN [host nation] government. Political, social, and economic programs are usually more valuable than conventional military operations in addressing the root causes of conflict and undermining an insurgency. COIN participants come from many backgrounds. They may include military personnel, diplomats, police, politicians, humanitarian aid workers, contractors, and local leaders. All must make decisions and solve problems in a complex and extremely challenging environment.[21]

The authors go on to spell out the basic services that must be provided to induce the local populace to share information with counterinsurgency forces:

COIN is fought among the populace. Counterinsurgents take upon themselves responsibility for the people's well-being in all its manifestations. These include the following:

Security from insurgent intimidation and coercion, as well as from nonpolitical violence and crime.

Provision for basic economic needs.

Provision of essential services, such as water, electricity, sanitation, and medical care.

Sustainment of key social and cultural institutions.

Other aspects that contribute to a society's basic quality of life.

Effective COIN programs address all aspects of the local populace's concerns in a unified fashion. Insurgents succeed by maintaining turbulence and highlighting local grievances the COIN effort fails to address. COIN forces succeed by eliminating turbulence and helping the host nation meet the populace's basic needs.[22]

The subsequent chapter on intelligence gathering reads like a sociology text, defining basic concepts such as identity, society, social capital, networks, beliefs, and even economy. It then uses these concepts to lay out a framework for winning sufficient loyalty from the local populace to induce them to share information about insurgents. The manual amounts to an informal argument for why the modus operandi laid out by the foreign special forces officers at the brainstorming session should work.

Knowing how religious radicals compete effectively with the government to provide services helps to clarify the handicap that Petraeus faced on his return to Iraq in early 2007. A constructive counterterrorism (or counterinsurgency) approach implies that to undermine radical Islamists such as al-Sadr who provide services, the government must directly compete with the rebels in service provision, which will increase pressure to defect and reduce attacks on high-value targets. Alternatively, in the view of current counterterrorism/counterinsurgency doctrine, service provision will induce information sharing by noncombatants. At this writing we are just beginning to see methodically collected evidence that this approach has been working in Iraq: local reconstruction spending began to have violence-reducing effects once the "surge" deployment was complete, in mid 2007.[23] The doctrine has not even begun to grapple with religious insurgents who provide services more effectively than the government and remains fuzzy on the mechanism by which service provision reduces insurgency.[24] Yet in the period before the occupation of Iraq and immediately after, U.S. policies *crippled* the Iraqi government that American forces later struggled to rehabilitate in order to quell the insurgency. A decade of sanctions left the public social service provision system badly depleted, causing alternative networks like Sadeq al-Sadr's to develop, especially among Iraqi Shiites who suffered most from the decline of government services. Immediately after the occupation, U.S. forces disbanded the military, which would have been capable of providing the most basic service—law and order. De-Baathifying the civil service effectively gave Shiite and Kurdish politicians license to fire Sunnis in the government and police, since Baath Party membership was necessary for promotion under Saddam. Finally, the United States arrived with a force large enough for conquest but far too small to begin the other 90 percent that Henry Crumpton spoke of, including providing law and order without a full strength Iraqi police force and with a gutted military, both depleted by the de-Baathification effort. The alternative networks of social service provision, like that developed by al-Sadr's father, became the organizational platforms from which rebel groups were launched.

The new approach to Afghanistan and Pakistan that President Obama announced in March 2009 is closer to constructive counterterrorism, but is dated.[25] The Taliban have a clublike element, so they are weakened by interventions that directly compete with services they provide. They will be little affected by a "hearts and minds" approach if noncombatants are not privy to useful intelligence.

Moreover, the U.S. government is struggling with the organizational implication of constructive counterterrorism, which requires simultaneously developing governance and the economy while providing security. Yet the military is not designed or trained to execute development projects, and the United States Agency for International Development (USAID) is not designed or trained to defend itself. The current solution is still being tested: a Provincial Reconstruction Team (PRT) jointly staffed by different government agencies, and sometimes by different governments!

The United Nations and the militaries of allied governments face the same organizational problem. The World Bank, USAID, and other international development and aid organizations currently lack even a theory of development in conflict situations, and have no mandate to intervene under fire. The U.S. military is already increasing its role in U.S. development efforts. It now directs 22 percent of U.S. development assistance, as opposed to 3.5 percent a decade ago.[26] The United States and her allies require a sort of armed Peace Corps, which can keep the peace in troubled countries and can operate with multinational partners. At the same time, it must also channel and direct reconstruction efforts in dangerous places, while protecting NGOs and civilians engaged in reconstruction.

In contrast, radical Islamists are extremely flexible institutionally. It is taking years for the U.S. military to build a social service provision organization onto a war-fighting institution, but recall that Hamas built a terrorist organization on top of a social service provision organization in months. The radical Islamists regularly carry out these transformations: they quickly field forces who speak the language, know how to augment existing social service provision networks to provide basic services, and can protect themselves. Hezbollah demonstrated all those abilities in the reconstruction of South Lebanon after their war with Israel in the summer of 2006. Muqtada al-Sadr's forces showed the same flexibility in Iraq within months of the occupation, quickly developing a religious social service provision network into a militia and political party. Various Islamist groups displayed similar flexibility in providing earthquake relief in Kashmir. At this writing Hamas is positioning itself to win the reconstruction of Gaza, following the destruction wrought by the Israeli incursion that ended in January 2009.

Returning to the conflicts in Iraq and Afghanistan, and the related insurgency in Pakistan, two important questions remain. First, how much security control is necessary before service provision is effective as a constructive counterinsurgency approach? That question is the subject of an ongoing debate.[27] Second, even if that strategy is effective and the counterinsurgency campaign is won, will the local government have the strength and legitimacy to retain power, or will it collapse anyway in the absence of permanent foreign support, as the government of South Vietnam did? That brings us again to a recurring theme, building the capacity of government to provide services. In Afghanistan and Pakistan that is a particularly vexing question. Given the Afghan government's difficulties with drug-linked corruption, it would seem that reducing the Taliban's revenue stream from opium is a prerequisite to any successful counterinsurgency or counterterrorism effort. This is not simply a matter of the Taliban winning a bidding war in bribing local officials. As we saw in chapters 4 and 5, clubs can make very effective use of outside subsidies in order to generate high levels of sacrifice among members.

The global threat of terrorism will be with us long after the last U.S. soldiers have left Iraq and Afghanistan, whenever that may be. Lessons learned now will be valuable in future conflicts. Capture, kill, and deter is an easy first step. It grabs headlines. It was emotionally satisfying and popular with voters. Yet social service provision creates the institutional base for most of the dangerous radical religious rebels. This implies that long-term reconstruction is a necessary part of any global effort to truly contain international terrorist threats emanating from countries exporting terrorism: building markets, generating tax revenue, improving the quality of government, and most important, helping allied governments compete with religious radicals in providing social services.

Will that be terribly expensive? Yes, that is the nature of improving governance. The question should be: compared to what? Protracted conflicts without effective reconstruction tie down massive armies of expensive troops from developed countries, as we have seen in Iraq and

Afghanistan. If the enemy is launching suicide attacks, the targets are already hard—defended with much more expensive and sophisticated equipment than the attackers have available. So once suicide attacks are in use, improving outside options is probably more useful in protecting targets than further hardening of targets, for two reasons. First, suicide attacks are effective even against hard targets. Second, hardening a single target will likely divert the attack to some other target—and hardening all targets so they are even moderately safe from suicide attacks is phenomenally expensive. If we in the West devoted some of our asymmetric advantage in resources and technology to economic and political development in a constructive counterterrorism strategy, the question should not be how expensive nation building is, but whether it is more cost-effective in protecting our troops and allies than the traditional approach.

In the meantime, the United States and other Western countries spend hundreds of billions annually protecting *domestic* targets from the terrorist fallout of rebellions abroad. These methods are expensive not only in tax dollars, but in time consumed (for example, at airports) and in freedoms subtly surrendered to surveillance cameras. While highly visible protection for domestic targets reassures the public, it is probably a much more expensive approach to protecting the homeland than undermining terrorism abroad. Recall that only a handful of terrorist organizations are responsible for most international terrorism. I argued earlier that the protective effect of improving outside options is particularly relevant for neighbors and allies of governments threatened by domestic terrorism. It stands to reason that if conspirators are willing to give up the life of an attacker, they are probably willing to go the trouble of finding a foreigner to target—and even a soft target abroad, perhaps in Europe or the United States. So weakening terrorist clubs through constructive approaches to counterinsurgency reduces the capacity of terrorists to attack Americans at home.

In the long run those constructive approaches may well be cost-effective for the United States and for other developed countries that are subject to international terrorism, because they are potentially sustainable. Conversely, an approach that is only coercive—concentrating on capturing or killing every last terrorist (or buying off some warlord to do so)—can probably only succeed in the short run, since the underlying conditions of weak governance and/or weak service provision will likely continue to generate new terrorist clubs. The challenge is then to find a way to *sustainably* stabilize allied governments in countries currently generating terrorism, not by merely improving their coercive capacity but by also enhancing the ability of local government to provide basic services that replace those provided by clubs.

Constructive approaches have two additional advantages. First, they carry no ideological baggage, so that allies, local governments, and nongovernmental organizations can wholeheartedly support them. Second, they play to a strength of western democracies—our resources and capacity for strong governance and economic growth. The next chapter will develop that theme, contrasting the Western experience with religious diversity in a period of rapid development to that of the Islamic world, and examining the development of radical Islam in that context.

St. Lambert's Cathedral in Münster, Germany. Above the clock are three cages where the bodies of Anabaptist rebel leader Jan Bockelson and others were left to rot (inset). The Münster rebellion established a theocracy in the city in 1532. It was violently suppressed in June 1535. (Rudiger Wolk, Münster).

8
Religious Radicals and Violence in the Modern World

Times of violent religious controversy have generally been times of equally violent political faction.
—Adam Smith, *An Inquiry into the Nature and Causes of the Wealth of Nations*, 1776[1]

It has been established in Pennsylvania, where, though the Quakers happen to be the most numerous sect, the law in reality favours no one sect more than another, and it is there said to have been productive of this philosophical good temper and moderation.
—Adam Smith, *An Inquiry into the Nature and Causes of the Wealth of Nations*, 1776[2]

We find in your houses and courts nothing but sparkling pomp and showy dress, boldness and presumptuousness of heart, insatiable avarice, hatred and envy, backbiting, betraying, harloting, seduction, gaming, carousing, dancing, swearing, stabbing, and violence.... The pitiful moaning and misery of the wretched men does not reach your ears. The sweat of the poor we find in your house, and the innocent blood on your hands.
—Menno Simons, *Foundation of Christian Doctrine*, 1539[3]

The author of that last quote is not Hassan al-Banna, who founded the Egyptian Muslim Brotherhood, or Sayyid Qutb, the twentieth-century theologian of violent political jihad who inspired Bin Laden. Those words come from the sixteenth century, the period Adam Smith was thinking of when he wrote the first quote above, linking religion and violence. They belong to Menno Simons of the Netherlands, sixteenth-century Christian radical reformer, contemporary of Martin Luther, and the original Mennonite. The Mennonites are pacifists today, though their fellow Anabaptists were often violent in the chaotic environment in which their sects first emerged. Anabaptist sects, even the pacifists among them, were cruelly repressed in Europe. Yet remarkably enough, many of those denominations survive to this day, mostly in North America, as Mennonites, Hutterites, Amish, and other modern Anabaptist radical religious communities.

I would like to use this final chapter to examine religious radicalism in a historical context. We've established why religious radicals can be lethal terrorists and especially effective rebels if they so choose. But where does religious radicalism come from? Why are some religious radicals always benign, like the present-day Amish, while others are sometimes so violent, like Hezbollah, Lashkar-e-Taiba, or Muqtada al-Sadr's Mahdi Army? To answer those questions, we return to Menno Simons and the sixteenth-century roots of modern religious radicalism in Europe.

Now is also a good time to reconsider the role of theology. Previous chapters have deemphasized or dismissed the spiritual and theological aspects of terrorism. In chapter 1 we saw that religious terrorists, even suicide bombers, are neither deranged nor poisoned by hate, but are also not particularly motivated by heavenly rewards. They are perhaps best thought of as altruists with their own view of the world—just like secular suicide bombers. Chapter 2 explored the organizational problems of terrorist operatives as they obsess over the possible defection of comrades—no mention of theology there. Religion reappeared in chapters 3 and 4, as I examined how religious radicals solve defection problems; they do so not by appealing to faith but by carefully selecting recruits for their mutual-aid networks and then using the leverage those social services provide to keep recruits from shirking their mutual-aid responsibilities to the community. Chapter 5 then applied that logic to reducing defection in insurgencies and terrorist organizations. Religious radicals who can control shirking in mutual aid—one form of cooperative production—are well positioned organizationally to engage in coordinated violence—cooperative production of a more deadly sort. Most radical religious communities are never violent, applying their cooperative capacity to providing spiritual services and mutual aid; yet when they turn to violence they are exceptionally lethal. Suicide terrorism, considered in chapter 6, is a special case of that argument. Theology briefly appeared here, because suicide attackers seldom target coreligionists, but a theological explanation was eventually dismissed; people of different religions merely tend to be dissimilar enough in appearance to make them harder targets, and hard targets explain the choice of suicide attacks over more conventional methods of killing. In chapter 7, on countering violence, religion was hardly mentioned; it was all about methods of undermining violent clubs (religious or secular) through competition with their benign organizational base: providing alternative services and creating outside options.

Where does that leave theology? What about the appeal to spiritual values so prominent in the rhetoric of radical Islamists, or the call to global jihad? So far a purely theological explanation has been dismissed: suicide attackers generally do not claim that their primary motivation is theological, as we have seen—even among those dispatched by religious radicals. Moreover, leaders like Mullah Omar of the Taliban change their stated goals so quickly that their theological objections to Western culture seem to be more reactive than anything else. The Taliban's goals have shifted quickly, from personal piety, protecting children on the way to school, and even the creation of a local Islamic state, to supporting an attack on Manhattan. What theological goal could that have served? Surely scaring New Yorkers into adopting a radical Islamic theology that limits their freedom and diversity is among the least feasible projects imaginable. Moreover, we have seen that theology alone does not guarantee success for terrorists. The Palestinian Islamic Jihad, for instance, is no more effective (i.e., lethal) than its secular rivals. Most theologically motivated terrorists fail quickly without a larger organization, like the ineffectual conspiracy of pickup soccer players in the suburbs of Toronto in June 2006, or the Jewish Underground of the 1980s. Theology by itself does not predict lethality, as we saw in the comparison between the Palestinian Islamic Jihad and Hamas; those two organizations share the same theological precepts, but Hamas, with an active service provision system, is far more lethal. That is a surprising but hopeful finding. People's core theological beliefs seldom change, so if their violent plans were really an expression of what they believe to be the will of the Almighty, how could those plans ever be foiled without the countervailing use of violence to capture or kill the perpetrators?

Yet despite the accumulated evidence that incentives within organizations matter, altogether ignoring the theological and spiritual aspects of radical religious violence cannot be right either. If al-Sadr's militia, the Taliban, Hezbollah, Hamas, and others are successful mainly because they have adopted a club structure, then why wouldn't secular organizations succeed in the same way? Why couldn't a club organize around Marxism, or environmental activism, or a profit motive, or no particular ideology at all, like a street gang does? To be sure, there are broad organizational similarities between street gangs, mafias, Marxist rebels, and radical religious terrorists—as we have seen. Yet today religious radicals constitute a far greater threat. Why are radical religious clubs more effective than secular clubs? The answer to that question takes us back to the sixteenth century, and to the surprising resilience of Christian religious radicals.

Radical Christians, Benign and Violent

Menno Simons, who railed against injustice and established the religious denomination that bears his name, was not the first Anabaptist. That distinction is generally attributed to Konrad Grebel, a radical reforming Catholic priest. Grebel was an early follower of Martin Luther's reformation in Switzerland. Zurich, in the early sixteenth century, was the eye of a hurricane of swirling economic and religious forces. The feudal system was challenged by evolving market economies in towns and cities. If the feudal structure were to be scattered by those winds, the tax base of the nobles and their religious allies, the Catholic Church, would be swept away with it. The competing order was an alliance of villages and princes, who had established enough independence to begin experimenting with alternative religious authorities outside the Church.

Into this brief vacuum of religious pluralism rushed a variety of new theologies. One stream of reformers believed that baptism as infants is insufficient; an additional baptism should be performed as an adult, when an individual is capable of making a religious commitment. Groups following that religious tradition are generally termed *Anabaptists* (the prefix is the Greek "ana", meaning "again"). Konrad Grebel, still a Catholic priest, first baptized adults in January 1525, in Zollikon, on lake Zurich. Martin Luther, who led the new Protestant Reformation, rejected the Anabaptist position as too radical and had Anabaptists priests expelled from their positions as clergy. Despite rejection by both the Catholic Church and the nascent Reformation, Anabaptism spread quickly to towns in the German-speaking parts of Switzerland and then to Germany and Austria. Within four years, Anabaptists could count over 3,600 converts in 507 communities.[4] Few of the new religious denominations of that time would survive, but the Anabaptists did, and they survive to this day in radical religious communities that include the Hutterites, Mennonites, and Amish.

One reason for the resilience of these communities is their economic structure. Anabaptist denominations from the outset were characterized not only by adult baptism but also by mutual aid. They emphasized "community of goods," a reference to Acts 2 of the New Testament, which taught that the first Christian denomination in Jerusalem "had all things in common," and that "they sold their possessions and goods and distributed them to all, as any had need."[5] The interpretation and application of this principle varied across Anabaptist denominations. Among the early Swiss Anabaptists and the Hutterites it implied communal property—that is, a functioning commune. Menno Simons would eventually interpret "community of goods" more restrictively; Mennonites practiced an active system of mutual aid and charity but were permitted to own private property.[6]

Mutual aid within Anabaptist communities was important because it allowed them to function independently of the feudal order, in which peasants were taxed by landowners and the Church authorities, in return for a safety net of services. As an example of this independence, the Anabaptist sect of Swiss Brethren forbade members to hold government office, swear oaths, sue in court, or fight in wars. Grebel also challenged the Church by fanning the flames of a tax revolt.[7] He objected to Church tithes to support its institutions, since much of the revenue was not spent in local parishes. Among the first villages to embrace Anabaptism was Zollikon, which had refused to pay tithes in 1523.[8] That tax revolt was not violent, but it constituted a serious challenge to government, since the Church and local government were so closely allied in sixteenth-century Switzerland. Moreover, Grebel's arguments struck a chord with a number of villages and parishes in the area, which were already grumbling about the excessive level of their tithes.[9] Ulrich Zwingli, a leader of the Protestant Reformation, cast the Anabaptists as potential rebels in a tract delivered in 1525: "The greater part of devout Christians will find no pleasure in the Anabaptist cause because they see at once that the Anabaptists are aiming at the community of goods and the abolition of government."[10] Whether Grebel and the early Swiss Anabaptists could actually have mounted and sustained a rebellion is unclear, but the rhetoric of the time and their subsequent persecution certainly indicate that the authorities were willing enough to see the new denomination as a threat. Of the 3,617 known converts within the first four years, at least 410 were executed by the authorities almost immediately. Entire congregations were effectively exterminated, especially those in the Hapsburg Empire.[11]

Konrad Grebel and Menno Simons were not violent, but their fellow radical reformer Thomas Müntzer was. Müntzer was a religious rebel, the Sayyid Qutb of his time. An early follower of Martin Luther, Müntzer had a falling out with Luther when Müntzer rejected infant baptism in 1521. The rift between Luther and his student ran deep. Müntzer fled to southern Germany, wrote scathing critiques of the clergy, and eventually endorsed a communal theocracy, including common property and equal sharing. He found political allies in the German city of Mühlhausen. Together they took control of the city council and declared an "eternal council."[12] Müntzer then joined the leadership of the so-called Peasants' War in South Germany in 1524, a massive insurgency against the feudal princes. Though that rebellion was social and economic in motivation—rather than religious—and lacked focus, Müntzer saw it as an attempt to create a single pan-national religious commune. The insurgency failed, in no small part because Martin Luther sided with the princes. Feudal armies quickly slaughtered the ill-prepared rebels, leaving an estimated hundred thousand people dead.[13]

Müntzer himself insisted on leading peasants in battle. The renegade minister was defeated and quickly beheaded. Friedrich Engels would later embrace Müntzer as a revolutionary leader of the masses in his book *The Peasant War in Germany*. Ironically, the East German communist government, which was virulently antireligious, followed Engels's lead and eventually declared Müntzer an early communist hero—even putting his face on the currency. Yet Müntzer was no communist. From today's perspective he looks more like a Christian jihadist, aiming at social reform through violent revolution and the establishment of a grand communal theocracy.

A decade later, in 1534, radical religious Anabaptists would again choose violence, expelling the rulers of the German city of Münster. The rebels declared a theocratic commune, legalized polygamy, and prepared to go forth from Münster, conquer the world, and spread theocracy. They managed to hold the city for eighteen months, until a siege organized by the local bishop broke their resistance. To make an example of the insurgents, the bodies of the executed leaders were hung in cages from the steeple of St. Lambert's Cathedral in the center of the city. Those cages, which can be seen in the photograph that opens this chapter, still hang from the steeple. The incongruous sight of cages that once held human remains, hanging from a church steeple, is a salient reminder of how seriously religious authorities treated challenges to their authority for hundreds of years after the rebellion.

The violent branch of Anabaptism died out quickly. Survivors fled as far as England; even there members were persecuted—sometimes burned at the stake. The nonviolent branches, including Simons's followers, survived as strict pacifists.

The Supernatural and Credibility

This historical episode of Anabaptist violence, isolated as it is, raises the very modern question of the special role of religion.[14] How did religious radicals succeed in organizing spectacular episodes of cooperative violence and survive as mutual-aid communities? Why are groups with some other common characteristic not equally successful? Guilds also had cooperative arrangements. Why were they less successful at leading rebellions and conquering cities? Ethnic minorities, regional coalitions, or groups organized around dialect or family ties could have, in principle, organized mutual aid, provided services, and rebelled against weak, ineffective, or exploitative governments. The club model explains why mutual aid and cooperative violence should go together, but why is religion necessary?

To answer that question requires thinking a little about the supernatural, an essential part of theology in most religions, radical and mainstream. So far I've discussed in detail the worldly content of religious services—schools, medical care, and welfare services—but avoided the spiritual, supernatural aspects. These are a huge and controversial part of human culture, debated passionately through the ages as they are today.[15] The special role that these aspects provide the clergy will be relevant to our discussion.

What can an economist say about the appeal of spirituality? The pervasive spiritual rhetoric in our culture suggests that spirituality is very basic to human psychology. It's not hard to imagine why. The human journey seems to be much more salient when associated with some higher, universal purpose that we hope will blow wind at our backs and grant us good judgment as we navigate through life. Mere mortals, we inevitably run up on the rocks of disappointment and failure, as our aspirations confront the laws of economics and medicine: most of us won't be very rich; we and our loved ones will eventually die, and we may face hardship and scarcity in the meantime. When aspiration meets failure we often seek solace in the spiritual and supernatural. I think that it really is consoling and inspiring to believe that a parental figure is watching over us in an uncertain world, that good deeds will be rewarded, and that we and our loved ones can somehow bargain to survive after death. Supernatural promises, which science cannot possibly refute, are tempting. So why not believe—at least a little—that some supernatural force can help, as Pascal's Wager[16] suggests? Demand for the supernatural is evident worldwide and dates back to ancient times.

Where there's a demand for the supernatural, suppliers are sure to appear. And indeed, the market for supernatural and spiritual services is one of the oldest in human culture. Our archeological and historical records are full of evidence that humans go to great lengths and invest tremendous efforts in imploring the deities to grant important needs: bountiful harvests, good health, fertility, victory in battle, and even blessings in the hereafter for ourselves and our loved ones. How else can we interpret the great pyramids of Egypt or the terracotta army of Shi Huang, if not as desperate attempts by rulers to avoid the laws of nature and buy an immortal place in the future with resources from the present (which perhaps some enterprising ancient contractors saw as a business opportunity)?

Yet marketing the supernatural is a challenge for suppliers. People's demand for supernatural services comes with healthy skepticism. Take supernatural promises about the hereafter, for example. Clergy offer what is essentially a contract: eternal salvation in return for ethical behavior in the present. It sound promising, but is it credible? (If customers are not satisfied in the hereafter, will they be in any position to complain?)

Since supernatural contracts (e.g., if I do good now, then I'll be rewarded later) are an essential component of religion, religious organizations must necessarily establish credibility. Clergy must be scrupulously ethical in their own conduct. Donations must go to the stated cause. Children entrusted to religious institutions must be gently and responsibly cared for. Hints of corruption or abuse of power will be taken very seriously by congregants, just as Jesus and Martin Luther took them seriously. Why do people treat corrupt clergy much more harshly than corrupt politicians, businesspeople, or even teachers? Perhaps because immoral behavior by clergy has deep implications beyond the particular act. It undermines a core belief: that followers can truly entrust their faith to clergy.

And so clergy really do go to great lengths to establish credibility. They are selected to be ethical in conduct. They surround themselves with community members who will vouch for their trustworthiness. They live frugal, pious lives devoted to study, prayer, and acts of charity. If they gain our trust, and we truly believe, then marvelous supernatural contracts can be made—and who can prove that we are not all better off for making the contract? In fact, the evidence of benefits in this life is strong. People who display religiosity, such as church attendance, are healthier, happier, and less likely to engage in self-destructive behaviors in their youth.[17]

Credibility also has practical implications in the here and now, which brings us back to mutual aid, communal property, and even rebellion. Once the clergy establish credibility—which they must—congregants can trust them not only with their afterlives, but also to organize soup kitchens, schools, hospitals, and all the other collective institutions that make tight communities thrive. These are all charitable activities that use volunteers who are typically happy to donate their time to a good cause.

Here, then, is one reason why theology strengthens communities in ways that other ideologies cannot. In principle, any group could establish clubs through relationships of trust and channel the healthy altruism of members to deliver charity and mutual aid. In practice, though, religious clergy have important advantages over leaders of other clubs. Congregants know that the clergy were carefully selected for their trustworthiness, and that they have strong incentives to behave honestly and fairly—all because their professional reputations are on the line. Should clergy get caught with their hand in the donation box, or in some other infraction, the public will dismiss the spiritual content of their work as well—the supernatural promises. And so populist religious leaders like Sheikh Ahmed Yassin of Hamas or Mohammed Sadeq al-Sadr (Muqtada al-Sadr's father) tend to live humbly, spend most of their revenues on visibly good causes, seldom get caught embezzling, and are extremely successful at organizing charitable activities, a form of cooperative production.

Credibility provides clergy with a *particular* advantage over secular charities (and governments) in countries were the legal system is weak, so that the threat of legal action cannot enforce honesty within nonprofit organizations. As we saw in the case of the Palestinian Islamic Jihad, merely espousing a radical religious theology is not enough, but the combination of clerical credibility and mutual-aid provision gives religious radicals a powerful organizational advantage.

The same arguments apply not only to charitable activity but also to political organization and coordinated violence. As sixteenth-century governments and Church officials may have feared, a religious club constitutes a far more potent opponent than a secular club, as the former is led by clergy whose credibility has already been established. Strong, well-funded governments have little to fear from religious clubs: they have the resources to provide basic health, education, welfare, and security by themselves, so that communities have no need for the mutual aid and communal services provided by religious clubs like the Anabaptists. Weak governments, on the other hand, might feel threatened.

Menno Simons spent most of his adult life fleeing, spreading the faith, and organizing scattered communities with a price on his head. Why were he and his followers persecuted so extensively? Considering their association with the Peasants' War, the subsequent brutal persecution of European Anabaptists by both governments and clergy is easier to explain—reprehensible as it was. Anabaptist communities were on record as declaring the clergy corrupt and tithing excessive, and had demonstrated that they could get by without the services of government. Against the late medieval background of weak states and a collapsing feudal system, governments feared a band of potential insurgents they could not control, and the established clergy—both Catholic and Protestant—shared those fears.

How did the Anabaptists survive at all? Many did not. Persecuted by authorities on all sides, Anabaptists were often drowned, tortured, or burned at the stake. Yet those dangers did create a sacrifice that easily distanced Anabaptists from mainstream culture, so that adult baptism could become the type of expensive sacrifice that demonstrated commitment, which is precisely what a mutual-aid club requires to control defection, as we saw in chapter 4. The Anabaptists illustrate a principle that remains relevant: radical religious communities that have successfully institutionalized signals of commitment can be remarkably resilient, even in the face of violent repression, and especially if they are led by credible clergy.

Markets and Denominations

The history of Anabaptism also raises additional questions that resonate today: Why do radical denominations exist at all? And why did Anabaptist religious clubs arise and prosper in the sixteenth century when they had not done so earlier? One set of answers we've explored already: the growth of town economies weakened feudal government. The Peasants' War of 1524–1525, the year before the first anabaptism was the largest single insurgency in Europe prior to the French Revolution. Its allies in government weakened, the Church was suddenly unable to repress competing denominations. In that sense, the same forces that enabled the Protestant Reformation also allowed a burst of theological pluralism among other religious innovators, which lasted until the Lutheran Protestants could consolidate political control.

A related explanation for the sudden appearance of radical denominations is that economic development in sixteenth-century Europe created a harsh environment for a traditional mutual-aid organization to survive in, if it did not somehow distance itself from evolving markets—as prohibitions and sacrifices do. The sixteenth century is the beginning of modern Europe for economic historians. The ascendant market economies of the towns and villages challenged the existing order by introducing a new type of competition: through mobility of individuals. Before markets beckoned, defection would not have been an issue in a feudal village; individuals were tied to the land; if they escaped they had nowhere to go, since the other feudal villages were typically closed to new entrants. Once defection to a town was possible, any possible religious commune or feudal village was threatened. Residents, newly empowered by the option of leaving, might be more demanding. Worse still, they might *selectively* defect, with the most talented leaving to try their luck in the towns. Selective attrition can set off a downward spiral in a village with a traditional collective support system. Once the most talented leave, the town becomes less attractive, so the next most talented leave, and so on . . ., until only the least able or the neediest remain for the feudal lord or the community mutual-aid system to care for. Prohibitions and sacrifices would have been necessary to defend a mutual-aid community or a communal society against selective attrition. And so the time was ripe for a modern radical religious club.

That sixteenth-century burst of denominational pluralism was short-lived. In the aftermath of the Peasants' War, and then the devastating Thirty Years' War, governments in Northern Europe reestablished their power, generally in partnership with the Protestant Reformers. They granted the Protestant churches the status of established (i.e., official state) religion, which had previously been held by the Catholic Church. This partnership of clergy and government then effectively repressed the new denominations, including the Anabaptist clubs. They would eventually thrive mostly in the more tolerant institutional setting of the

American Colonies and the Canadian prairie provinces, where fertile land was available far from the nearest town that might tempt followers to defect. Those communities grew and thrived as they do to this day, not because government is too weak to repress them or to provide competing services, but because government is tolerant, allowing members to peacefully express their preference for a separate, communal, and religious lifestyle.

Jewish and Muslim Denominations

Economic opportunity again generated radical religious denominations in the late eighteenth century, this time among European Jews. Jewish religious practice had been fairly uniform for over a thousand years when economic emancipation began in the eighteenth century. Until that time European Jews had not been as restricted as feudal peasants in closed villages; they could travel and migrate between Jewish communities, but they were not generally permitted to live and work among gentiles. Economic emancipation began gradually for Jews in the towns and cities of Germany and elsewhere in Central Europe. As earnings increased time became more precious, so it is hardly surprising (at least to an economist) that the upwardly mobile Jewish communities of Germany invented Reform Judaism—a denomination that demands less of members in time spent in prayer and in other religious obligations. What *is* surprising is that at the same time, Orthodoxy and ultra-Orthodoxy were invented. These denominations made greater demands on members' time than traditional Judaism did. Ultra-Orthodoxy even introduced a new time-intensive form of practice: the yeshiva. The first of these religious seminaries was established in 1802 by the Lithuanian Hassidic denomination, a form of ultra-Orthodoxy.

Who would join a denomination that makes increasing demands on one's time? Emancipation was making time more *precious* by expanding opportunities to work at higher wages and to consume the goods made available by urban markets. The logic of clubs can explain the apparent contradiction. As in the case of the Anabaptists, the incursion of market opportunities into traditional society carried with it an increased need within mutual-aid communities to observe signals of commitment by members. Otherwise selective defection could undermine mutual aid by removing the most talented community members. Religious sacrifices could fill the role of signals. Rather than adult baptism, which would have been at odds with Jewish tradition, the ultra-Orthodox created a new set of sacrifices, such as protracted yeshiva attendance.

The major modern Jewish denominational forms evolved out of the reaction to emancipation in the early nineteenth century. Reform, Orthodox, and ultra-Orthodox Judaism originated in that period, while Conservative Judaism was added in the early twentieth century in the United States as a middle ground between Orthodoxy and Reform.

This interpretation of Jewish denominationalism is consistent with the subsequent development of religious practice among the Jews of North Africa and the Middle East (the Sephardi communities mentioned in chapter 4). They did not experience emancipation and indeed retained a single traditional form of Judaism until those communities emigrated to Israel in the 1950s. When they did, the new immigrants experienced an accelerated version of the same denominational split, with some traditional families becoming secular, and others choosing Orthodoxy and ultra-Orthodoxy.

The beginnings of denominationalism among modern Jews have another interesting economic characteristic: charity flowing from the liberal end of the denominational spectrum to the conservative end. The high-commitment, low-income ultra-Orthodox denomination successfully solicited donations from the emancipating, high-income, low-commitment Reform communities to assuage feelings of guilt the latter had about abandoning tradition.

Viewed in the context of the Christian and Jewish histories of denominationalism, when Hassan al-Banna founded the Muslim Brotherhood in Egypt in the 1920s, he raised the curtain on a familiar drama. Economist Timur Kuran points out that, like Christians and Jews, Muslims eventually transitioned from collective to individualistic communities, but much later, not until the nineteenth and twentieth centuries.[18] As market opportunities improved, the temptations that markets provided—high-wage labor and new consumption opportunities—posed a threat to the mutual-aid organizations that characterized traditional collective communities. The market had the ability to cherry-pick the most talented members, leaving only those members with the greatest needs, or the shirkers, to take care of each other—a disaster for a community practicing mutual aid. Faced with that threat, a traditional mutual-aid community could either unravel or erect barriers. Twentieth-century radical Islam can be understood as the erection of those barriers, just as assimilated, individualistic Islamic communities are the unraveling.

By and large, the transition to market economies has tended to occur in fits and starts in the Middle East, and in an environment with very weak government provision of basic services. The reasons for slow economic development in the Middle East (putting the oil economy aside) are anxiously debated by scholars and would provide more distraction than insight at this point.[19] The reasons for weak governance, though, are worth pursuing. Part of the problem is institutional. The waqf system of charitable trusts, which I described in chapter 5 in the context of Hamas's capture of public resources in Gaza, has been well entrenched for centuries in Muslim communities, both because of tradition and because it facilitates avoiding high inheritance taxes—as Kuran shows. Over time, communities have come to rely on waqf provision of basic services, crowding out the need to organize municipal provision that would have required tax collection—besides inheritance taxes.[20] (Unfortunately, the waqf may not reform their charters, making them extremely conservative institutions that have a hard time adjusting to changes in community needs.) Moreover, the legal system has been slow to recognize corporations, which has not only hampered economic development but has also deprived governments of an easy target for taxation. Between stagnant economies, lack of corporations, and waqf provision of services, local governments in the Middle East have been starved for a tax base, so that public service provision has tended to be weak—especially in comparison to the standards of currently developed economies.[21]

Against this background, modern radical Islam developed first in the 1920s in Egypt, in the presence of a nascent market-oriented economy and a weak government, in the form of the Muslim Brotherhood. Under similar conditions, and quite independently, radical Islam also developed in the early 1940s in British India, in the form of Jamaat-e-Islami, founded by Sayyid Abul A'ala Maududi. In both cases, provision of social services to communities was accompanied by some increase in the stringency of religious prohibitions, evoking Anabaptist and ultra-Orthodox histories.

In a further historical parallel, since oil prices first soared in the 1970s, Islamic religious charities have enjoyed a windfall that echoes the cross-denominational donations of European Jews. Oil-rich Arab families and governments have assuaged the guilt that comes with their sudden material wealth (and very materialist consumption habits) by donating to Muslim charities, which are disproportionately controlled by low-income, high-commitment radical religious denominations.[22]

The parallel history of religious radicalism among Christians, Jews, and Muslims suggests that the incursion of markets into traditional societies encourages the development of religious denominations—including extreme radicals. Before markets provided attractive outside opportunities, the parents in my suitor-at-the-door example didn't have to worry. The prospective son-in-law could not abscond with their daughter and grandchildren when it was his turn to donate his time to the community, because he had nowhere else to go. Once defection was possible, that calculation changed: a sacrifice became necessary to signal commitment. Radical religious clubs developed the necessary sacrifices to fit themselves into that new cultural niche.

These parallel histories also suggest that *weak governments* can play an important role in the development of denominations, for two reasons. First, strong governments that provide social services leave less opportunity for competition from a radical religious club serving the same function. Where we do see strict denominations, such as the Muslim Brotherhood in Egypt, or the JUI in Afghan refugee camps in Pakistan, they deliver social services that the government does not. The Lebanese and Palestinian governments have been too weak to successfully suppress political challenges from Hezbollah and Hamas, respectively. These groups can be found delivering basic services such as education and healthcare, and sometimes even collect the garbage. Strict denominations have thrived in Israel, though not because public social service provision is weak; rather, ultra-Orthodox politicians have managed to co-opt a politically weak government—engineering publicly funded services and subsidies that discriminate in favor of their followers.

Second, in the presence of an established (i.e., state) religious denomination, only a weak government will fail to suppress competitors to the established denomination. While that argument clearly applies to medieval Christian Europe, it would not have been a factor for Jews. European and Middle Eastern governments were indifferent to Jewish denominations; they could easily collect taxes regardless of Jewish denominational affiliations. In the twentieth-century Muslim case the picture is more complex. Most governments such as the Egyptian and the Indian (under the British) were secular and allowed strict denominations such as the Muslim Brotherhood to organize as long as they posed no political threat. The Saudi Arabian government continues an old tradition of nominal power-sharing with clergy reminiscent of the state religions of medieval Europe. The Wahhabi denomination was established as the religion of the House of Saud by an agreement between Ibn Abd al-Wahhab and Ibn Saud in the mid-eighteenth century. Since the 1970s Saudi Arabia has allowed Muslim Brotherhood members (many of them Egyptians) to staff universities and operate charities so long as they further the Wahhabi agenda. The Islamic revolution in Iran provides an example of a weak government—the Shah's—failing to repress a radical religious group that offered competing services, including political representation. Once in power, though, Ayatollah Khomeini and the Islamists of Qom have governed according to a strict theocratic model, in which a single denomination monopolizes control of the state, allowing nominal political representation but granting elected legislators little power.

These historical parallels also recall the early Christian period when the first known Jewish radical religious club originated. The Essenes sect of Qumran—made famous by the Dead Sea Scrolls—were an active commune and had clear sacrifices as entry requirements. They also developed in a time of changing economic opportunities and a collapsing theocracy. Those conditions also generated the period of religious pluralism from which early Christianity arose.

Returning to modern times, religious groups providing practical social services are fairly common worldwide when government services are inadequate or discriminatory. In Vietnam under French rule, for example, one of the initial benefits that Catholic missionaries could offer peasants was intervention on their behalf to counterbalance the coercive power of landlords. Two new religious denominations quickly gained a following once a weakened (roughly) feudal system allowed religious pluralism. The Cao Dai, a popular denomination that fused Buddhism, Confucianism, and Taoism, intervened on behalf of peasants as the Catholics did, but also collected taxes, provided welfare services, and adjudicated disputes—virtually a government. Even more popular were the Hoa Hao, a Buddhist denomination that not only provided welfare services and settled disputes, but also protected members from pirates and criminals. The Hoa Hao were also political entrepreneurs, exceeding the cultural patriotism of the Cao Dai in their explicitly nationalist anticolonial stance. The Hoa Hao were so successful that they virtually freed peasants from the authority of landlords and the French authorities. Their leader, Huynh Phu So, was considered such a political threat by the ascendant communist party that they assassinated him in 1946. Though their theologies differed vastly, the Catholics, Cao Dai, and Hoa Hao were quite similar in the social services they provided.[23]

Religious groups practicing mutual aid and providing social services should be familiar to residents of Western countries. They are just an extreme version of something Americans once experienced daily. If you find yourself entering a building named for a saint or a holy site in Boston or New York today, you're most likely walking into the lobby of a hospital. In the nineteenth century, hospitals with names like St. Elizabeth's, Holy Cross, or Mount Sinai were built by religious communities to meet the medical needs of poor immigrant coreligionists. These institutions are generally secular today, a reflection of the expansion of government provision of health services in the twentieth century,[24] but their names recall a recent past when religious communities were segregated and took care of their own. When the Mount Sinai Hospital in New York was founded in 1852, its name was simply "The Jews' Hospital." Today Muslim religious communities in cities such as Beirut and Baghdad fund hospitals to care for refugees and immigrants from rural areas in the absence of adequate healthcare by government. This is not merely an elaborate cover for some violent organization. The vast majority of the activities of most radical Islamist communities are entirely benign. Moreover, their charitable activity would have been quite familiar to Americans in the nineteenth century.

What's Wrong with Religion in Government? Competition and Pluralism

What can medieval European history teach us about religious radicalism? The story has some familiar elements. Emerging market forces generated high wages and new consumption possibilities, threatening traditional community provision of mutual aid. Exclusionary clubs organized to preserve and expand mutual aid, creating more extreme religious denominations. The government was too weak, corrupt, or just plain inept to guarantee the established clergy a monopoly on the one hand, or to compete in provision of services to the common people, on the other. The resulting religious pluralism created a new reforming clergy who were more credible than the government in providing social services, among them the Anabaptists. People asked themselves: If I trust the clergy with my salvation, why shouldn't I trust their charities to feed the poor, clothe the naked, and educate the children? Why not let their scholars adjudicate family law and commercial law? And while we're at it, wouldn't they do a better job of enforcing the law than the government does? Why not let the clergy run the government altogether? That question—which the residents of Münster grappled with five centuries ago—resonates today in Gaza, Kabul, Tehran, and throughout the Muslim world.

European history provides cautionary answers to the question of religion in government. Religious charities providing welfare services have traditionally performed admirably in meeting the needs of communities, just as Islamist groups excel at doing so today. In this sense they preceded the twentieth-century expansion of the welfare state by at least two millennia. On the other hand, reforming, entrepreneurial, politically motivated clergy in an environment with weak government can be an incredibly toxic combination, as it was during in the Peasants' War. The Reformation broke the hegemony of Catholicism on the European continent; yet within towns, cities, and states, princes and nobles generally tried to grant a monopoly to a single denomination, either Protestant or

Catholic. Lutheran and Catholic clergy (and eventually Calvinists) competed to become the favored religion, taking charge of tithing and delivering basic services. The result in Germany was disastrous. Regional disputes over territory and sovereignty became religious wars, drawing in mercenaries in the pay of coreligionists, first from the rest of the country and eventually from other European countries. The resulting bloodbath was the Thirty Years' War, a catastrophic religious-political civil war that engulfed Germany from 1618 until 1648. Ruthless mercenaries destroyed entire villages and towns. Battles, massacres, and disease eventually claimed between 15 and 20 percent of German lives, exceeding the German casualty rate in World War I and World War II combined.[25]

Before drawing our own lessons about the relevance of European history, it's worth exploring what two intellectual giants of the eighteenth century had to say about religious pluralism, violence, and governance. Philosopher David Hume and economist Adam Smith debated how to avoid repeating the religious carnage that followed the Protestant Reformation. To be sure, the stakes were high for the English as well, who had themselves suffered three bloody civil-religious wars between 1642 and 1651. Hume knew his material; the greatest philosopher and historian of his time, he had spent fifteen years writing *The History of England*.

Hume offered a straightforward diagnosis of religious conflict: Religious radicals compete by promoting superstition and heaping scorn on the clerics of competing denominations. Their theological hatemongering can lead to civil strife, political instability, and even civil war. Smith, writing in the *Wealth of Nations*, agreed with Hume's analysis. In the conditions of contemporary Europe, religious competition led to hatemongering. In Smith's words, "Each ghostly practitioner, in order to render himself more precious and sacred in the eyes of his retainers, will inspire them with the most violent abhorrence of all other sects."[26]

Yet the two greatest social scientists of their time disagreed on the solution to violent denominational competition. David Hume proposed a state-funded established religion, which "bribes the indolence" of the clergy, turning them into staid civil servants with safe jobs and no particular incentive to rabble-rouse for a living. Hume's suggestion recalls Yasir Arafat's method of domesticating Black September terrorists in the

1970s, easing them into quiet domestic lives by finding them wives and apartments, as we saw in chapter 7.

Smith agreed with Hume's prediction, that the clergy of a state-funded established religion would give "themselves up to indolence," yet Smith had a different proposal. He objected that Hume was missing the larger picture. Smith argued that the reason competition led to dangerous bad-mouthing of competing denominations in the first place was that clergy were competing to be monopolists. As the established (state) religion, they would be able to suppress competitors using the power of the state, locking in their power and status.

Smith imagined a better solution: religious pluralism in which competition was constructive. In his words,

The interested active zeal of religious teachers can be dangerous and troublesome only where there is, either but one sect tolerated in the society, or where the whole of a large society is divided into two or three great sects; the teachers of each acting by concert, and under a regular discipline and subordination. But that zeal must be altogether innocent where the society is divided into two or three hundred, or perhaps into as many thousand small sects, of which no one could be considerable enough to disturb the publick tranquillity. The teachers of each sect, seeing themselves surrounded on all sides with more adversaries than friends, would be obliged to learn that candour and moderation which is so seldom to be found among the teachers of those great sects, whose tenets [are] supported by the civil magistrate.[27]

In other words, Smith conjectured that pluralism would beget tolerance. His argument is worth illustrating with an example. Say a preacher promises salvation but only on the condition that you excommunicate your Catholic cousins and distinguish yourself by wearing strange-looking hats. A competing preacher, also seeking your allegiance, will promise salvation at a lower personal cost, allowing you to remain friendly with your cousins and only requiring that you attend regular services, dressed however you like. With a few hundred competing denominations bidding for followers, preachers will eventually bid down the price of salvation, until one of them promises salvation virtually for free—with no requirement of intolerance toward members of other denominations.

In terms of our brief sketch of the violence that accompanied the Reformation, Smith would be conceding to Hume that making Lutheranism a state religion might have averted the Peasants' War by giving rabble-rousing clergy such as Müntzer safe jobs as civil servants. Yet it was the very existence of state religions that catalyzed the much more devastating Thirty Years' War.

Smith advocated religious pluralism as a solution to sectarian violence. A brilliant solution but difficult to implement: How would one keep politicians from seeking the support of religious allies, favoring one sect over another, creating a political alliance, and stifling constructive, pluralistic competition? Smith's answer was simple: *Forbid government discrimination on the basis of religion or denomination.* That would be hard to implement, admitted Smith, but he hopefully mentioned Pennsylvania, where (to repeat one of the quotations introducing this chapter) "the law in reality favours no one sect more than another, and it is there said to have been productive of this philosophical good temper and moderation."

True to form, the greatest economist of all time was arguing for competition: remove discriminatory barriers that impede the entry of competitors and two good things will happen. First, producers will stop spending their time lobbying government for protection against competition (through tariffs in the case of imported cars, say, or through violent repression in the case of the imported denominations—such as the abused Anabaptists). Second, competition will force producers to improve the product, reduce prices, or both. The same way that deregulating telephone markets reduced prices and improved the quality of telephone service, deregulating the market for religion would increase tolerance (the cost to community members) and improve the quality of religious services for members.

That seems a rather crude way to treat religion—comparing religious denominations to competing phone companies. Yet history has favored Smith's argument. A few years after Smith wrote those words, the United States became the first country to introduce a constitutional ban on discrimination by government on the basis of religion. By the nineteenth century visitors from Europe were surprised to find high levels of religious participation among Americans, and the very unusual combination of abundant religious sects and little religious conflict.[28] Modern evidence reveals that the second benefit of Smith's recommendation is also evident: countries and regions where people have abundant religious denominations to choose from tend to have higher rates of church attendance, a good indicator of higher-quality service provision.[29]

Why are religious groups generally not a source of conflict in the United States, as they had been historically in Europe? The answer, following Smith's logic, is nondiscrimination. Religious groups today generally don't bother organizing political parties in the United States, Canada, and most European countries. Why would they? The law precludes spending government funds disproportionately on their own members, so that members' time is better spent in charitable work and spiritual services, their core activities. Once there are no public funds to compete over, the benefits of intolerance toward other denominations diminish. Moreover, taking a public political stand on a controversial issue is as likely to antagonize a congregant for life as it is to influence voters in a single election, so clergy become largely apolitical, the polar opposite of their role in the Thirty Years' War. Tolerance cannot be legislated directly, but a law that removed incentives to discriminate made competition a powerful force for tolerance.

Americans and Western Europeans might find it odd to be portrayed as cultures free of religious interference in politics. This is a matter of proportion. True, church-state separation and the role of religion in politics are debated with passion in these countries. In the United States under debate are issues such as school prayer, the teaching of creationism in public schools, public funding of religious schools, or even the role of religious groups in supporting secular political candidates. In Europe those debates also involve the role of religious law (including Sharia) in the legal system. Yet, it is no longer possible in these countries for the government to grant a monopoly over civil law to a particular denomination, as it does in many Middle Eastern countries. It is hardly conceivable that in Europe or the United States a domestic religious scholar would grant divine permission to assassinate a president or prime minister in order to reverse some policy, as occurred in Egypt and in Israel, for instance.

The United States was in an ideal position to constitutionally ban discrimination, because there was no state religion to disestablish, and the descendants of refugees from religious persecution surely argued their case passionately. Nevertheless, over the last century the American experiment with nondiscrimination has been successfully replicated in most Western countries, which have reduced both state support for religion and state regulation of religion while increasing religious competition. When Japan prohibited government discrimination toward religions after World War II, the resulting outburst of religious denominations and movements was dubbed "the rush hour of the gods." In those countries political-religious parties are now uncommon.

In contrast, in the Middle East and other parts of the developing world, political-religious parties are widespread. Politicians seek the support of religious leaders and repay them with resources directed to their own religious constituencies. Clubs and credibility are powerful instruments. They allow religious politicians to coordinate action, persuade voters, and deliver blocks of votes. In organizing opposition to the government, mosques and churches are ideal locations; in repressive regimes, they are sometimes the only safe places to organize. There is nothing inherently wrong with religious politicians, but *they are symptoms of a political system that allows discrimination*, and that, in turn, creates toxic incentives. Once discrimination is allowed, it tempts politicians to make bargains that trade state support for discriminatory policy, as ultra-Orthodox politicians have done in Israel. In the Israeli case, as we saw, those discriminatory policies not only distance the ultra-Orthodox from the general culture in their religious practices, but they also increase the size of the ultra-Orthodox voting base, making the process self-reinforcing.Worse than that, a political system that allows discrimination tempts religious leaders like Müntzer, al-Sadr, Khomeini, and Qutb to capture power through violence, confident that should they succeed they will be free to discriminate in favor of their followers.

Once in power the record of religious politicians is mixed. In Turkey at this writing the Justice and Development Party (AKP) holds power, in what should be viewed by other countries as a democratic success. This Islamist party won election in 2002 and reelection in 2007 by moderating its positions to appeal to a broader constituency, rather than discriminating in favor of followers. Yet mosque-state separation is enforced by the military in Turkey, and Europe beckons with its own rules against discrimination, so that the voters' possible worries about the discriminatory use of the government's resources can be contained. In Iran, on the other hand, a broad-based revolution was organized and then captured by a narrow sect of Khomeini's followers, who discriminate legally and fiscally in favor of their own. In Gaza, Hamas won a parliamentary election, entered a power-sharing arrangement with their secular rivals from Fatah, and then seized absolute power in a violent action that Palestinian President Abbas termed a "coup." At this writing it is too early to judge the quality of their governance, though their assassination of Fatah cadres bodes ill for future experiments with Hamas in government. The Iranian and Gazan examples may be telling; the institutions blocking discriminatory abuse of power in most developing countries are feeble, especially in the Middle East, so that the temptation for religious politicians to organize politically and capture power must be strong indeed.

Aside from competition and religious pluralism, Adam Smith had other interesting recommendations. He advocated imposing educational standards in science and philosophy, and encouraging state support of what he called "public diversions": painting, poetry, music, and dance.[30] Can it be a coincidence that Smith advocated government support for the same cultural and educational activities that the Taliban repressed and banned?

Not about Us

In the tense days after 9/11 Americans asked: "Why do they hate us?" Reviewing European history yields a surprising answer: *Maybe it's not about us.* It could be a much older story about something else: about the incursion of markets into traditional communities; about the weakness of governments, both to suppress rebels and to provide basic services; and about governments discriminating among their own citizens on the basis of religion or religious denomination. In the Middle East, the past few centuries have witnessed the arrival of modern market economies, breaking up traditional community structures—mostly feudal villages. The market provides a great opportunity for individuals to meet their needs and pursue their aspirations, but it also threatens traditional mutual-aid arrangements through selective attrition of the least needy and most talented. These same forces also weakened government, which in the Middle East generally meant the replacement of a colonial Ottoman Empire with colonial European powers and eventually with weak monarchies and republics.

An opening of religious plurality allowed the Muslim Brotherhood in Egypt and the Jamaat-e-Islami in Muslim India, among others, to organize religious social service provision and political-religious movements. These religious radicals, without allies in government to protect them, were suppressed. Yet political Islamists were not suppressed nearly as effectively by the religious and civil authorities in the Muslim world as were the Anabaptists in Europe. Twentieth-century radical Islamists created a broader and more populist movement, perhaps because they managed to draw on the resources of religious charities and trusts, which were more independent of the official clergy in the Muslim world than were the charities of the Catholic Church or the Lutherans. With a social service provision base in place, the Egyptian Muslim Brotherhood, for example, could vie for political power, first through elections, then through their support for the Free Officers' coup, just as Thomas Müntzer supported the Peasants' rebellion four centuries earlier, with the intention of creating a theocracy.

The Muslim Brotherhood was betrayed by Nasser in Egypt, spurring Qutb to develop a theocratic solution. He justified jihad even against Muslims, doubtlessly influenced by the torture he endured in prison at the hands of the regime's secular thugs. Political radical Islam had by that time spread to other countries with the same starting conditions: social upheaval generated by the incursion of markets, and governments competing poorly with Islamic charities in providing basic services. In some Muslim countries the challenge to government was political, with Islamist parties running for office, as in Turkey and Pakistan; in others it was violent insurgency, as in Iran in 1979 and Palestine in 1987 and again in 2006. When insurgency was ineffective its proponents turned to terrorism, as did the Egyptian Islamic Jihad, first domestically and then internationally. The Egyptian Islamic Jihadists would form the core of Al Qaeda. Those are not battles in a "War of Civilizations" with the West, as the title of Samuel Huntington's famous book suggests; they are rather instances in somebody else's civil war, the title of a work by Michael Scott Doran.[31]

Could it really not be "about us"? Didn't radical Islamists attack civilians in Western countries? Yes, and they will continue to try, since the logic of terrorism requires capturing headlines. Once insurgency fails, and rebels run out of soft military targets in their own country, they often turn to civilian targets, which could be domestic or foreign. Al Qaeda does not aim to conquer New York, London, and Madrid any more than the PLO aspired to liberate Munich during the bloody summer Olympics of 1972. The point of terrorism is not to win territory, as in conventional insurgency, but to demonstrate a violent capability in order to extort concessions. The violence may as well be in a Western city as in a domestic capital; it will be carried out wherever it is most feasible to extort the authorities and their allies.

If it is someone else's civil war, why did radical Islamist terrorists declare a global jihad, in which Americans, Christians, Jews, Hindus, and all unbelievers are considered legitimate targets for terrorism? They did, and it is natural to feel threatened, but Müntzer also declared a religious war: "For the godless have no right to live, unless by the sufferance of the elect. . . . So be bold! He to whom all power is given in heaven and on earth is taking the government into his own hands."[32] That kind of rhetoric plays well with the terrorists' constituency and captures the attention and imagination of the media. Did he really believe it? And even if he did, should anyone else have taken him seriously? Müntzer lost quickly and is long forgotten, as is his threat to fight the godless.

If we ignore their rhetoric and just pay attention to what today's radical Islamic terrorists actually *do*, they demonstrate a clear behavioral pattern. When given a choice between attacking the far Satan (Western governments and civilians) and the near Satan (domestic secular governments), they almost always choose to attack the near Satan, the target from which they can possibly aspire to seize power. Like the violent Anabaptists of the sixteenth century, radical Islamists may be just another gang of rebels suffering delusions of grandeur. Or perhaps they are not deluded at all, but skillfully recasting their mundane quest for local power as a cosmic struggle.

To suggest that it is "not about us" is not to dismiss or delegitimize the grievances Muslims have about foreign occupation, support for repressive governments, or the seedy underside of Western culture that reaches their shores and satellite dishes. It's just that given an opportunity to seize power, religious radicals would have rebelled anyway.

The analogy of today's religious radicals to those of the Protestant Reformation is far from perfect. The Peasants' War was a geographically dispersed insurgency that claimed scores of civilian lives but never developed into international terrorism, as far as we know. Terrorism today truly is global because international travel and global media make foreign civilians feasible substitutes for domestic targets. Furthermore, international alliances make the Western allies of domestic governments worth extorting. What better way for Al Qaeda to embarrass the Saudi Arabian royal family in the West than to organize some Saudi nationals to kill American civilians?

Another important difference is in the abundance of charitable resources at stake. While radical Islamists are mainly competing over their declared goal—the power that comes with being a state religion or theocracy—competing for contributions from wealthy Muslim sympathizers and Islamic charities is a rewarding intermediate objective. These charitable institutions fill a legitimate role, providing basic services to Muslim communities as they have since the earliest days of Islam. Yet since the 1970s, pumped full of oil revenues and poorly regulated, these charities represent an inviting target for rebels who can wrap themselves in holiness in order to gain funding.

Nevertheless, these are differences in tactics and resources rather than in the substantive historical process. The sixteenth and twenty-first centuries share strong common threads of political-religious violence: the arrival of markets, the vulnerability of weak governments, opposition by radical denominations, the inability of government to commit to nondiscrimination, and the potential for long religious-political civil wars like the Thirty Years' War.

What's Our Role?

Can these historical analogies provide guidance about useful reactions to modern radical religious terrorism? I think so. They should provide perspective, patience, and confidence.

First, understanding the historical process allows us the perspective to put the radical Islamist terrorist threat in context. Radical Islam does not threaten Western civilization. Its proponents are a minority in most Muslim countries. Western countries and their allies can protect their citizens without themselves amplifying the rhetoric of radical Islamists by overstating the threat or demonizing the perpetrators. Global terrorism is far less dangerous than many other challenges humankind faces, including poverty, climate change, disease, uncontrolled civil wars, environmental degradation, violent crime, and nuclear proliferation.

Second, considering how long it took Europeans to endorse Adam Smith's solution—religious pluralism and strong nondiscriminatory government, patience is obviously necessary as new democracies develop their own versions of tolerant, nondiscriminatory governance in the contemporary world. The European transition from the feudal system to nation-states was slow and awful; the evolution of religious pluralism took even longer. A full century passed between the Protestant Reformation in the early sixteenth century and the English Independent Party first proposing religious pluralism as policy, toward the end of the English Civil War. Their proposal was rejected. A century and a half later, on a different continent, the American experiment with nondiscriminatory national government began with the constitutional amendments of the late eighteenth century. Over the next two centuries U.S. state governments and most Western governments followed suit. True, the Islamic empire was tolerant and prosperous while Europe was slogging through the Dark Ages, but that was long ago and hard to replicate. Discriminatory governments create vested interests and political alliances that are self-reinforcing and hard to displace. The state religions of Northern European countries, for instance, were only disestablished in the last few decades.

Finally, the historical analogy should give us confidence that religious pluralism and tolerance are a winning combination, so attractive that developing democracies will eventually choose to embrace them, just as they have embraced competition in markets—the current recession notwithstanding. To achieve long-term political stability developing democracies will likely have to replicate a key achievement of Western governments: competing successfully with the clergy in providing basic social services to residents in a nondiscriminatory way.

The great ideological competitions of the twentieth century were over the form of government that should take precedence. The Western democratic model prevailed. Economists tend to think that the Cold War was won, not by bleeding the Soviet Union by sponsoring jihadists in Afghanistan, but by generously enabling a cultural and economic juggernaut in Western Europe that Eastern Europeans could only ogle with increasing envy. It was not *Charlie Wilson's War* (a 2007 film written by Aaron Sorkin about covert support for the Mujaheddin) as much as the eventual victory of George Marshall's reconstruction plan. We could take the same approach to radical religious clubs, who after all are on the wrong side of history. They run remarkably efficient mutual-aid communities but cannot compete with markets in generating services and tax revenue to support strong, competent, generous governments. Viewed in a historical context, countries that have followed Adam Smith's advice about competitive markets and religious tolerance have created a shared culture of prosperity, diversity, technological progress, and cultural creativity that the world has never seen the equal of. To surrender any of that in the name of some echo of a remote threat from late medieval times would be a foolish tragedy for the West, and would undermine the demonstrative value of this remarkable success for developing countries.

Beyond setting an example, a second action developed countries can take to promote a peaceful transition to tolerance is to share our good fortune with allies in the developing world. We can protect our own citizens against terrorism and protect our allies against rebellion by helping those governments with the constructive as well as the coercive technology of governance: not just providing technical assistance in suppressing insurgency, but also helping to improve the quality of governance so that rebel clubs and other insurgents cannot gain a foothold. Developed countries can help allies thrive the same way we have, by providing the services that make governments secure and popular with their constituencies: security, education, welfare, justice, and responsive and representative government, as well as the occasional "public diversion" that Adam Smith recommended.

Analytical Appendix

Economists like diagrams. Not everyone does, but for those who do, diagrams can really clarify an argument. Some of the more technical arguments in the text are reproduced here for the diagrammatically inclined.[1] If you enjoy this appendix more than the text, you might consider graduate school in economics.

The Defection Constraint

The defection constraint, which first appears in the section "Trade Routes and Defection" in chapter 2, is illustrated in figure A.1. On the horizontal axis is the value of the project, in this case the convoy, which increases as we move to the right, for increasingly valuable convoys. On the vertical axis is the well-being of Taliban operatives, the guards at the checkpoint. For the moment think of well-being as simply a result of their payoffs. The line with the steep slope illustrates the payoff to defectors, which increases quickly with the value of the convoy: $5,000 each for a $10,000 convoy, $50,000 each for a $100,000 convoy, and so on. The serrated line with the shallow slope is the payoff to loyal guards. It increases as the value of the project increases, but at a much slower rate, because the Taliban share of revenues must be shared among all their personnel (all 100 in the example). On the other hand, the payoff for the loyal guards starts at a higher value—representing the value of being able to go home, remaining loyal to friends, and preserving the reputation of the family—which loyal members receive regardless of the convoy's size.[2]

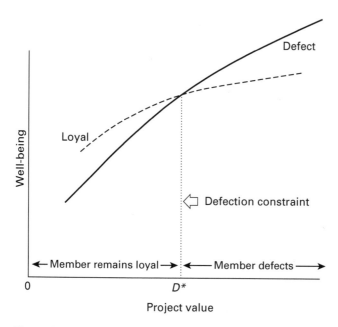

Figure A.1
The defection constraint.

Why aren't these lines straight? Well, there's an important economic regularity in play called *diminishing returns*, which means that additional equal increments of payoff give successively less pleasure to the recipient, as the additional money available is spent on successively less necessary items, or saved for less valuable investments.

The key point about this graph is that the two lines cross. To the left of the intersection point guards remain loyal, because they value the combination of home, loyalty, friends, family, reputation, and their 1/100th of revenues to the payoff if they defect—half the value of the convoy. To the right of the intersection point guards will defect, because half the value of the convoy is worth more to them than all the benefits of loyalty. (What if loyalty can't be valued? That's either a semantic issue, which is dealt with in note 2, or the reader should imagine a very, very valuable convoy.) The intersection point is where the *defection constraint* binds exactly, telling us how large a convoy (reading the value D* off the horizontal axis) can be run down the road without the guards stealing it.

Clubs, Loyalty, and Outside Options

The central argument of chapter 5 is that clubs can effectively engage in militia activity because of their ability to limit defection. That idea is illustrated in figure A.2. As in figure A.1, on the vertical axis is a measure of how good the Taliban operative feels (discounted over his entire future and including even complex emotions such as loyalty). Higher is happier. On the horizontal axis is the value of the convoy or hill. Right is more valuable. The dashed line with the shallow slope represents how an operative feels if he's loyal while the steep solid lines represent how he feels if he defects.

What distinguishes this diagram from the last is the difference between operatives with strong and weak outside options. Operatives with strong outside options are, for example, the ones who attended a good school. They have a secular education and will do just fine running a little grocery store in exile (or in witness protection). If they decide to defect

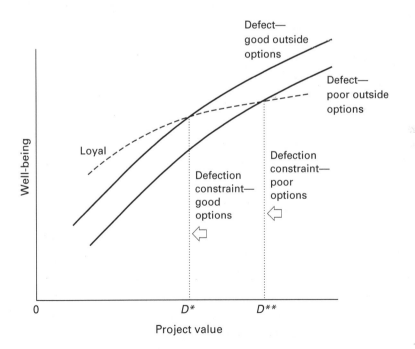

Figure A.2
The defection constraint and outside options.

they are represented by the upper of the two steep solid lines. Operatives with weak outside options might have attended the radical religious school in the refugee camp. If they decide to defect, their well-being is represented by the lower of the two steep lines.

As before, the defection constraint is given by the intersection of the solid "loyal" line and the serrated "defect" line. The key point is this: for operatives with good outside options the intersection point, which indicates the minimum project value D^* at which they choose to defect, is further to the left, at lower-value projects. Operatives with good outside options can be trusted only with smaller projects. Operatives with poor outside options, on the other hand, allow the organization to run bigger convoys down the road, capture larger hills, and attack higher value targets as terrorists, all because they can be trusted not to defect until the project value reaches D^{**}, a higher level of potential bribe or loot to be stolen.

This argument is very general and is the core concept in understanding the internal economies of radical religious communities, in both their violent and their nonviolent activity. If a group can selectively recruit members with low outside options it can gain the advantages of increased loyalty, allowing cooperative production in benign activities that are sensitive to defection, such as mutual aid or smuggling across borders. By the same token it has an advantage in cooperative production for violent activities sensitive to defection, such as guarding a trade route, capturing a hill, or committing terrorist acts. Chapter 5 also reports evidence corroborating the key prediction of the diagram, that radical religious clubs (those providing social services) are indeed more lethal.

Suicide Attacks vs. Hard Targets

Chapter 6 introduces the idea of a hard target, as illustrated in figure A.3. The upper serrated line with the shallow slope represents the well-being (*utility* for economists) of a member who chooses to remain loyal when attacking a soft target. Since targets are soft, rebels have a wide range of feasible target values. If the government has the resources and is so inclined, it can harden targets, which we can think of as improving airport security, or of raising the probability of a combat helicopter

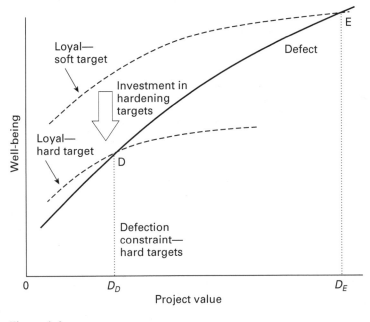

Figure A.3
Hardening targets.

arriving to defend the hill—in the example in chapter 6. The lower serrated line with the shallow slope is the expected well-being of a loyal member attacking a hard target. It is lower because it averages in the probability of the attack failing. (The lower line is not quite parallel to the upper. It is flatter because defenders will wisely invest more in hardening high-value targets, increasingly depressing the expectation of success the further the target is to the right.[3]) Hardening the target shifts the defection constraint inward from point E to point D, removing many high-value targets from the reach of insurgents. The diagram is meant to reflect the unfavorable conditions increasingly faced by insurgents in the late twentieth century.

A new diagram (figure A.4) should help illustrate why suicide attacks are chosen against hard targets. It starts with the hardened target defection constraint (point D) from the previous diagram, but adds an extra dotted line to illustrate the payoffs for a new option for rebels that remain loyal: the suicide attack. The dotted line lies below the serrated

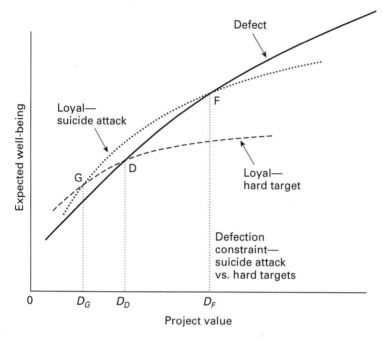

Figure A.4
Suicide attacks vs. hard targets.

"soft-target" line from figure A.3 (not shown) because the suicide attack carries the expense of giving up a member, the suicide attacker. For low-value targets it lies below the serrated conventional attack line for hard targets as well (assuming that members remain loyal), since the value of the target doesn't justify giving up a member's life. Yet for larger-value hard targets (to the right of point G) the suicide attack has a higher payoff than the conventional attack, because the tactical benefits make a successful suicide attack much more likely than a conventional attack.

Suicide attacks allow higher-value targets to be taken on without fear of defection by operatives, since the probability of failure is lower, increasing the chances of a net gain for operatives. In figure A.4 that's illustrated by the suicide-attack defection constraint at intersection point F, to the left of which attacks can be carried out without fear of operatives defecting. From the rebels' point of view that's an improvement over point D, which allowed only lower-value targets. Suicide attacks would never be chosen against soft targets (the upper line, not shown) or low-value targets (those with a lower value than D_G in the diagram), because conventional attacks will be effective against those without losing the attacker. The availability of suicide attacks expands the range of targets that can be attacked without defection (to the right of D_D) to include higher-value targets. Chapter 6 discusses evidence that suicide attacks are the tactic of choice against hard targets.

A diagram can also help illustrate why clubs have a particular advantage at suicide attacks. Figure A.5 combines the hard-target logic of suicide attacks with the organizational logic of clubs.

In a hard-target environment clubs can be more lethal than other terrorists because their higher defection constraint applies particularly to the high-value targets that require suicide attacks. In the diagram, terrorists not organized as clubs can only attack targets smaller than D_F in

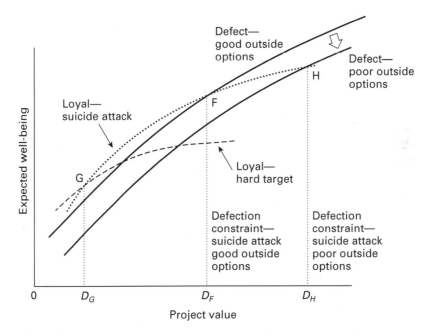

Figure A.5
Clubs and suicide attacks.

value, even if they choose suicide attacks. A club will use suicide attacks without fear of defection in a much larger range, from D_G to D_H, because it has more confidence in its operatives' loyalty. The reason is this: the highest-value targets attainable without defection require suicide attacks, whether the attack comes from a club or not. Introducing clubs shifts out the defection constraint—they have operatives available who are less likely to defect—allowing higher-value targets to be attacked. Thus, if clubs choose terrorism, and suicide attacks are being used, clubs will use suicide attacks more than other terrorist organizations do, and their suicide attacks will be more lethal. Chapter 6 provides evidence that clubs (i.e., religious radicals that provide social services—a sign of selective recruitment) choose suicide attacks more often than other terrorist organizations, and are more lethal when they do.

Protecting Hard Targets by Improving Outside Options

Chapter 7, on constructive counterterrorism, analyzes the environments in which we can expect to see suicide attacks. The setting is this: a government with adequate resources has hardened targets (shifting down the serrated line, as in figure A.3), and a club has responded by resorting to suicide attacks. In that environment the highest-value targets—those liable to be targets of suicide attacks—will benefit the most from a policy of enhancing outside options.

This conclusion is important enough to warrant one last diagram, figure A.6, which illustrates how enhanced outside options reduce the ability of rebels to attack high-value targets. When education and jobs are available, for instance, the outside options of members are described by the solid upper line with the steep slope, rather than the solid lower line. Shifting to the upper line reduces the range of targets that an organization can attack without fear of defection (from D_H to D_F) using suicide attacks.

Two points are worth stressing about the "hard"-target scenario in this diagram, in which suicide attacks are in use. First, improving outside options is more effective in protecting targets than is further hardening of targets, since suicide attacks are being used anyway. To see this, imagine shifting the serrated line downward; that does not reduce the

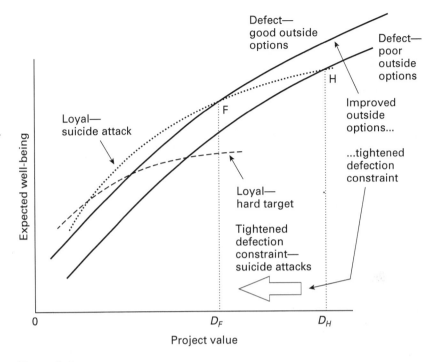

Figure A.6
Improving outside options protects against suicide attacks.

range of targets vulnerable to attack. Second, the attacks prevented by improving outside options are primarily suicide attacks, since those are preferred to conventional attacks for high value targets. (In the diagram the dotted line lies above the serrated line in the range for which the defection constraint is tightened first.) This is particularly relevant for neighbors and allies with well-defended targets, since we've learned that suicide attacks are more likely to target nationals of developed countries, both at home and abroad.

Notes

Chapter 1

1. The Memorial Institute for the Prevention of Terrorism tracked terrorist incidents worldwide from 1998 through December 2007. It was established after the 1995 bombing of the Murrah federal building in Oklahoma City, carried out by Timothy McVeigh. For more information see the MIPT Terrorism Knowledge Base at www.tkb.org. These data were transferred in 2008 to the National Consortium for the Study of Terrorism and Responses to Terrorism (START) at the University of Maryland, where they are being subsumed into the Global Terrorism Database.

2. These figures were calculated using the final version of the MIPT database, provided to me in early 2008.

3. Though the Reagan administration did not assign responsibility, a U.S. District Court judge ruled in 2003 that Hezbollah and Iranian agents carried out the Marine barracks attack.

4. Waddah Sharara, *Dawla Hizbullah: Lubnan Mujtama'an Islamiyyan* (Beirut: Dar al-Nahar, 1996).

5. Ahmed Rashid, *Jihad: The Rise of Militant Islam in Central Asia* (New Haven, Conn.: Yale University Press, 2002). Historian Richard English, in his comprehensive history of the Irish Republican Army, points on that the IRA initially established a following among Irish Catholics, and then entrenched it, by providing security that the government did not. See Richard English, *Armed Struggle: The History of the IRA* (New York: Oxford University Press, 2003), 108, 136.

6. These figures are calculated using the MIPT dataset referred to in note 1. The twenty religious terrorist organizations in this calculation include the Taliban (which the State Department has not yet placed on its list of international terror organizations). The others are the Abu Sayyaf Group, Ansar al-Islam, Armed Islamic Group, Asbat al-Ansar, Aum Shinrikyo / Aleph, Hamas, Harakat ul-Mujahidin, Hezbollah, Islamic Movement of Uzbekistan, Jaish-e-Mohammad, Jemaah Islamiya, Kahane Chai, Lashkar-e-Jhangvi, Lashkar-e-Taiba, Palestinian

Islamic Jihad, al-Gama'a al-Islamiyya, al-Qaeda, al-Qaeda in the Islamic Maghreb, and al-Qaeda Iraq.

7. President George W. Bush at the Pentagon following a briefing on January 4, 2006: "We talked about the areas of concern in this global war on terror, recognizing that the enemy, which has an ideology of hate and a desire to kill, lurks in parts around the world" (White House, Office of the Press Secretary, January 4, 2006, www.whitehouse.gov/news/releases/2006/01/20060104.html).

8. Ariel Merari, "Suicide Terrorism in the Context of the Israeli-Palestinian Conflict," presentation at the Suicide Terrorism Research Conference, National Institute of Justice, Washington, D.C., October 25–26, 2004.

9. Eli Berman and David D. Laitin, "Religion, Terrorism and Public Goods: Testing the Club Model," *Journal of Public Economics* 92, no. 10–11 (October 2008): 1942–1967. Data are from the Interdisciplinary Policy Institute for Counterterrorism (ICT), www.ict.org.il and Robert A. Pape, "The Strategic Logic of Suicide Terrorism," *American Political Science Review* 97 (2003): 343–361.

10. The list of Foreign Terrorist Organizations was last updated in October 2005 and is available at http://www.state.gov/s/ct/rls/fs/37191.htm. Suicide attacks account for only a small fraction of deaths due to terrorism, but they are relatively easy to record and give an indication of the danger posed by different organizations. Of the forty-two organizations on the list, only six had been responsible for more than 100 fatalities by suicide attacks through 2003: Al-Qaeda, Al-Qaeda Iraq, the LTTE, Hezbollah, Hamas, the Palestinian Islamic Jihad, and the Al Aqsa Martyrs (affiliated with the Palestinian Fatah). Iraqi and Chechen organizations not on the Foreign Terrorist Organization list also accounted for more than 100 fatalities due to suicide attacks. Thus by this measure there are only eight organizations worldwide that constitute an extremely serious threat. These data are from Pape and ICT. For details see Eli Berman and David D. Laitin, "Hard Targets: Theory and Evidence on Suicide Attacks," mimeo, UC San Diego, December 2006.

11. Chris Kraul, "FARC Commander Surrenders in Colombia," *Los Angeles Times*, May 20, 2008, http://articles.latimes.com/2008/may/20/world/fg-rebel20.

12. Though the media and the general public tend to focus on the psychology and motivation of terrorists, scholars have emphasized an organizational approach for at least twenty years. The interested reader might explore the articles in David C. Rapoport, ed., *Inside Terrorist Organizations* (New York: Columbia University Press, 1988), especially the contributions of Martha Crenshaw and Zeev Ivianski. Crenshaw explains that organization is more important than individual motivation: "The incentives that the organization provides for its members are critical to its survival. However, the relationship between actual rewards for membership and the organization's stated objectives is not straightforward, since recruits often join for reasons other than ideological commitment. . . . The popular image of the terrorist as an individual motivated exclusively by deep and intransigent political commitment obscures a more complex reality"

(Martha Crenshaw, "Theories of Terrorism: Instrumental and Organizational Approaches," 19). Ivianski traces the history of terrorism, finding that—when faced with strong states—secrecy and loyalty are crucial to a terrorist organization. He traces those ideas to the pamphlet *Terrorist Struggle*, written by the Russian revolutionary Nicholas Morozov in 1890 while in exile in Geneva. Morozov argued that insurgency was infeasible in largely rural Russia, against the powerful central government: "Against the omnipotent government, with its army, its spies, its prisons and its millions of police, there was to be set up a small fighting group . . . this small group would be armed with an impenetrable secrecy, an unassailable loyalty of one member towards the others" (Zeev Ivianski, "The Terrorist Revolution: Roots of Modern Terrorism," 138).

13. Note 12 reviews this scholarship.

14. Rosabeth Moss Kanter, *Commitment and Community: Communes and Utopias in Sociological Perspective* (Cambridge, Mass.: Harvard University Press, 1972).

15. Rodney Stark and William S. Bainbridge, *The Future of Religion: Secularization, Revival, and Cult Formation* (Berkeley: University of California Press, 1985).

16. Laurence R. Iannaccone, "Sacrifice and Stigma: Reducing Free-riding in Cults, Communes, and other Collectives," *Journal of Political Economy* 100 (1992): 271–291.

17. A good general introduction to the theory of clubs is available in Richard Cornes and Todd Sandler's book, *The Theory of Externalities, Public Goods and Club Goods* (New York: Cambridge University Press, 1986). For early application to social and business groups see Allan C. DeSerpa, "A Theory of Discriminatory Clubs," *Scottish Journal of Political Economy* 24 (February 1977): 33–41, and also Jack L. Carr and Janet Landa, "The Economics of Symbols, Clan Names and Religion," *Journal of Legal Studies* 12 (January 1983): 135–156.

18. Eli Berman, "Sect, Subsidy and Sacrifice: An Economist's View of Ultra-Orthodox Jews," *Quarterly Journal of Economics* 115, no. 3 (2000): 905–953.

19. Those findings come from my joint research with economist Ara Stepanyan.

20. Lindsay Heger, "In the Cross-Hairs: The Targets of Terrorism," doctoral dissertation draft, UC San Diego, 2008, chaps. 1, 4.

21. See for example Selva Benhabib, "Unholy Wars," *Constellations* 9, no. 1 (March 2002): 34–45.

Chapter 2

1. Popkin returned from Vietnam skeptical about the conventional wisdom on the politics of rural villages. Investigating those doubts became a major research

project, producing a book, *The Rational Peasant: The Political Economy of Rural Society in Vietnam* (Berkeley: University of California Press, 1979), in which Popkin argued against a kind view of feudal villages as supportive communities that peasants would fight to defend. He claimed that peasants choose sides between feudal lords, rebels, colonial powers, and government by a very concrete calculation of which side will most likely improve their quality of life, or at least extort less from them.

2. Samuel Popkin, presentation at the conference "Terrorist Organizations," University of California Institute on Global Conflict and Cooperation, La Jolla, April 2007.

3. Strictly speaking, *madrassa* is Arabic for school, including religious schools of any religion. In English the term has come to mean a Muslim religious school. That is how it will be used here.

4. The cost figures for U.S. and Soviet efforts are from Samuel Huntington, *The Clash of Civilizations and the Remaking of World Order* (New York: Simon & Schuster, 1996).

5. Ahmed Rashid, *The Taliban: Militant Islam, Oil, and Fundamentalism in Central Asia* (New Haven, Conn.: Yale University Press, 2000), 19.

6. Rashid, *The Taliban*, 21.

7. Rashid, *The Taliban*, 27. Anthony Davis, relying on several sources, also emphasizes the role of Pakistani economic interests in the formation of the Taliban. See his "How the Taliban Became a Military Force," in William Maley, ed., *Fundamentalism Reborn? Afghanistan and the Taliban* (New York: New York University Press, 1999).

8. Ahmed Rashid, "Pakistan and the Taliban," in William Maley, ed., *Fundamentalism Reborn? Afghanistan and the Taliban* (New York: New York University Press, 1998).

9. Rashid, "Pakistan and the Taliban."

10. Shaul Mishal and Avraham Sela, *The Palestinian Hamas: Vision, Violence, and Coexistence* (New York: Columbia University Press, 2000); Mark Juergensmeyer, *Terror in the Mind of God: The Global Rise in Religious Violence* (Berkeley: University of California Press, 2000), 78.

11. Karen Armstrong, *The Battle for God* (New York: Ballantine, 2000), 351. Hamas would eventually have a leadership in exile in the United States that raised funds among the Palestinian diaspora as well. The Israel Security Agency estimated foreign support at about $1 million per month in the spring of 2003, following international pressure on donors to stop that support. "Only a fraction" of those funds go to the military wing (ISA director Avi Dichter, *Ha'Aretz*, July 4, 2003 (in Hebrew)).

12. Zeev Schiff and Ehud Ya'Ari, *Intifada: The Palestinian Uprising—Israel's Third Front* (New York: Simon & Schuster, 1989).

13. Hamas's shift to violence may have been under discussion for some time within the organization. Kim Cragin points out that members of the Congress had already been arrested for smuggling weapons in 1983, including Salah Shehade, who would eventually lead the military wing of Hamas. For details see Kim Cragin, "Al-Mujama and the Resistance, 1973–1986," draft dissertation chapter, Cambridge University, 2008, 47, 87.

14. Steven Erlanger, "Hamas Seizes Broad Control in Gaza Strip," *New York Times,* June 13, 2007, A1.

15. The impatient reader is welcome to skip ahead, but will end up going back to read chapter 3 to figure it out.

16. Ehud Sprinzak, *Brother against Brother: Violence and Extremism in Israeli Politics from Altalena to the Rabin Assassination* (New York: Free Press, 1999). The Jewish Underground is well described by Israeli political scientist Ehud Sprinzak and by one of the members. David Weisburd, in *Jewish Settler Violence: Deviation as Social Reaction* (University Park: Pennsylvania State University Press, 1989), describes Gush Emunim.

17. Weisburd, *Jewish Settler Violence.*

18. Sprinzak, *Brother against Brother*, 169, discussing the report of Deputy Attorney General Yehudit Carp.

19. Sprinzak, *Brother against Brother*, 169.

20. Josh Meyer, "Records Show Man in LAX Plot Gave U.S. Key Terrorist Details," *Los Angeles Times*, April 27, 2005, Section A1.

21. Jane Mayer, "Junior," *New Yorker*, September 11, 2006: http://www .newyorker.com/archive/2006/09/11/060911fa_fact (accessed March 16, 2009).

22. Mark Bowden "The Ploy," *Atlantic Monthly*, May 2007: 54–68. Other sources credit Jordanian intelligence agents with information leading to Zarqawi's demise.

23. Though the United States never accused Hezbollah, and it never claimed responsibility, a District Court judge ruled in 2003 that Hezbollah and Iranian agents were responsible. For a discussion of responsibility for the Marine barracks and U.S. Embassy attacks, and the connection of Hezbollah to terrorist Imad Mugniyeh (a Lebanese Shiite who trained with Fatah), see Judith Palmer Harik, *Hezbollah: The Changing Face of Terrorism* (New York: Palgrave Macmillan, 2004), chap. 11, and Magnus Ranstorp, *Hizballah in Lebanon: The Politics of the Western Hostage Crisis* (London: Macmillan Press, 1997).

24. Naim Qassem, *Hizbullah: The Story from Within* (Beirut: Saqi Books, 2005), 18–20.

25. Shimon Shapira, *Hizbullah between Iran and Lebanon* (Tel Aviv: Hakibbutz Hameuchad, 2000) (in Hebrew), 12.

26. Qassem, *Hizbullah.*

27. Norton, in Harik, *Hezbollah*, 210.

28. Shapira, *Hizbullah between Iran and Lebanon*, 106.

29. A U.S. House resolution in July 2004 declared a Hezbollah member from southern Lebanon, Ibrahim Hussein Berro, to be the suicide attacker.

30. Qassem, *Hizbullah*, 70.

31. Qassem, *Hizbullah*, 69.

32. Qassem, *Hizbullah*, 69.

33. International Crisis Group, "Iraq's Muqtada al-Sadr: Spoiler or Stabilizer?", *Middle East Report 55* (Brussels: icg.org, July 2006).

34. Toby Dodge, in "Political Mobilisation in the Absence of Civil Society or a State: Islamic Nationalism in Post-Saddam Iraq" (mimeo, University of London, 2004), describes current insurgent groups in Iraq, including al-Sadr's militia.

35. Vali Nasr, *The Shia Revival: How Conflicts within Islam Will Shape the Future* (New York: Norton, 2006), 191.

36. An arrest warrant for Muqtada was issued for that killing but never served. Two of his lieutenants were arrested for that murder in March 2004, but were released as part of a political compromise in August 2005.

37. Paul Bremer, *My Year in Iraq* (New York: Simon & Schuster, 2006), 313, quoted in International Crisis Group, "Iraq's Muqtada al-Sadr: Spoiler or Stabilizer?"

38. Bremer, *My Year in Iraq*, 129; quoted in ICG.

39. If allegations about the Mahdi Army are correct, it received at least some Iranian funding, as do Hamas and Hezbollah, creating another commonality across the groups. The Taliban had Pakistan as a foreign sponsor.

Chapter 3

1. Though Smith was religious he may have had unusual views for his time. Scholars disagree over whether he believed that the Almighty intervenes in daily life.

2. Adam Smith, *An Inquiry into the Nature and Causes of the Wealth of Nations* (New York: Modern Library, [1776] 1965), 788–814.

3. Iannaccone's girlfriend was also researching a compelling question involving religion. Raised as a Mormon, Carrie Miles was writing a doctoral dissertation in the social psychology department about how the Mormon church dealt with women's rights. Iannaccone listened carefully, analyzed the problem, and returned with some mathematical calculations and graphs. The two would soon be married, and the ideas that Miles inspired would form the basis of Iannaccone's first major publication. Nevertheless, that particular moment did not go so well. Miles understood the technical argument, but at the time math and graphs weren't going to fit any better into the nontechnical field that was then social

psychology than religion was fitting into economics. In Iannaccone's words, "She told me I should go write my own dissertation on religion!"

4. One of the difficult issues Iannaccone tackled is how people make choices they know will change their character, and in turn influence future choices. For example, choosing to learn to like sushi, or classical music, are choices that affect future choices. Iannaccone was interested because learning about religion will affect how we make future choices about our personal and spiritual lives. Interestingly, this approach has become most famous in analyzing the economics of addiction.

5. James Hurd, "The Shape of High Fertility in a Traditional Mennonite Population," mimeo, Bethel University, May 2006: 4.

6. Economists Jonathan Gruber and Daniel Hungerman confirm that secular activities and worship are substitutes. U.S. states that repealed "blue laws" prohibiting retail trade on Sundays experienced declines in church attendance. For details see Jonathan Gruber and Daniel Hungerman, "The Church vs the Mall: What Happens When Religion Faces Increased Secular Competition?", *Quarterly Journal of Economics*, 123 (2008): 831–862.

7. Laurence R. Iannaccone, "Looking Backwards: A Cross-National Study of Religious Trends," working paper, George Mason University, 2003.

8. Yeshiva attendance may be somewhat, but not grossly, exaggerated. A government commission reports that among yeshiva students suspected of violating the deferment agreement, 40 percent were indeed in violation, either by working or by simply being in a different yeshiva. The Israel Defense Forces claim that figure to be 20 percent, which is probably an overestimate of the violation rate in general, since this sample is of suspected violators. See Shahar Ilan, "Deceit," *Ha'Aretz*, May 19, 1998 (in Hebrew).

9. Menachem Friedman, in *The Haredi (Ultra-Orthodox) Society—Sources, Trends and Processes*, Research Series No. 41 (Jerusalem: Jerusalem Institute, 1991), describes the history of yeshiva attendance in Central and Eastern Europe.

10. A survey of the Montreal Hassidic community in the mid-1990s found that only 6 percent of men over the age of twenty-five attended yeshiva full time. For details see Charles Shahar, Morton Weinfeld, and Randal F. Schnoor, *Survey of the Hassidic and Ultra-Orthodox Communities in Outremont and Surrounding Areas* (Outremont, Quebec: Coalition of Outremont Hassidic Organizations, 1997).

11. Klinov and I examined the draft-deferral rule and made a mistaken policy recommendation, which we would later regret. Only *full-time* yeshiva students qualify for a draft deferral. They revert to being draft eligible if they work even part time. So if a yeshiva student in his twenties even experimented with working, he would be liable for three years of military service and decades of subsequent reserve duty. That seemed like a huge disincentive to experimenting with work for yeshiva students. We circulated a research paper in 1996 explaining that if

the "penalty" of draft eligibility were reduced, it would be easier for yeshiva students to experiment with work and transition into the workforce, allowing the ultra-Orthodox community to become more self-sufficient. (Eli Berman and Ruth Klinov, "Human Capital Investment and Nonparticipation: Evidence from a Sample with Infinite Horizons (Or: Mr. Jewish Father Stops Going to Work)." Discussion Paper No. 97.05. (Jerusalem: The Maurice Falk Institute for Economic Research in Israel, 1997).) We realized the mistake not long after the paper circulated, and published the counterargument (as explained in the text): If it were only the draft deferral, then ultra-Orthodox men would have left yeshiva when the deferral became an exemption. Unfortunately, by then it was too late—the argument had legs of its own. By the year 2000 a strong lobby arose for reform, and the policymakers among the reformers found the "penalty" argument compelling. The government introduced a policy of the form we had mistakenly recommended in 2001, giving yeshiva students the option of experimenting with work for a year before deciding whether to return to yeshiva or face limited military service (or national service). A few dozen yeshiva students accepted the option of experimenting with work. The vast majority ignored it. The dependence of the ultra-Orthodox community on subsidies deepened as an opportunity for constructive reform was squandered. The only benefit of the exercise was that it provided further evidence that yeshiva students are not studying primarily in order to dodge the Israeli draft.

12. Julia A. Ericksen, Eugene P. Ericksen, John Hostetler, and Gertrude E. Huntington, "Fertility Patterns and Trends among the Old Order Amish," *Population Studies* 33, no. 2 (July 1979): 274.

13. Menachem Friedman, quoted in David Landau, *Piety and Power: The World of Jewish Fundamentalism* (New York: Hill and Wang, 1993), 255.

14. Landau, *Piety and Power*, 255.

15. Landau, *Piety and Power*, 262.

16. Landau, *Piety and Power*, 255.

17. Landau, *Piety and Power*, 259.

18. Josephus, *War*, II, viii, 3, cited by Adolfo Roitman in "From Dawn to Dusk among the Qumran Sectarians," in Adolfo Roitman, ed., *A Day at Qumran: The Dead Sea Sect and Its Scrolls* (Jerusalem: Israel Museum, 1997).

19. Community document (XIV, 11–15), cited in Roitman, *A Day at Qumran*.

20. Damascus document (XIII, 14–15), cited in Eyal Regev, "Comparing Sectarian Practice and Organization: The Qumran Sects in Light of the Regulations of the Shakers, Hutterites, Mennonites and Amish," *Numen* 51, no. 2 (2004): 146–181.

21. Daniel Chen, "Club Goods and Group Identity: Evidence from Islamic Resurgence during the Indonesian Financial Crisis," mimeo, University of Chicago, 2005.

22. As reported in Laurence R. Iannaccone, "Sacrifice and Stigma: Reducing Free-Riding in Cults, Communes, and Other Collectives," *Journal of Political Economy* 100 (1992): 271–291, the data sources are the Northern California Church Membership Survey of 1963, conducted by Charles Glock and Rodney Stark; as well as the General Social Surveys, 1984–1987, conducted by the National Opinion Research Center. The full list of denominations is as follows. Most churchlike: Congregationalists, Methodists, Episcopalians, Disciples of Christ; churchlike: Presbyterians, American Lutherans, American Baptists; sect-like: Missouri Lutherans, Southern Baptists; sects: Assemblies of God, Church of God, Church of Christ, Nazarene, Seventh-Day Adventists, Gospel Lighthouse, Foursquare Gospel.

23. Claus-Peter Clasen, *Anabaptism, A Social History, 1525–1618* (Ithaca, N.Y.: Cornell University Press, 1972), 244. That population estimate is a lower bound. An upper bound would be around 50,000.

24. The TFR measure isn't perfect either. For instance, it tends to understate predicted fertility if women are in the process of shifting to older ages of birth.

25. As recorded by sociologists Joseph W. Eaton and Albert J. Mayer in "The Social Biology of High Fertility among the Hutterites: The Demography of a Unique Population," *Human Biology* 25, no. 4 (December 1953): 206–264.

26. Hurd, "The Shape of High Fertility in a Traditional Mennonite Population."

27. Ericksen, Ericksen, Hostetler and Huntington, "Fertility Patterns and Trends among the Old Order Amish," 255–276. Some 258 interviews were conducted between 1969 and 1973 in and around the four largest Amish settlements in North America: Lancaster County, Pennsylvania; Elkhart County, Indiana; and Holmes and Geauga Counties, Ohio.

28. Ruth Klinov and I discuss the implied social welfare issues for Israeli ultra-Orthodox Jews in "Human Capital Investment and Nonparticipation: Evidence from a Sample with Infinite Horizons (Or: Mr. Jewish Father Stops Going to Work)," Discussion Paper No. 97.05 (Jerusalem: Maurice Falk Institute for Economic Research in Israel, 1997), and in Eli Berman, "Subsidized Sacrifice: State Support of Religion in Israel," *Contemporary Jewry* 20 (December 1999): 167–200.

29. A minor denomination that is explicitly antinatalist is the Shakers, a communal sect established in England in 1747. A number of members emigrated to the United States in 1774, where they eventually established thriving communal settlements in northern New England. Their furniture factories made them quite prosperous, which led to a tightening of requirements for entry. As clubs go, they seem to have hit on the wrong sacrifice from an evolutionary point of view. They started by encouraging members to adopt children, then shifted to a ban on fertility. At this writing there are believed to be four surviving Shakers in Maine.

30. T. W. Schultz, ed., *Economics of the Family: Marriage, Children, and Human Capital* (Cambridge, MA:. National Bureau of Economic Research, 1974). For a clear exposition of modern literature see David N. Weil, *Economic Growth* (New York: Addison-Wesley, 2004).

31. Ronald Freedman and P. K. Whelpton, "Social and Psychological Factors Affecting Fertility: X. Fertility Planning and Fertility Rates by Religious Interest and Denomination," *The Milbank Memorial Fund Quarterly* 28 (3) (July 1950):. 294–343.

32. Eli Berman and Ara Stepanyan, "How Many Radical Islamists? Evidence from Asia and Africa," mimeo, UC San Diego, 2003.

33. The differential is 0.81 for Côte D'Ivoire but not precisely estimated for the oldest group of women, age forty to forty-nine. For some reason the differential is larger for the thirty- to thirty-nine-year-old cohort, and precisely estimated at 1.34.

34. The phrase "after accounting for the effects . . ." means that the reported coefficients are from a multiple regression of the number of surviving children on the "religious radical" indicator, which also included variables measuring education as well as indicators for religion and rural location. For details see Berman and Stepanyan, "How Many Radical Islamists?"

Chapter 4

1. Community (*Yahad*) Rule, column VI, lines 16–23 (Frank Moore Cross and Esther Eshel, "The Yahad (Community) Ostracon," in Adolfo Roitman, ed., *A Day at Qumran: The Dead Sea Sect and Its Scrolls* (Jerusalem: Israel Museum, 1997)). The italics are my own. The Qumran sect apparently lived near the site where the Dead Sea Scrolls were discovered and may have written the scrolls. The Community Rule, which is one of the Dead Sea Scrolls, presumably describes the rules of the same Qumran sect.

2. Whether early Christians living at the same time as the Qumran sect were communal is open to debate. Luke does write in the Book of Acts (2:44), "And all who believed were together and had all things in common; and they sold their possessions and goods and distributed them to all, as any had need." Whether he is describing an ideal of friendship, an ideal of charity, or an actual commune is unclear.

3. Eyal Regev, "Comparing Sectarian Practice and Organization: The Qumran Sects in Light of the Regulations of the Shakers, Hutterites, Mennonites and Amish," *Numen* 51, no. 2 (2004): 147, 153.

4. Rosabeth Moss Kanter, *Commitment and Community: Communes and Utopias in Sociological Perspective* (Cambridge, Mass.: Harvard University Press, 1973): 63–64.

5. Adam Smith *did* come first, discussing sects in the *Wealth of Nations*.

6. Shahar Ilan, "Reconciling Conscription," *Ha'Aretz*, April 22, 2008 (in Hebrew).

7. Shahar Ilan, "The Yeshiva-Bocher Basket: 17 Thousand Shekel Gross," *Ha'Aretz*, March 2, 1998 (in Hebrew), estimates that an ultra-Orthodox family with six children and a father studying in yeshiva is eligible for 6,500 NIS ($1,850) per month in government support from all sources.

8. Economist Yoram Weiss of Tel Aviv University raised a related question: By the time people are forty, why isn't their level of commitment obvious to the community? A possible answer comes from an older *kollel* (yeshiva) student I interviewed. His explanation for his own yeshiva attendance was that it insulated him from the corrupting influences of the secular world. When asked if at the age of forty, with six children, he was still a candidate for defection or backsliding, he answered: "Of course, I haven't been tested until I leave."

9. Forty is an age at which a demonstration of commitment may be the most valuable, because a father will soon depend on the community to raise funds for apartments to allow his children to marry. Menachem Friedman, in *The Haredi Society*, reports on articles in the ultra-Orthodox press documenting the stress faced by middle-aged yeshiva graduates who must finance their children's marriage. In his book *Piety and Power* (1993), David Landau describes a massive philanthropic effort to provide fathers with such funds. Before their bankruptcy the Reichmann brothers, ultra-Orthodox real estate magnates from Toronto, reportedly provided thousands of dollars to ultra-Orthodox newlyweds. In conversation, a number of sources estimated that a needy ultra-Orthodox father could solicit about $30,000 on a fundraising tour of the Diaspora, with the proper letter from a respected ultra-Orthodox rabbi.

10. I'm indebted to Edward Glaeser, my editor at the *Quarterly Journal of Economics*, for encouraging me to look for further testable implications. Glaeser and his anonymous referees also helped sharpen the arguments made here in various ways.

11. Sephardi is a misnomer suggesting Spanish origin, but is commonly used. The Shas party self-identifies as Sephardi.

12. These estimates are subject to sampling error because of inherent variation in the data. The difference between the two changes in yeshiva attendance is 10.3 percentage points, with a standard error of 6.0. The standard error is a measure of that inherent variation, which you might recall from an introductory statistics course. The ratio of the difference to the standard error is 1.7, indicating that the chance that the pattern reported is due to sampling error (in other words, is just a fluke) is less than 10 percent.

13. The attempted policy reform of 2003, referred to in note 11 of the previous chapter, provides some additional evidence. The reformers gave yeshiva students the opportunity to test the labor market for a year, without risk of military service, but were surprised to find that they failed to draw more than a few yeshiva students into the workforce. The standard logic of price theory predicts that reducing the cost of work would draw students out of yeshiva into the work force. Yet these reforms also *reduced* the economic cost of yeshiva attendance by providing the option of working for a year. The logic of sacrifice dictates that

if the government reduces the economic cost of yeshiva, making sacrifice easier, the individual must *increase* the number of years of yeshiva attendance in order to demonstrate the same commitment. In terms of our anecdote, lowering the cost of sacrifices (yeshiva) only adds more young men (potential shirkers) to your doorstep, who will compete for your daughter and club membership by bidding up yeshiva attendance, not reducing it, as proponents of the policy had hoped. (Or, in terms of the classics, it would be like Penelope improving the quality of food served to her suitors, reducing the inconvenience for them of waiting around for her to give up on Odysseus and finally choose.)

14. For completeness, here are the estimated returns for the other three countries. In Uttar Pradesh and Bihar the estimated return on general schooling is 12.2 percent; the return on religious schooling is 1.2 percent higher, with a standard error (SE) of 4.8 percent; and the estimated intercept is—5.1 percent. In Pakistan the estimates are as follows: general schooling, 8.2 percent; religious schooling, 0.2 percent lower (SE 1.8 percent); intercept, 10 percent (SE 19 percent). In Côte D'Ivoire the estimates are as follows: general schooling, 17.5 percent; religious schooling, 2.9 percent lower (SE 7.0 percent); intercept, 10.5 percent (SE 28.5 percent). In nontechnical terms, this means that in two of the other three cases the returns on an additional year of religious schooling were lower, while the returns on the first year were higher in two of the three cases. Yet the main point is that these estimates are not precise enough to tell us whether any of the findings are more than a statistical fluke.

15. L. Choon Wang, "The Effects of Education on the Amish," mimeo, UC San Diego, June 2008.

16. The difference between fertility growth among Sephardi and Ashkenazi ultra-Orthodox women is estimated fairly precisely. Technically speaking, the standard error of the difference in birth-rate changes is 0.82, so that a 95 percent confidence interval excludes the number zero. In other words, the finding is unlikely to be a fluke.

17. Census and household surveys in Pakistan reveal that in 2001 less than 1 percent of students were enrolled in madrassas. Even in the districts of Pakistan bordering Afghanistan, where madrassa enrollment is highest, it averaged less than 7.5 percent. For details see Tahir Andrabi, Jishnu Das, Asim Ijaz Khwaja and Tristan Zajonc, "Religious School Enrollment in Pakistan: A Look at the Data," *Comparative Education Review* 50, no. 3 (August 2006): 446.

18. Statistical agencies take note: this simple, unobtrusive and innocuous question would make a terrific addition to any household survey in any country where domestic religious radicalism is interesting.

19. Through the efforts of Iannaccone and others, an analysis of religious activity from the perspective of markets and competition has become an active field of study not only in economics, but also in the sociology of religion. Sociologists Rodney Stark and Roger Finke call this approach the "New Paradigm" in their book *Acts of Faith: Explaining the Human Side of Religion* (Berkeley: University of California Press, 2000).

Chapter 5

1. Cited in Shaul Mishal and Avraham Sela, *The Palestinian Hamas: Vision, Violence, and Coexistence* (New York: Columbia University Press, 2000), 71.

2. Susanne Koelbl, "Islamic Extremists Gain Upper Hand in Kashmir Relief Efforts," *Der Spiegel International*, February 25, 2006. http://www.spiegel.de/international/spiegel/0,1518,403726,00.html (accessed March 16, 2009).

3. Ibid.

4. Ibid.

5. Whether the Jaish-e-Mohammed (Army of Mohammed) is a strong economic club like the Taliban with both violent and benign wings, or just a charity with links to Islamist terrorists, is hard to say. Work is certainly done by volunteers, as in Iannaccone's conception of a radical religious club, though many of the benefits flow to nonmembers. Some of the funding reportedly comes from the outside, because the article states that these Islamist militants are "generously funded by Muslims from Saudi Arabia and by overseas Pakistanis." The Jaish-e-Mohammed is one of an increasing number of violent Islamist groups in Asia now being associated with the "Hamas model." Zachary Abuza, a political scientist at Simmons College in Boston, argues that the Jemaah Islamiah (JI) in Indonesia is trying to transition to a "Hamas model" to build an organizational base. The JI is responsible for a string of bomb attacks in Indonesia, including the Bali bombings of October 2002, which killed more than two hundred people. As evidence, he points to internal documents and JI-linked charities that participated in humanitarian relief after the cataclysmic tsunami of December 2004. See Zachary Abuza, "Jemaah Islamiyah and the Inverse Triangle," *Middle East Quarterly* 16(1) (Winter 2009): 15–26.

6. Karen Armstrong provides a clear history of the Muslim Brotherhood in *The Battle for God* (New York: Ballantine, 2000).

7. Ziad Munson, "Islamic Mobilization: Social Movement Theory and the Egyptian Muslim Brotherhood," *Sociological Quarterly* 42, no. 4 (2001): 487–510, p. 501.

8. Richard P. Mitchell, *The Society of Muslim Brothers* (London: Oxford University Press, 1969). Other estimates are higher.

9. Munson, "Islamic Mobilisation," 501; my italics.

10. Mitchell, *The Society of Muslim Brothers*.

11. John L. Esposito, *Unholy War: Terror in the Name of Islam* (New York: Oxford University Press, 2002), 27.

12. For excerpts and interpretation of Al Qaeda leader Ayman al-Zawahiri's answers to questions posed to him on the Internet, see Jarret Brachman, Brian Fishman, and Joseph Felter, *The Power of Truth: Questions for Ayman al-Zawahiri* (West Point, N.Y.: United States Military Academy Combating Terrorism Center, 2008).

13. Timur Kuran, *Islam and Mammon: The Economic Predicaments of Islamism* (Princeton, N.J.: Princeton University Press, 2005).

14. Yassin was arrested by the Egyptian authorities in 1965 as part of a general crackdown on the Muslim Brotherhood. See Kim Cragin, "Al-Mujama' and the Resistance, 1973–1986," draft dissertation chapter, Cambridge University, 2008, 72.

15. Mishal and Sela, *The Palestinian Hamas*, 44.

16. Mishal and Sela, *The Palestinian Hamas*.

17. Former FBI analyst Matthew Levitt presents Hamas this way in "Hamas from Cradle to Grave," *Middle East Quarterly* 11, no. 1 (Winter 2004): 3–15. He quotes then Israeli Prime Minister Shimon Peres, who told the Israeli Knesset (parliament) in 1996 that "Hamas has established charitable organizations in order to camouflage its true nature." While Levitt is correct in emphasizing that the violent and benign "wings" of Hamas have a single leadership, share personnel, and complement each other, he ignores the fact that the religious and social service provision networks predate the terrorist wing.

18. Reuven Paz, address to the Washington Institute, July 19, 2001. Reproduced as "Special Forum Report: Islamic Palestine or Liberated Palestine? The Relationship between the Palestinian Authority and Hamas" (rapporteur's summary of his remarks), Peace Watch No. 337, www.washingtoninstitute.org/templateC05.php?CID=2028. Paz is academic director of the International Policy Institute for Counter-Terrorism at the Interdisciplinary Center, Herziliya, Israel.

19. An interview conducted by the International Crisis Group reports that Pakistani residents donate about $1.1 billion to mosques and madrassas annually. See International Crisis Group, "Pakistan: Madrasas, Extremism and the Military," *Asia Report* 36 (Islamabad/Brussels: icg.org, July 2002).

20. Ahmed Rashid, "Pakistan and the Taliban," in William Maley, ed., *Fundamentalism Reborn? Afghanistan and the Taliban* (New York: New York University Press, 1998), 75.

21. Anthony Davis, "How the Taliban Became a Military Force," in Maley, *Fundamentalism Reborn?*, 43.

22. David Kilcullen, *The Accidental Guerrilla: Fighting Small Wars in the Midst of a Big One* (New York: Oxford University Press, 2009), 47.

23. These data cover international terrorist incidents for the eight major organizations that carried out terrorist attacks in Lebanon or Israel between 1968 and 2006, as compiled by the Terrorism Knowledge Base of the Memorial Institute for the Prevention of Terrorism. As of 2008 most of these data are being subsumed into the Global Terrorism Database managed by the National Consortium for the Study of Terrorism and Responses to Terrorism at the University of Maryland.

24. This difference is statistically significant.

25. Yateendra Singh Jafa, "Defeating Terrorism: A Study of Operational Strategy and Tactics of Police Forces in Jammu & Kashmir (India)," *Police Practice and Research* 6, no. 2 (May 2005): 148.

26. Saeed Shafqat, "From Official Islam to Islamism: The Rise of Dawat-ul-Irshad and Lashkar-e-Taiba," in Christophe Jaffrelot, ed., *Nationalism without a Nation: Pakistan Searching for Its Identity*. (New Delhi: Zed Books, 2002), 131.

27. Shafqat, "From Official Islam to Islamism," 142.

28. Shafqat, "From Official Islam to Islamism," 144.

29. Jafa, "Defeating Terrorism," 150.

30. The figures are from MIPT data, as in chapter 1, note 1.

31. Jafa, "Defeating Terrorism," 153.

32. Shafqat, "From Official Islam to Islamism," 145.

33. The U.S. Treasury Office of Foreign Assets Control lists JuD and LeT as acronyms on its *Specially Designated Nationals List*, www.ustreas.gov/offices/enforcement/ofac/sdn/sdnlist.txt.

34. Jan McGirk, "Kashmir: The Politics of an Earthquake," October 19, 2005, www.OpenDemocracy.net. McGirk also reports that LeT members are not entirely altruistic in earthquake relief. After they rescued a fourteen-year-old-boy from the rubble, the child tragically discovered he was an orphan. They claimed the child, told the neighbors, "He's ours," and drove him off to a madrassa.

35. Hunter Thompson, *Hell's Angels: The Strange and Terrible Saga of the Outlaw Motorcycle Gangs* (New York: Random House, 1966).

36. "Gang Member Tells Jurors about Initiation in Double Murder Trial," WRAL-TV, www.lochaltechwire.com/news/local/story/139973, March 7, 2000.

37. John Kobler, *Capone* (New York: Putnam, 1971), 308.

38. George A. Akerlof and Janet L. Yellen develop a model of street gangs with this quality in "Gang Behavior, Law Enforcement, and Community Values," in Henry J. Aaron, Thomas E. Mann, and Timothy Taylor, eds., *Values and Public Policy* (Washington, D.C.: Brookings Press, 1994). My coauthors and I take a similar approach to analyzing insurgencies in Iraq in Eli Berman, Jacob Shapiro, and Joseph Felter, "Can Hearts and Minds Be Bought? The Economics of Counterinsurgency in Iraq," mimeo, UC San Diego, October 2008.

39. Daniel A. Metraux, "Religious Terrorism in Japan: The Fatal Appeal of Aum Shinrikyo," *Asian Studies* 35, no. 12 (December 1995): 1140–1154 (quote on 1142).

40. Yoshiyuki Kogo, "Aum Shinrikyo and Spiritual Emergency," *Journal of Humanistic Psychology* 42 (2002): 82–101, p. 88.

41. Thomas F. O'Dea, "Sects and Cults," in David L. Sills, ed., *International Encyclopedia of the Social Sciences*, vol. 14 (New York: Macmillan/Free Press), 130–135, cited in Metraux, "Religious Terrorism in Japan," 1142.

42. Metraux, "Religious Terrorism in Japan," 1142.

43. Metraux, "Religious Terrorism in Japan," 1142.

44. Metraux, "Religious Terrorism in Japan," 1153.

45. International Crisis Group, "Where Is Iraq Heading? Lessons from Basra," *Middle East Report* 67 (Damascus/Amman/Brussels ICG.org, June 25, 2007), 3.

46. Ahmed Rashid, *Taliban: Militant Islam, Oil, and Fundamentalism in Central Asia* (New Haven, Conn.: Yale University Press, 2000), 106, 111.

47. Rashid, *Taliban*, 101–105.

48. See, for example, Alan B. Krueger and Jitka Maleckova, "Education, Poverty and Terrorism: Is There a Causal Connection?", *Journal of Economic Perspectives* 17, no. 4 (2003): 119–144. In a later book Krueger puts these findings in context and discusses the policy implications for education and poverty reduction as a counterterrorism strategy. He argues that poverty reduction should be pursued as a moral obligation, but cautions against "drawing a false connection between poverty and terrorism," based on his analysis of individual data on terrorists' characteristics as well as findings on the characteristics of terrorists' countries of origin. See Alan B. Krueger, *What Makes a Terrorist: Economics and the Roots of Terrorism* (Princeton, N.J.: Princeton University Press, 2007), 51.

49. In his book *Understanding Terror Networks* (Philadelphia: University of Pennsylvania Press, 2004), Marc Sageman says that 62 percent of Al Qaeda members are university educated.

50. Efraim Benmelech and Claude Berrebi, "Attack Assignment in Terror Organizations and the Productivity of Suicide Bombers," NBER Working Paper No. 12910 (Cambridge, MA: National Bureau of Economic Research, February 2007).

51. Shawn Teresa Flanigan, "Nonprofit Service Provision by Insurgent Organizations—the cases of Hizballah and the Tamil Tigers," *Studies in Conflict and Terrorism* 31(6) (2008): 499–519, p. 507.

52. Ibrahim al-Yazuri, *Filastin al-Muslima* (London, January 1998), cited in translation in Dale L. Watson, "Holy Land Foundation for Relief and Development, International Emergency Economic Powers Act, Action Memorandum," memorandum to R. Richard Newcomb, director of the Office of Foreign Assets Control, U.S. Department of the Treasury, November 5, 2001; included in Levitt, "Hamas from Cradle to Grave," p. 7.

Chapter 6

1. "The Twilight Zone: A Dead Man Walking," *Ha'Aretz*, March 26, 2004 (in Hebrew). Gideon Levy's question was not about suicide attacks but about targeting civilians, yet Zubeidi's response invokes asymmetry of violent capacity as an answer. The al-Aqsa Martyrs' Brigade carried out thirty-one of the thirty-three suicide attacks attributed to Fatah through 2003. In July 2007 Zubeidi was removed from Israel's "hit or capture list" in return for disavowing armed

resistance as part of a negotiated deal between Israel and Fatah, though at the time of the interview Zubeidi was very much a wanted man.

2. This chapter draws heavily on my joint paper with political scientist David D. Laitin of Stanford University, "Religion, Terrorism, and Public Goods: Testing the Club Model," *Journal of Public Economics* 92, no. 10–11 (October 2008): 1942–1967.

3. For a precise definition of what's termed an internal war, see James D. Fearon and David D. Laitin, "Ethnicity, Insurgency, and Civil War," *American Political Science Review* 97, no. 1 (February 2003): 75–90.

4. Fearon and Laitin, "Ethnicity, Insurgency and Civil War."

5. These results are from a suicide attack database David Laitin and I assembled from various sources. For details see Berman and Laitin, "Religion, Terrorism, and Public Goods."

6. These calculations are from the Fearon-Laitin data on civil wars. For details see Fearon and Laitin, "Ethnicity, Insurgency, and Civil War."

7. Nadav Shragai, "Two out of Five," *Ha'Aretz*, September 26, 2003 (in Hebrew).

8. Gambetta, Diego. "Epilogue," in Diego Gambetta, ed. *Making Sense of Suicide Missions* (Oxford: Oxford University Press, 2006), 309.

9. These data differ slightly from the previous sources in that they separately report on four Fatah-affiliated organizations: Tanzim, the al-Aqsa Martyrs' Brigade, Force 17, and Fatah itself.

10. Valery Tishkov, *Chechnya: Life in a War-Torn Society* (Berkeley: University of California Press, 2004), 172–176.

11. Gambetta, *Making Sense of Suicide Missions*, 309.

12. Robert A. Pape, *Dying to Win: The Srategic Logic of Suicide Terrorism*, (New York: Random House, 2005), chapter 6.

Chapter 7

1. David Kilcullen, "Twenty-Eight Articles: Fundamentals of Company-Level Counterinsurgency," *Iosphere*, 1, (Summer 2006): 1–11.

2. Bruce Hoffman. "All You Need Is Love: How the Terrorists Stopped Terrorism," *Atlantic Monthly*, December 2001: 36–37.

3. Ahmed Rashid, *Jihad: The Rise of Militant Islam in Central Asia* (New Haven, Conn.: Yale University Press, 2002).

4. A. Heather Coyne, presentation at Panel on Aid, Governance and Counterinsurgency: Mindanao, Iraq, Afghanistan, UC Institute on Global Conflict and Cooperation conference on Terrorist Organizations, May 2007.

5. Judith Palmer Harik, *Hezbollah: The Changing Face of Terrorism* (New York: Palgrave Macmillan, 2004), 85.

6. Harik, *Hezbollah*, chap. 6.

7. Richard English, *Armed Struggle: The History of the IRA* (New York: Oxford University Press, 2003), 108, 136.

8. Kilkullen, "Twenty-Eight Articles."

9. Michael Keating, "Dilemmas of Humanitarian Assistance in Afghanistan," in William Maley, ed., *Fundamentalism Reborn? Afghanistan and the Taliban* (New York: New York University Press, 1999).

10. Ahmed Rashid, *Taliban: Militant Islam, Oil, and Fundamentalism in Central Asia* (New Haven, Conn.: Yale University Press, 2000), 190.

11. Ambassador Henry A. Crumpton, Coordinator for Counterterrorism, "Islamist Extremism in Europe," Testimony before the Senate Committee on Foreign Relations, Subcommittee on European Affairs, April 5, 2006.

12. Robert Thompson, *Defeating Communist Insurgency: The Lessons of Malaya and Vietnam* (New York: Praeger, 1966).

13. James E. Dougherty "The Guerilla War in Malaya," in Franklin Mark Osanka, ed., *Modern Guerilla Warfare: Fighting Communist Guerilla Movements 1941–1961* (New York: Free Press of Glencoe, 1963), 298–308.

14. National Archives of Australia, "Review of the Emergency in Malaya from June 1948 to August 1957 by the Director of Operations, Malaya" (Secret), Item 1968/4248, Series A452/2.

15. This figure was calculated by assuming that the 1957 estimate was in current British pounds, applying the UK domestic price index and the 2006 rate of exchange.

16. The estimated population of Malaya is from Fearon and Laitin 2003. The proportion of ethnic Chinese is estimated using the 1966 figure in P. K. Chattopadhyay and D. Ganeson, "An Anthropological Study of the Malay and the Chinese of Malaysia," *Annals of Human Biology* 4, no. 4. (July 1977): 379–381. The number of MRLA rebels is reported by Robert O. Tilman, "The Non-Lessons of the Malayan Emergency," *Asian Survey* 6, no. 8 (August 1966): 407–419.

17. A. J. Stockwell estimates the cost of repressing the insurgency over and above standard costs of colonial administration in "Chin Peng and the Struggle for Malaya," *Journal of the Royal Asiatic Society*, series 3, vol. 16, no. 3 (2006): 279–297.

18. Stephen A. Cheney, *The Insurgency in Oman, 1962–1976* (Quantico, Va.: Marine Corps Command and Staff College, April 1984).

19. David P. Fridovich and Fred T. Krawchuk, "Winning the Global War on Terrorism in the Pacific Region: Special Operations Forces' Indirect Approach to Success," *Joint Forces Quarterly* 44, 1st quarter, 2007: 24–27.

20. Abu Sayyaf has not been defeated. It remains active in the neighboring islands of Sulu and Jolo, and clashed with Philippine troops in Basilan in the

summer of 2007. They continue to kidnap for ransom, including the highly publicized kidnapping in June 2008 of Philippine journalist Ces Driscol, her television crew, and Professor Octavio Dinampo of Mindanao State University, which took place on Sulu. The captives were released, apparently in exchange for ransom.

21. David Petraeus and James Amos, *Counterinsurgency*, Field Manual 3–24 (Washington, D.C.: Department of the Army, December 2006), 2–1.

22. Petraeus and Amos, *Counterinsurgency*, 2–2.

23. While most reconstruction spending seems to have no violence-reducing effect, funds allocated by U.S. officers through the Commanders Emergency Response Program (CERP) appear to reduce the incidence of violence against coalition and Iraqi forces at the district level, beginning in mid 2007, once a district's propensity for violence is controlled for. For details see Eli Berman, Jacob Shapiro, and Joseph Felter. "Can Hearts and Minds Be Bought? The Economics of Counterinsurgency in Iraq." Working Paper No.14606, (Cambridge, Mass.: National Bureau of Economic Research, 2008).

24. At this writing the most recent version of doctrine is the U.S. Government Counterinsurgency Guide, drafted at the State Department and issued by the Interagency Counterinsurgency Initiative. That document endorses a "population-centric" approach (as opposed to "capture and kill"), but does not recognize the special capabilities of clubs in providing services and the need of government to compete directly in service provision or the ability of insurgents to capture government projects. United States Government Interagency Counterinsurgency Initiative, U.S. Government Counterinsurgency Guide, January 2009. www.state.gov/t/pm/ppa/pmppt 2009 (downloaded March 29, 2009).

25. Barack Obama, "Remarks by the President on a New Strategy for Afghanistan and Pakistan," March 27, 2009, www.whitehouse.gov/the_press_office/Remarks-by-the-President-on-a-New-Strategy-for-Afghanistan-and-Pakistan/ (accessed March 29, 2009).

26. Refugees International, as reported by Tom Shanker in the article "Command for Africa Is Established by Pentagon," *New York Times*, October 4, 2008, p. A8, New York edition.

27. At this writing, a good current reference is "Building Legitimate States After Civil Wars," February 2008, a working paper by UC San Diego political scientist David A. Lake.

Chapter 8

1. Adam Smith, *An Inquiry into the Nature and Causes of the Wealth of Nations* (New York: Modern Library, [1776] 1965), 313.

2. Smith, *An Inquiry into the Nature and Causes of the Wealth of Nations*, 315.

3. Menno Simons, *Foundation of Christian Doctrine* (1539), in *Complete Writings*, p. 195; quoted in Thomas Heilke, "Locating a Moral/Political Economy: Lessons from Sixteenth-Century Anabaptism," *Polity* 30, no. 2 (Winter 1997): 199–229.

4. Claus-Peter Clasen, *Anabaptism, A Social History, 1525–1618: Switzerland, Austria, Moravia, South and Central Germany* (Ithaca, N.Y.: Cornell University Press, 1972), 20.

5. Acts 2: 44–45 (Revised Standard Version), as explained in James M. Stayer, *The German Peasants' War and the Anabaptist Community of Goods* (Montreal and Kingston: McGill–Queen's University Press, 1991), 9.

6. Stayer, *The German Peasants' War and the Anabaptist Community of Goods*, 8.

7. Clasen, *Anabaptism: A Social History, 1525–1618*, 32.

8. Stayer, *The German Peasants' War and the Anabaptist Community of Goods*, 95.

9. Heilke, "Locating a Moral/Political Economy."

10. *Huldrych Zwinglis samtliche Werke* (Berlin, 1905), vol. 4: 432. Leland Harder, ed. and trans., *The Sources of Swiss Anabaptism* (Scottdale, Ariz.: Herald Press, 1985), 409; in Stayer, *The German Peasants' War and the Anabaptist Community of Goods*, 97.

11. Clasen, *Anabaptism: A Social History, 1525–1618*, 437.

12. Encyclopedia Britannica Online, *Thomas Müntzer*.

13. Hajo Holborn, *A History of Modern Germany, Volume 2: 1648–1840* (Princeton, N.J.: Princeton University Press, 1982), 73–174.

14. The idea of an economic demand for the supernatural and argument that cooperative production in religious communities encourages that their clergy nurture credibility should be attributed to Laurence Iannaccone. A more complete and careful version of the arguments in this section is developed in Laurence R. Iannaccone and Eli Berman, "Religious Extremists: The Good, the Bad, and the Deadly," *Public Choice* 128, no. 1–2 (2006): 109–129.

15. Fascinating contributions include Pascal Boyer's *Religion Explained: The Evolutionary Origins of Religious Thought* (New York: Basic Books, 2001), and Scott Atran's *In Gods We Trust: The Evolutionary Landscape of Religion* (New York: Oxford University Press, 2002). While I've given a club-based model for prohibitions and sacrifices, Atran and Boyer offer an explanation for prohibitions, sacrifices, and faith based on evolutionary biology. These are complementary rather than competing explanations. Clubs do a better job of explaining why sacrifices and prohibitions respond to subsidies (chapters 3 and 4) and to market and political conditions (below). Evolutionary biology excels at explaining the appeal of faith and the supernatural.

16. Pascal's Wager is a favorite of mathematically inclined believers. At the risk of oversimplifying, it goes like this: Since the existence of the Almighty cannot

be refuted by reason or evidence, one must admit some probability that the Amighty exists. The rewards to belief are infinite (as they include the hereafter), and the cost of believing is finite, so a self-interested agnostic should "wager, then, without hesitation, that He exists." Blaise Pascal, *Pensées*, (trans.) A. J. Krailsheimer, Part III, note 233 (London: Penguin, 1995 [1670]).

17. For evidence on the correlation between religiosity and well-being see, for example, Christopher G. Ellison, "Religious Involvement and Subjective Well-Being," *Journal of Health and Social Behavior* 32, no. 1 (1991): 80–99, and Christopher. G. Ellison, "Religion, the Life Stress Paradigm, and the Study of Depression," in J. S. Levin, ed., *Religion in Aging and Mental Health*, 78–121 (Thousand Oaks, Calif.: Sage, 1993). For a survey of this evidence see Laurence Iannaccone, "Introduction to the Economics of Religion," *Journal of Economic Literature* 36 (1998): 1465–1496.

18. Timur Kuran, "Islam and Underdevelopment," in Timur Kuran, *Islam and Economics*, unpublished manuscript, University of Southern California, 1999.

19. The interested reader might refer to Timur Kuran, "Islam and Economic Underdevelopment: Legal Roots of Organizational Stagnation in the Middle East" Unpublished manuscript, Duke University, 2009, or to Charles Issawi, *The Middle East Economy, Decline and Recovery* (Princeton: Markus Wiener, 1995). For raw statistics measuring the relative economic position of majority Arab countries, see United Nations Development Program, *The Arab Human Development Report 2002: Creating Opportunities for Future Generations*, (New York: United Nations Publications, 2002).

20. Kuran, "Islam and Economic Underdevelopment," 2009, chapter 5.

21. For a clear explanation of all these arguments, see Kuran, "Islam and Economic Underdevelopment," 2009.

22. Timur Kuran, *Islam and Mammon: The Economic Predicaments of Islamism* (Princeton, N.J.: Princeton University Press, 2005).

23. Samuel L. Popkin, *The Rational Peasant: The Political Economy of Rural Society in Vietnam* (Berkeley: University of California Press, 1979), chap. 5.

24. Increased government relief spending under the New Deal accounts for much of the decline in church-provided welfare services during the 1930s, according to the estimates of Jonathan Gruber and Daniel Hungerman in "Faith-Based Charity and Crowd-Out during the Great Depression," *Journal of Public Economics* 91, no. 5–6 (June 2007): 1043–1069.

25. Stephen J. Lee, *The Thirty Years War* (New York: Routledge, 2001), 55.

26. Smith, *An Inquiry into the Nature and Causes of the Wealth of Nations*, 312.

27. Smith, *An Inquiry into the Nature and Causes of the Wealth of Nations*, 314.

28. Roger Finke and Rodney Stark, *The Churching of America, 1776–1990: Winners and Losers in Our Religious Economy* (New Brunswick, N.J.: Rutgers University Press, 1992), 17–20, 39–40.

29. Laurence R. Iannaccone, "Introduction to the Economics of Religion," *Journal of Economic Literature* 36 (1998): 1465–1496.

30. Smith, *An Inquiry into the Nature and Causes of the Wealth of Nations*, 318.

31. Samuel Huntington, *The Clash of Civilizations and the Remaking of World Order*. (New York: Simon & Schuster, 1996); Michael Scott Doran, "Somebody Else's Civil War," *Foreign Affairs* 81, no. 3 (January/February 2002): 22–42.

32. Thomas Müntzer, "Sermon to the Princes," 1524, http://http-server.carleton.ca/~jopp/3850/6–1.htm.

Analytical Appendix

1. A reader seeking more precision may be interested in the original research papers, where these arguments and more are expressed using equations.

2. If you feel uncomfortable about expressing the value of relationships with colleagues, friends, and family in dollars, don't worry, you're in good company. Economist Gerard Debreu worked out a lovely "representation theorem" in 1954. Debreu's theorem implies that this way of thinking is just a convenient shortcut for a more general approach without the dollar signs or even the numbers applied. Just about anytime one is capable of choosing between options, there's no harm in attaching a numerical value to each option and comparing the numbers as long as the rank order is preserved. The numerical values don't even have to be denominated in money.

3. The extent to which governments should invest disproportionately in defending their most valuable targets depends on whether they think terrorists will respond by attacking undefended targets. This and other insights are pointed out by Robert Powell, a political scientist at Berkeley, in his analysis of optimal counterterrorism methods in "Defending against Terrorist Attacks with Limited Resources," *American Political Science Review* 101, no. 3 (August 2007): 527–541.

References

Abuza, Zachary. "Jemaah Islamiyah Adopts the Hezbollah Model." *Middle East Quarterly*, 16(1) (Winter 2009): 15–26.

Akerlof, George A., and Janet L. Yellen. "Gang Behavior, Law Enforcement, and Community Values." In Henry J. Aaron, Thomas E. Mann, and Timothy Taylor, eds., *Values and Public Policy*. Washington, D.C.: Brookings Press, 1994.

Allen, Charles. *God's Terrorists: The Wahhabi Cult and the Hidden Roots of Modern Jihad*. London: Little, Brown, 2006.

Andrabi, Tahir, Jishnu Das, Asim Ijaz Khwaja, and Tristan Zajonc. "Religious School Enrollment in Pakistan: A Look at the Data." *Comparative Education Review* 50, no. 3 (August 2006): 446–477.

Armstrong, Karen. *The Battle for God*. New York: Ballantine, 2000.

Atran, Scott. *In Gods We Trust: The Evolutionary Landscape of Religion*. New York: Oxford University Press, 2002.

Aziz, Ahmad. *Islamic Modernism in India and Pakistan*. London: Oxford University Press, 1967.

Azzi, Corry, and Ronald G. Ehrenberg. "Household Allocation of Time and Church Attendance." *Journal of Political Economy* 83, no. 1 (February 1975): 27–56.

Barro, Robert J., and Gary S. Becker. "Fertility Choice in a Model of Economic Growth." *Econometrica* 57, no. 2 (March 1989): 481–501.

Becker, Gary S. "An Economic Analysis of Fertility." In A. J. Coale, ed., *Demographic and Economic Change in Developed Countries*. Princeton, N.J.: Princeton University Press, 1960.

Becker Gary S. "Crime and Punishment: An Economic Approach." *Journal of Political Economy* 76, no. 2 (March 1968): 169–217.

Becker, Gary S. *The Economic Approach to Human Behavior*. Chicago: University of Chicago Press, 1976.

Becker, Gary S. *A Treatise on the Family*. Cambridge, Mass.: Harvard University Press, 1991.

Beito, David T. "Mutual Aid, State Welfare and Organized Charity: Fraternal Societies and the 'Deserving' and 'Undeserving' Poor, 1900–1930." *Journal of Political History* 5 (1993): 419–434.

Benhabib, Selya. "Unholy Wars." *Constellations* 9, no. 1 (March 2002): 34–45.

Benmelech, Efraim, and Claude Berrebi. "Human Capital and the Productivity of Suicide Bombers." *Journal of Economic Perspectives* 21, no. 3 (2007): 223–238.

Benmelech, Efraim, and Claude Berrebi. "Attack Assignment in Terror Organizations and the Productivity of Suicide Bombers." Working Paper 12910. Cambridge, MA: National Bureau of Economic Research, February 2007.

Ben-Porath, Yoram. "The Production of Human Capital and the Life Cycle of Earnings." *Journal of Political Economy* Vol. 75 (August 1967): 352–365.

Ben-Porath, Yoram. "The F-Connection: Families, Friends and Firms and the Organization of Exchange." *Population and Development Review* 6 (1980): 1–29.

Berman, Eli. "Sect, Subsidy and Sacrifice: An Economist's View of Ultra-Orthodox Jews." *Quarterly Journal of Economics* 115, no. 3 (2000): 905–953.

Berman, Eli. "Subsidized Sacrifice: State Support of Religion in Israel." *Contemporary Jewry* 20 (1999): 167–200.

Berman, Eli. "Hamas, Taliban and the Jewish Underground: An Economist's View of Radical Religious Militias." Working Paper No. 10004. Cambridge, MA: National Bureau of Economic Research, 2003.

Berman, Eli, and Ruth Klinov. "Human Capital Investment and Nonparticipation: Evidence from a Sample with Infinite Horizons (Or: Mr. Jewish Father Stops Going to Work)." Discussion Paper No. 97.05. Jerusalem: Maurice Falk Institute for Economic Research in Israel, 1997.

Berman, Eli, and David D. Laitin. "Hard Targets: Theory and Evidence on Suicide Attacks." Mimeo, UC San Diego, December 2006.

Berman, Eli, and David D. Laitin. "Religion, Terrorism, and Public Goods: Testing the Club Model." *Journal of Public Economics* 92, no. 10–11 (October 2008): 1942–1967.

Berman, Eli, Jacob Shapiro, and Joseph Felter. "Can Hearts and Minds Be Bought? The Economics of Counterinsurgency in Iraq." Working Paper No. 14606, Cambridge: National Bureau of Economic Research, 2008 (December).

Berman, Eli, and Ara Stepanyan. "How Many Radical Islamists? Evidence from Asia and Africa." Mimeo, UC San Diego, 2003.

Berrebi, Claude. "Evidence about the Link between Education, Poverty, and Terrorism among Palestinians." Princeton University Industrial Relations Section, Working Paper No. 477. Princeton, N.J.: Princeton University, September 2003.

Black, Antony. *The History of Islamic Political Thought.* New York: Routledge, 2001.

Bloom, Mia. *Dying to Kill.* New York: Columbia University Press, 2005.

Bowden, Mark. "The Ploy." *Atlantic Monthly*, May 2007: 54–68.

Boyer, Pascal. *Religion Explained: The Evolutionary Origins of Religious Thought.* New York: Basic Books, 2001.

Brachman, Jarret, Brian Fishman, and Joseph Felter. *The Power of Truth: Questions for Ayman al-Zawahiri.* West Point, N.Y.: United States Military Academy Combating Terrorism Center, 2008.

Camerer, Colin. "Gifts as Economic Signals and Social Symbols," *American Journal of Sociology* 44 (1988): S180–S214.

Carr, Jack L., and Janet Landa. "The Economics of Symbols, Clan Names and Religion." *Journal of Legal Studies* 12 (January 1983): 135–156.

Central Bureau of Statistics. *Israel Income Survey*, Jerusalem (various years).

Central Bureau of Statistics. *Statistical Abstract of Israel*, Jerusalem (various years).

Chattopadhyay, P. K., and D. Ganeson. "An Anthropological Study of the Malay and the Chinese of Malaysia." *Annals of Human Biology* 4, no. 4 (July 1977): 379–381.

Chen, Daniel. "Club Goods and Group Identity: Evidence from Islamic Resurgence during the Indonesian Financial Crisis." Mimeo, University of Chicago, 2005.

Cheney, Stephen A. *The Insurgency in Oman, 1962–1976.* Quantico, Va.: Marine Corps Command and Staff College, 1984.

Chiswick, Carmel Ullman, "The Economics of American Judaism." *Shofar* 13 (1995): 1–19.

Clasen, Claus-Peter. *Anabaptism, A Social History, 1525–1618: Switzerland, Austria, Moravia, South and Central Germany.* Ithaca, N.Y.: Cornell University Press, 1972.

Collier, Paul, and Anke Hoeffler. "Greed and Grievance in Civil War." World Bank mimeo, 2001, http://econ.worldbank.org/programs/library.

Cornes, Richard, and Todd Sandler. *The Theory of Externalities, Public Goods and Club Goods.* New York: Cambridge University Press, 1986.

Coyne, A. Heather. Presentation at Panel on Aid, Governance, and Counterinsurgency: Mindanao, Iraq, Afghanistan, UC Institute on Global Conflict and Cooperation conference on Terrorist Organizations, May 2007.

Cragin, Kim. "Al-Mujama' and the Resistance, 1973–1986." Draft dissertation chapter, Cambridge University, 2008.

Crenshaw, Martha. "Theories of Terrorism: Instrumental and Organizational Approaches." In David C. Rapoport, ed., *Inside Terrorist Organizations*, 13–31. New York: Columbia University Press, 1988.

Cross, Frank Moore, and Esther Eshel. "The Yahad (Community) Ostracon." In Adolfo Roitman, ed., *A Day at Qumran. The Dead Sea Sect and Its Scrolls.* Jerusalem: Israel Museum, 1997.

Crumpton, Henry A. "Islamist Extremism in Europe." Testimony before the Senate Committee on Foreign Relations, Subcommittee on European Affairs, April 5, 2006. Washington, DC.

Davis, Anthony. "How the Taliban Became a Military Force." In William Maley, ed., *Fundamentalism Reborn? Afghanistan and the Taliban*. New York: New York University Press, 1999.

Dekmejian, R. Hrair. *Islam in Revolution: Fundamentalism in the Arab World*. Syracuse, N.Y.: Syracuse University Press, 1995.

DeSerpa, Allan C. "A Theory of Discriminatory Clubs." *Scottish Journal of Political Economy* 24 (February 1977): 33–41.

Dodge, Toby. "Political Mobilisation in the Absence of Civil Society or a State: Islamic Nationalism in Post-Saddam Iraq." Mimeo, University of London, 2004.

Doran, Michael Scott. "Somebody Else's Civil War." *Foreign Affairs* 81, no. 3 (January/February 2002): 22–42.

Dougherty, James E. "The Guerilla War in Malaya." In Franklin Mark Osanka, ed., *Modern Guerilla Warfare: Fighting Communist Guerilla Movements 1941–1961*, 298–308. New York: Free Press of Glencoe, 1963.

Durkheim, E. *The Elementary Forms of Religious Life*. New York: Free Press, 1965.

Eaton, Joseph W., and Albert J. Mayer. "The Social Biology of VERY High Fertility among the Hutterites: The Demography of a Unique Population." *Human Biology* 25, no. 4 (December 1953): 206–264.

Ekelund, Robert B., Robert F. Hebert, Robert D. Tollison, Gary Anderson and Audrey B. Davidson. *Sacred Trust: The Medieval Church as an Economic Firm*. New York: Oxford University Press, 1996.

Ellenson, David. "German Jewish Orthodoxy: Tradition in the Context of Culture." In Jack Wertheimer, ed., *The Uses of Tradition*. Cambridge, Mass.: Harvard University Press, 1992.

Ellison, Christopher G. "Religious Involvement and Subjective Well-Being." *Journal of Health and Social Behavior* 32, no. 1 (1991): 80–99.

Ellison, Christopher G. "Religion, the Life Stress Paradigm, and the Study of Depression." In J. S. Levin, ed., *Religion in Aging and Mental Health*, 78–121. Thousand Oaks, Calif.: Sage, 1993.

Enders, Walter, and Todd Sandler. *The Political Economy of Terrorism*, New York: Cambridge University Press, 2006.

Engels, Frederich. *The Peasant War in Germany* (2nd edition) London: Allen & Unwin, 1927.

English, Richard. *Armed Struggle: The History of the IRA*. New York: Oxford University Press, 2003.

Ericksen, Julia A., Eugene P. Ericksen, John Hostetler, and Gertrude E. Huntington. "Fertility Patterns and Trends among the Old Order Amish." *Population Studies* 33, no. 2 (July 1979): 255–276.

Erlanger, Steven. "Hamas Seizes Broad Control in Gaza Strip." *New York Times*, June 14, 2007, p. A1 of New York Edition.

Esposito, John L. *Unholy War: Terror in the Name of Islam.* New York: Oxford University Press, 2002.

Faith, Roger L., and Stephen K. Happel. "The More the Merrier: The Economics of Mob Goods." Manuscript, Arizona State University, Tempe, 1989.

Faksh, Mahmud A. *The Future of Islam in the Middle East: Fundamentalism in Egypt, Algeria, and Saudi Arabia.* Westport, Conn.: Praeger, 1997.

Fandy, Mamoun. *Saudi Arabia and the Politics of Dissent.* New York: St. Martin's Press, 1999.

Fearon, James D., and David D. Laitin. "Ethnicity, Insurgency, and Civil War." *American Political Science Review* 97, no. 1 (February 2003): 75–90.

Filatov, S. "On Paradoxes of the Post-Communist Russian Orthodox Church." In R. Cipriani, ed., *Religions Sans Frontiers? Present and Future Trends of Migration, Culture, and Communication,* 117–125. Rome: Rome University, 1993.

Finke, Roger, and Rodney Stark. *The Churching of America, 1776–1990: Winners and Losers in Our Religious Economy.* New Brunswick, N.J.: Rutgers University Press, 1992.

Flanigan, Shawn Teresa. "Nonprofit Service Provision by Insurgent Organizations—the Cases of Hizballah and the Tamil Tigers." *Studies in Conflict and Terrorism* 31 (6) (2008): 499–519.

Freedman, Ronald, and P. K. Whelpton, "Social and Psychological Factors Affecting Fertility: X. Fertility Planning and Fertility Rates by Religious Interest and Denomination," *The Milbank Memorial Fund Quarterly* 28 (3) (July 1950): 294–343.

Fridovich, David P., and Fred T. Krawchuk. "Winning the Global War on Terrorism in the Pacific Region: Special Operations Forces' Indirect Approach to Success." *Joint Forces Quarterly* 44, 1st quarter, 2007: 24–27.

Friedman, Menachem. *The Haredi (Ultra-Orthodox) Society—Sources, Trends and Processes.* Research Series No. 41. Jerusalem: Jerusalem Institute, 1991.

Fritsch, P. "Religious Schools in Pakistan Fill Void—and Spawn Warriors." *Wall Street Journal*, Oct. 2, 2001, A1, A24.

Gambetta, Diego. "Epilogue," in Diego Gambetta, ed., *Making Sense of Suicide Missions.* New York: Oxford University Press, 2006.

"Gang Member Tells Jurors about Initiation in Double Murder Trial." WRAL-TV, March 7, 2000. www.lochaltechwire.com/news/local/story/139973.

Glaeser, Edward L., and Spencer Glendon. "The Demand for Religion." Mimeo, Harvard University, 1997.

Glaeser, Edward L., Bruce Sacerdote, and Jose A. Scheinkman. "Crime and Social Interactions." *Quarterly Journal of Economics* 111, no. 2 (May 1996): 507–548.

Glock, Charles Y., and Rodney Stark. *Christian Beliefs and Anti-Semitism*. New York: Harper and Row, 1966.

Greif, Anver. "Cultural Beliefs and the Organization of Society: A Historical and Theoretical Reflection on Collectivist and Individualist Societies." *Journal of Political Economy* 102 (1994): 912–950.

Gruber, Jonathan, and Daniel Hungerman. "Faith-Based Charity and Crowd-Out during the Great Depression." *Journal of Public Economics* 91, no. 5–6 (June 2007): 1043–1069.

Gruber, Jonathan, and Daniel Hungerman. "The Church vs the Mall: What Happens When Religion Faces Increased Secular Competition?" *Quarterly Journal of Economics* 123 (2008): 831–862.

Harik, Judith Palmer. *Hezbollah: The Changing Face of Terrorism*. New York: Palgrave Macmillan, 2004.

Hassan, Nasra. "An Arsenal of Believers: Talking to the 'Human Bombs.'" *New Yorker*, November 19, 2001. 77 (36): 36–41.

Heger, Lindsay. "In the Cross-Hairs: The Targets of Terrorism." Doctoral dissertation draft, UC San Diego, 2009.

Heilke, Thomas. "Locating a Moral/Political Economy: Lessons from Sixteenth-Century Anabaptism." *Polity* 30, no. 2 (Winter 1997): 199–229.

Heilman, Samuel C. *Defenders of the Faith: Inside Ultra-Orthodox Jewry*. New York: Schocken Books, 1992.

Hine, Robert V. *California's Utopian Colonies*. Berkeley: University of California Press, 1983.

Hoffman, Bruce. "All You Need Is Love: How the Terrorists Stopped Terrorism." *Atlantic Monthly*, December 2001. 288 (5): 36–37.

Hoffman, Bruce. "The Logic of Suicide Terrorism." *Atlantic Monthly*, June, 2003. 291(5): 1–10.

Holborn, Hajo. *A History of Modern Germany, Volume 2: 1648–1840*. Princeton, N.J.: Princeton University Press, 1982.

Hume, David. "Of Superstition and Enthusiasm." In David Hume, *Essays: Moral, Political and Literary*, 73–79. New York: Liberty Classics, 1989. Originally published by Henry Frowde, Edinburgh and Glasgow, 1903–1904

Huntington, Samuel. *The Clash of Civilizations and the Remaking of World Order*. New York: Simon & Schuster, 1996.

Hurd, James. "The Shape of High Fertility in a Traditional Mennonite Population." Mimeo, Bethel University, May 2006.

Hyman, Paula E. "Traditionalism and Village Jews in 19th-Century Western and Central Europe: Local Persistence and Urban Nostalgia." In Jack Wertheimer, ed., *The Uses of Tradition*. Cambridge, Mass.: Harvard University Press, 1992.

Iannaccone, Laurence R. "A Formal Model of Church and Sect." *American Journal of Sociology* 94, suppl. (1988): s241–s268.

Iannaccone, Laurence R. "Religious Participation: A Human Capital Approach." *Journal for the Scientific Study of Religion* 29 (September 1990): 297–314.

Iannaccone, Laurence R. "Sacrifice and Stigma: Reducing Free-Riding in Cults, Communes, and Other Collectives." *Journal of Political Economy* 100 (1992): 271–291.

Iannaccone, Laurence R. "Why Strict Churches Are Strong." *American Journal of Sociology* 99, no. 5 (1994): 1180–1211.

Iannaccone, Laurence R. "Toward an Economic Theory of Fundamentalism." *Journal of Institutional and Theoretical Economics* 15 (1997): 100–116.

Iannaccone, Laurence R. "Introduction to the Economics of Religion." *Journal of Economic Literature* 36 (1998): 1465–1496.

Iannaccone, Laurence R. "Looking Backwards: A Cross-National Study of Religious Trends." Working paper, George Mason University, 2003.

Iannaccone, Laurence R., and Eli Berman, "Religious Extremists: The Good, the Bad, and the Deadly." *Public Choice* 128, no. 1–2 (2006): 109–129.

Ilan, Shahar. "Deceit." *Ha'Aretz*, May 19, 1998. (In Hebrew.)

Ilan, Shahar. "The Yeshiva-Bocher Basket: 17 Thousand Shekel Gross." *Ha'Aretz*, March 2, 1998. (In Hebrew.)

Ilan, Shahar. *Haredim Ltd.* Jerusalem: Keter, 2000. (In Hebrew.)

Ilan, Shahar. "Reconciling Conscription." *Haaretz*, April 22, 2008. (In Hebrew.)

International Crisis Group. "Pakistan: Madrasas, Extremism and the Military." *Asia Report* 36. Islamabad/Brussels: icg.org, July 2002.

International Crisis Group. "Iraq's Muqtada al-Sadr: Spoiler or Stabilizer?" *Middle East Report* 55. Brussels: icg.org, July 2006.

International Crisis Group. "Where Is Iraq Heading? Lessons from Basra." *Middle East Report* 67. Damascus/Amman/Brussels icg.org, June 25, 2007, 3.

Issawi, Charles, *The Middle East Economy, Decline and Recovery.* Princeton: Markus Wiener, 1995.

Ivianski, Zeev. "The Terrorist Revolution: Roots of Modern Terrorism." In David C. Rapoport, ed., *Inside Terrorist Organizations*, 129–149. New York: Columbia University Press, 1988.

Jafa, Yateendra Singh. "Defeating Terrorism: A Study of Operational Strategy and Tactics of Police Forces in Jammu & Kashmir (India)." *Police Practice and Research* 6, no. 2 (May 2005): 141–164.

Juergensmeyer, Mark. *Terror in the Mind of God: The Global Rise in Religious Violence.* Berkeley: University of California Press, 2000.

Kalyvas, Stathis, and Ignacio Sánchez-Cuenca. "Killing without Dying: The Absence of Suicide Missions." In Diego Gambetta, ed., *Making Sense of Suicide Missions*, 209–232. Oxford: Oxford University Press, 2006.

Kandel, Eugene, and Edward P. Lazear. "Peer Pressure and Partnerships." *Journal of Political Economy* 100, no. 4 (1992): 801–817.

Kanter, Rosabeth Moss. *Commitment and Community: Communes and Utopias in Sociological Perspective.* Cambridge, Mass.: Harvard University Press, 1972.

Karoly, Lynn A., and Elizabeth Frankenberg. *1993 Indonesia Family Life Survey.* Santa Monica, Calif.: RAND, 1996.

Keating, Michael. "Dilemmas of Humanitarian Assistance in Afghanistan." In William Maley, ed., *Fundamentalism Reborn? Afghanistan and the Taliban.* New York: New York University Press, 1999.

Kenney, Michael. *From Pablo to Osama: Trafficking and Terrorist Networks, Government Bureaucracies and Competitive Adaptation.* University Park: Pennsylvania State University Press, 2007.

Kifner, John. "Israel Arrests Settlers It Says Tried to Bomb Palestinians." *New York Times,* May 19, 2002. Section 1, page 10, New York edition.

Kilcullen, David. "Twenty-Eight Articles: Fundamentals of Company-Level Counterinsurgency." *Iosphere* 1, (March, 2006): 1–11.

Kilcullen, David. *The Accidental Guerrilla: Fighting Small Wars in the Midst of a Big One.* New York: Oxford University Press, 2009.

Kobler, John. *Capone.* New York: Putnam, 1971.

Koelbl, Susanne. "Islamic Extremists Gain Upper Hand in Kashmir Relief Efforts." *Der Spiegel International,* February 25, 2006, http://www.spiegel.de/international/spiegel/0,1518,403726,00.html (accessed March 16, 2009).

Kogo, Yoshiyuki. "Aum Shinrikyo and Spiritual Emergency." *Journal of Humanistic Psychology* 42 (2002): 82–101.

Kraul, Chris. "FARC Commander Surrenders in Colombia." *Los Angeles Times,* May 20, 2008. http://articles.latimes.com/2008/may/20/world/fg-rebel20.

Krueger, Alan B. *What Makes a Terrorist: Economics and the Roots of Terrorism.* Princeton, N.J.: Princeton University Press, 2007.

Krueger, Alan B., and Jitka Maleckova. "Education, Poverty and Terrorism: Is There a Causal Connection?" *Journal of Economic Perspectives* 17, no. 4 (2003): 119–144.

Kruglanski, Arie. "Inside the Terrorist Mind." National Academy of Sciences presentation, April 2002.

Kuran, Timur. "Islam and Underdevelopment." In Timur Kuran, *Islam and Economics.* Unpublished manuscript, University of Southern California, 1999.

Kuran, Timur, "Islam and Economic Underdevelopment: Legal Roots of Organizational Stagnation in the Middle East" Unpublished manuscript, Duke University, 2009.

Kuran, Timur. *Islam and Mammon: The Economic Predicaments of Islamism.* Princeton, N.J.: Princeton University Press, 2005.

Lake, David A. "Building Legitimate States After Civil Wars." Mimeo, UC San Diego, February 2008.

Landau, David. *Piety and Power: The World of Jewish Fundamentalism*. New York: Hill and Wang, 1993.

Landers, Renee M., James B. Rebitzer, and Lowell J. Taylor. "Rat Race Redux: Adverse Selection in the Determination of Work Hours in Law Firms." *American Economic Review* 86 (June 1996): 329–348.

Lee, Stephen J. *The Thirty Years War*. New York: Routledge, 2001.

Levitt, Matthew. "Hamas from Cradle to Grave." *Middle East Quarterly* Volume 11, No. 1 (Winter 2004): 3–15.

Levy, Gideon. "The Twilight Zone: A Dead Man Walking." *Ha'Aretz*, March 26, 2004. (In Hebrew.)

Maimonides, Moses. *The Guide for the Perplexed*. (1904 trans. from the twelfth-century Arabic *Dalalāt al-Hairin* by M. Friedländer, 2nd ed.) New York: Dover, 1956.

Marty, M. E., and R. S. Appleby, eds. *Fundamentalism Observed*. Chicago: University of Chicago Press, 1991.

Mayer, Jane. "Junior: The clandestine life of America's top Al Qaeda source." *New Yorker*, September 11, 2006: http://www.newyorker.com/archive/2006/09/11/060911fa_fact (accessed March 16, 2009).

McGirk, Jan. "Kashmir: The Politics of an Earthquake." October 19, 2005. www.OpenDemocracy.net.

Merari, Ariel. "Suicide Terrorism in the Context of the Israeli-Palestinian Conflict." Presentation at the Suicide Terrorism Research Conference, National Institute of Justice, Washington, D.C., October 25–26, 2004.

Metraux, Daniel A. "Religious Terrorism in Japan: The Fatal Appeal of Aum Shinrikyo." *Asian Studies* 35, no. 12 (December 1995): 1140–1154.

Meyer, Josh. "Records Show Man in LAX Plot Gave U.S. Key Terrorist Details." *Los Angeles Times*, April 27, 2005. Section A1.

Mishal, Shaul, and Avraham Sela. *The Palestinian Hamas: Vision, Violence, and Coexistence*. New York: Columbia University Press, 2000.

Mitchell, Richard P. *The Society of Muslim Brothers*. London: Oxford University Press, 1969.

Munson, Ziad. "Islamic Mobilization: Social Movement Theory and the Egyptian Muslim Brotherhood." *Sociological Quarterly* 42, no. 4 (2001): 487–510.

Nasr, Vali. *The Shia Revival: How Conflicts within Islam Will Shape the Future*. New York: Norton, 2006.

National Archives of Australia. "Review of the Emergency in Malaya from June 1948 to August 1957 by the Director of Operations, Malaya" (Secret). Item 1968/4248, Series A452/2.

Obama, Barack, "Remarks by the President on a New Strategy for Afghanistan and Pakistan," March 27, 2009, www.whitehouse.gov/the_press_office/Remarks-by-the-President-on-a-New-Strategy-for-Afghanistan-and-Pakistan/ (accessed March 29, 2009).

Pape, Robert A. "The Strategic Logic of Suicide Terrorism." *American Political Science Review* 97 (2003): 343–361.

Pape, Robert A. *Dying to Win: The Srategic Logic of Suicide Terrorism*, New York: Random House, 2005.

Pascal, Blaise. *Pascal's Pensées*. Trans. Alban J. Krailsheimer. New York: Penguin, 1995 [1670].

Paz, Reuven. Address to the Washington Institute, July 19, 2001. Reproduced as "Special Forum Report: Islamic Palestine or Liberated Palestine? The Relationship between the Palestinian Authority and Hamas" (rapporteur's summary of his remarks). Peace Watch No. 337. www.washingtoninstitute.org/templateC05.php?CID=2028.

Petraeus, David, and James Amos. *Counterinsurgency*. Field Manual 3–24. Washington, D.C.: Department of the Army, December 2006.

Popkin, Samuel L. "Pacification: Politics and the Village." *Asian Survey* 10, no. 8, (August 1970): 662–671.

Popkin, Samuel L. *The Rational Peasant: The Political Economy of Rural Society in Vietnam*. Berkeley: University of California Press, 1979.

Powell, Robert. "Defending against Terrorist Attacks with Limited Resources." *American Political Science Review* 101, no. 3 (August 2007): 527–541.

Qassem, Naim. *Hizbullah: The Story from Within*. Beirut: Saqi Books, 2005.

Rahman, Omar, Jane Menken, Andy Foster, Christine E. Peterson, Mohammed Nizam Khan, Randall Kuhn, and Paul Gertler. *The 1996 Matlab Health and Socioeconomic Survey: Overview and User's Guide*. Santa Monica, Calif.: RAND, 1999.

Ranstorp, Magnus. *Hizballah in Lebanon: The Politics of the Western Hostage Crisis*. London: Macmillan Press, 1997.

Rashid, Ahmed. "Pakistan and the Taliban." In William Maley, ed., *Fundamentalism Reborn? Afghanistan and the Taliban*. New York: New York University Press, 1998.

Rashid, Ahmed. *Taliban: Militant Islam, Oil and Fundamentalism in Central Asia*. New Haven, Conn.: Yale University Press, 2000.

Rashid, Ahmed. *Jihad: The Rise of Militant Islam in Central Asia*. New Haven, Conn.: Yale University Press, 2002.

Regev, Eyal. "Comparing Sectarian Practice and Organization: The Qumran Sects in Light of the Regulations of the Shakers, Hutterites, Mennonites and Amish." *Numen* 51, no. 2 (2004): 146–181.

Reuter, C. *My Life Is a Weapon: A Modern History of Suicide Bombing*. Princeton, N.J.: Princeton University Press, 2004.

Richman, B. D. "How Communities Create Economic Advantage: Jewish Diamond Merchants in New York." Duke Law School Legal Studies Research

Paper No. 65; Harvard Law and Economics Discussion Paper No. 384, 2005. http://ssrn.com/abstract=349040.

Roitman, Adolfo. "From Dawn to Dusk among the Qumran Sectarians." In Adolfo Roitman, ed., *A Day at Qumran: The Dead Sea Sect and Its Scrolls*. Jerusalem: Israel Museum, 1997.

Sageman, Marc. *Understanding Terror Networks*. Philadelphia: University of Pennsylvania Press, 2004.

Schiff, Zeev, and Ehud Ya'Ari. *Intifada: The Palestinian Uprising—Israel's Third Front*. New York: Simon & Schuster, 1990.

Schultz, T. W., ed. *Economics of the Family: Marriage, Children, and Human Capital*. Cambridge, MA: National Bureau of Economic Research, 1974.

Segal, Haggai. *Dear Brothers: The West Bank Jewish Underground*. Woodmere, N.Y.: Beit-Shamai Publications, 1988.

Shafqat, Saeed. "From Official Islam to Islamism: The Rise of Dawat-ul-Irshad and Lashkar-e-Taiba." In Christophe Jaffrelot, ed., *Nationalism without a Nation: Pakistan Searching for Its Identity*. New Delhi: Zed Books, 2002.

Shahar, Charles, Morton Weinfeld, and Randal F. Schnoor. *Survey of the Hassidic and Ultra-Orthodox Communities in Outremont and Surrounding Areas*. Outremont, Quebec: Coalition of Outremont Hassidic Organizations, 1997.

Shanker, Tom. "Command for Africa Is Established by Pentagon." *New York Times*, October 4, 2008. Section A8, New York Edition

Shapira, Shimon. *Hizbullah between Iran and Lebanon*. Tel Aviv: Hakibbutz Hameuchad, 2000. (In Hebrew.)

Sharara, Waddah. *Hezbollah State*. Beirut: Dar Al-Nahar, 1996. (In Arabic.)

Shragai, Nadav. "Two out of Five." *Ha'Aretz*, September 26, 2003. (In Hebrew.)

Silber, Michael K. "The Emergence of Ultra-Orthodoxy: The Invention of a Tradition." In Jack Wertheimer, ed., *The Uses of Tradition*. Cambridge, Mass.: Harvard University Press, 1992.

Smith, Adam. *An Inquiry into the Nature and Causes of the Wealth of Nations*. New York: Modern Library, [1776] 1965.

Spence, A. Michael. *Market Signaling: Informational Transfer in Hiring and Related Screening Processes*. Cambridge, Mass.: Harvard University Press, 1974.

Sprinzak, Ehud. *Brother against Brother: Violence and Extremism in Israeli Politics from Altalena to the Rabin Assassination*. New York: Free Press, 1999.

Sprinzak, Ehud. "Rational Fanatics." *Foreign Policy* issue 120 (September/October 2000): 66–74.

Stark, Rodney, and William S. Bainbridge. *The Future of Religion: Secularization, Revival, and Cult Formation*. Berkeley: University of California Press, 1985.

Stark, Rodney, and Roger Finke. *Acts of Faith: Explaining the Human Side of Religion*. Berkeley: University of California Press, 2000.

Stayer, James, M. *The German Peasants' War and the Anabaptist Community of Goods*. Montreal and Kingston: McGill–Queen's University Press, 1991.

Stockwell, A. J. "Chin Peng and the Struggle for Malaya." *Journal of the Royal Asiatic Society*, series 3, vol. 16, no. 3 (2006): 279–297.

"Thomas Müntzer." *Encyclopædia Britannica*. 2008. Encyclopædia Britannica Online. http://www.britannica.com/EBchecked/topic/397713/Thomas-Muntzer.

Thompson, Hunter. *Hell's Angels: The Strange and Terrible Saga of the Outlaw Motorcycle Gangs*. New York: Random House, 1966.

Thompson, Robert. *Defeating Communist Insurgency: The Lessons of Malaya and Vietnam*. New York: Praeger, 1966.

Tilman, Robert O. "The Non-Lessons of the Malayan Emergency." *Asian Survey* 6, no. 8 (August 1966): 407–419.

Tishkov, Valery. *Chechnya: Life in a War-Torn Society*. Berkeley: University of California Press, 2004.

Trajtenberg, Manuel. "Defense R&D in the Anti-Terrorist Era." *Defense and Peace Economics* 17 (2006): 177–199.

United Nations Development Program, *The Arab Human Development Report 2002: Creating Opportunities for Future Generations*. New York: United Nations Publications, 2002.

United States Department of the Treasury, Office of Foreign Assets Control. *Specially Designated Nationals List*. www.ustreas.gov/offices/enforcement/ofac/sdn/sdnlist.txt.

United States Government Interagency Counterinsurgency Initiative, *U.S. Government Counterinsurgency Guide*, www.state.gov/t/pm/ppa/pmppt 2009 (January).

Wang, L. Choon. "The Effects of Education on the Amish." Mimeo, UC San Diego, June 2008.

Weber, Max. "The Protestant Sects and the Spirit of Capitalism." in Max Weber, *From Max Weber: Essays in Sociology*, trans. and ed. H. H. Gerth and C. Wright Mills. New York: Oxford University Press, 1946.

Weber, Max. *The Sociology of Religion*. Boston: Beacon Press, 1963.

Weber, Max. *Economy and Society*. Berkeley: University of California Press, 1978.

Weil, David N. *Economic Growth*. New York: Addison-Wesley, 2004.

Weinstein, Jeremy. *Inside Rebellion: The Politics of Insurgent Violence*. New York: Cambridge University Press, 2006.

Weisburd, David. *Jewish Settler Violence: Deviation as Social Reaction*. University Park: Pennsylvania State University Press, 1989.

Wintrobe, Ronald. "Can Suicide Bombers Be Rational?" Mimeo, University of Western Ontario, 2003.

Wintrobe, Ronald. *Rational Extremism: The Political Economy of Radicalism*. New York: Cambridge University Press, 2006.

Index

9/11. *See* Attacks on United States, September 2001